Language and the Law

Language and the Law

By Sanford Schane

With a Foreword by Roger W. Shuy

continuum
LONDON • NEW YORK

Continuum

The Tower Building
11 York Road
London SE1 7NX

80 Maiden Lane
Suite 704
New York NY 10038

© Sanford Schane and Foreword, Roger W. Shuy 2006

British Library Cataloguing-in-Publication Data
A catalogue record for this book is available from the British Library.

ISBN: HB: 0-8264-8828-5
    PB: 0-8264-8829-3

Library of Congress Cataloguing-in-Publication Data
To come

Typeset by Servis Filmsetting Ltd, Manchester
Printed and bound in Great Britain by MPG Books, Cornwall

To the memory of my parents

Acknowledgements

Sanford Schane
La Jolla, California

Foremost, I wish to recognize all the students, throughout the years, who participated in my course on language and the law. They experienced first-hand much of the material presented here. Their questions and comments led to a clarification of ideas in my own mind and compelled me to discover how to present most effectively this interdisciplinary subject to an audience of diverse backgrounds and training.

Jennifer Lovel of the Continuum International Publishing Group was instrumental in initially bringing my proposal for a book on law and language to the attention of this publishing house. I appreciate her support in moving the manuscript through the appropriate channels. Joanna Taylor, also at Continuum, provided editorial assistance. I enjoyed working with her on improving the structure and content of the book, and I thank her for prompt replies to my numerous enquiries.

Finally, I am grateful to my wife, Marjorie, for her patience and understanding while I was working on the manuscript and especially for her willingness to wait her turn in 'sharing' a computer that I was dominating most of the time.

Contents

Foreword

Roger W. Shuy
Distinguished Research Professor of Linguistics, Emeritus
Georgetown University

One of the major contributions of science is the ability of its leading members to see how its theory and research connect with the pressing problems of the real world. Unfortunately, this pathway from knowledge to practical application usually stays inside the individual disciplines, seldom crossing the deep moats that academic fields construct around themselves. Thus, applied linguists tend not to venture beyond problems close to linguistics proper, such as language learning and teaching. Nor has it been characteristic of most linguists to transport their field into other areas, such as medical communication, politics or law. Similarly, legal theory and its practice tend to stay pretty close to home, dealing with the specific issues of individual law cases. It is not characteristic of law to reach out to the practitioners of other disciplines for help, other than as expert witnesses in cases involving medical, engineering or other technical areas. It takes creative scholars to bridge disciplinary boundaries, even when it is broadly apparent that the neighbouring disciplines could contribute a great deal to each other. It also takes a certain amount of courage to venture into foreign territory and to risk being considered naive or just plain wrong about one's efforts to see interdisciplinary relationships.

But when scholars have the will to make a concerted effort, they can see how the route from theory to practice in their own field relates also to the practical concerns of another field. Sometimes this discovery begins serendipitously. My own introduction to the intersection of language and law took place on an aeroplane while I was chatting with a lawyer sitting next to me. For Sanford Schane, it was the result of leafing through his wife's law books. For others, the cross-disciplinary relationship is consciously planned. They have taken their linguistic training with them to lawschool, realizing that the two fields had much in common. By whatever means the decision to apply one's knowledge to another field takes place, it is a very welcome development. Law has much to offer linguistics and linguistics has much to offer law.

For linguists, as the author of this book explains, the study of legal theory and individual law cases provides 'a goldmine of issues' to explore, and linguists are gradually awakening to this opportunity. Even though many linguists are now participating in lawsuits as consultants to attorneys and as expert witnesses, it has not always been easy to convince the legal profession that linguistics can be of help. One way to attract and accommodate lawyers is to begin from their own perspective by addressing the issues that they face concerning laws, statutes, decisions and individual cases. If linguists are to make an impact in law, they need to capture the law's professional vision, and not the vision of linguistics alone. This means, before adding linguistic contributions to the legal repertoire, linguists first need to speak lawyers' language, see their problems, and know their values and beliefs. Any potential success in the cross-fertilization of ideas demands not only shared vision but also mutual respect and dignity.

Language and the Law is a book written for linguists who want to learn more about law and for lawyers who want to learn about linguistics. In the world of publishing it can be a difficult task for a book to address two different audiences. Readers from one field commonly want a book to focus on their own discipline. Even though lawyers may tend to prefer case analysis and linguists may prefer to read about how linguistic principles work, for cross-disciplinary topics such as language and law, it is necessary to write for two simultaneous groups of readers. As Professor Schane illustrates in this book, the secret is to start where both fields operate and to teach what each needs to know about the other with respect and dignity.

Although the two fields have much to say to each other, they have gone their singular paths alone for far too long. For example, both fields are deeply concerned about ambiguity, precision, promising, offering, defining, metaphor, indirectness and many other overlapping matters that this book treats. One of the difficulties linguists have in reading books about law is that it can seem daunting to plough through the style and presentation conventions of the law. Lawyers are used to legal language and the details of lawsuits, whereas linguists prefer to go straight to the language issues involved in them. The reverse is true for lawyers reading books about linguistics, which may often seem irrelevant to their individual cases and the way laws and statutes are drafted. This book avoids both extremes. At the same time, it brings together the thinking of both areas in a number of specific law cases, where the two fields conveniently mesh, whether or not this was their original intention. It deals with four major issues that have attracted the attention of linguists: ambiguity, metaphor, speech acts and promises. Professor Schane shows how numerous civil and criminal lawsuits centre on these current linguistic issues. This book is the product of a distinguished linguist's many years of fruitful thinking about important areas in both language and the law.

Introduction

> The law is a profession of words.
>
> *David Mellinkoff*[1]

By means of written language, national constitutions come into existence, laws and statutes are enacted, and contractual agreements between private individuals take effect. Spoken language is just as indispensable to the legal process. One need look no further than the courtroom, whether it be the interrogation of plaintiffs and defendants, the testimony of witnesses, the pleadings by attorneys, or the instructions from a judge to a jury. The legal implications of language continue to extend far beyond the courtroom – to interactions between police and suspects, to conversations between lawyers and their clients, to law enforcement's use of surreptitious recordings, and to such unlawful speech acts as offering a bribe, or issuing a threat, or making a defamatory statement. A little reflection suffices to reveal just how essential language is to the legal enterprise. Yet academic research on the intersection of language and the law is a relatively recent phenomenon, with much of the work dating from the 1980s.[2]

Personal background

My own introduction to the topic began in the early years of that decade. I was leafing through some textbooks belonging to my wife, a law student back then. I could see that within those pages lay a goldmine of issues, not just concerning the law, but dealing also with the use of language. Perhaps it should not be so surprising that I would be fascinated by legal language. After all, I am a professional linguist. I was curious to know more about this area of study and interested in doing some research, but I was unsure where to turn. As yet there was no professional organization or journal devoted exclusively to the language and law interface, and the term 'forensic linguistics', which would become one of the names for what was to blossom into a vibrant discipline, had not yet been invented. (There is now a professional organization, the International Association of Forensic Linguists (IAFL), and a publication, *International Journal of Speech, Language, and the Law*, formerly called *Journal of Forensic Linguistics*.)

If I were serious about delving further into the subject of law and language, I felt I needed to know much more about the 'law' side of the coin, and so I considered dedicating part of a forthcoming sabbatical year to legal studies. A colleague urged me to apply to the Harvard Law School for one of its Liberal Arts Fellowships. The one-year grants were intended to enable faculty from other institutions to acquire a basic law background for undertaking legal research and for creating interdisciplinary courses after returning to their home campuses. In order to accomplish these goals, the recipients, of whom I was one of four, were encouraged to pursue the first-year programme, to attend other classes and seminars, and to begin a personal research project. One of the lectures in a civil procedures course dealt with the concept of 'the corporation as a person' and I decided to take on that topic as my project. It eventually burgeoned into a full-scale article that was published in a law review. In Chapter 2, the reader will find some of these ideas.

Investigation into law and language is quite extensive, emanating not only from the field of linguistics, but also from other social sciences. Three principal strands of research have evolved.[3] For some researchers, the primary concern centres on language, and the law provides relevant data for linguistic analysis and the testing of theories about language. For others, the law becomes the main ingredient, and language serves as a vehicle for understanding the legal process and the workings of that system. For still other researchers, the major interest resides in the disciplines of psychology, sociology or anthropology, and language as it operates within the legal system functions as a means for investigating psychological processes, societal interactions or cultural traits.[4] Because my own academic training has been in linguistics, my approach to law and language tends to fall into the first category. Here are some topics directly concerned with the language of the law that have been of personal interest. I do not treat all of them in the following chapters, as some have been extensively dealt with elsewhere.

Legal English

The mention of legal language tends to conjure up in the mind of the layperson 'legalese' – that often incomprehensible verbiage found in legal documents, as well as an arcane jargon used among attorneys. To elucidate how this 'special dialect' came about and how it differs from 'ordinary English', researchers have turned to the language of the law as a linguistic phenomenon in its own right, tracing its evolution and noting the peculiarities of its vocabulary and sentence structure. In fact, one of the first scholarly publications about law and language that I consulted was David Mellinkoff's monumental work, *The Language of the Law*, published in 1963, nearly two decades before linguists would turn to legal language.[5] Mellinkoff was not a linguist; he was a law professor at the UCLA School of Law, where he taught until his death in 1999. In his book he covers the historical development of legal English, beginning with its Anglo-Saxon roots and continuing on through the Middle English period right up to the present day, while acknowledging along the way the contributions from Latin and French. He considers, too, some of the grammatical features of this style of language, as well as the social and cultural significances. Although clearly indispensable as a source for serious research into the language of the law, this nearly 500-page tome probably contains more information than the casual reader may need to know.

A more accessible account of the history of legal English is Peter Tiersma's recent book, *Legal Language*.[6] Tiersma too is a professor of law, but he also holds an advanced degree in linguistics; hence, his text appeals to both linguists and law professionals. In addition to treating the historical developments, he thoroughly explains why legal language is so often difficult for non-lawyers to comprehend. It is full of wordiness, redundancy and specialized vocabulary and it often contains lengthy, complex and unusual sentence structure.

Plain English

In an endeavour to counteract the negative effects of legalese, there has developed a trend towards 'plain English'. It began as a consumer movement to simplify the language of the law so that the public can understand documents that they may be required to sign, such as apartment rental leases, insurance policies or promissory notes.

The plain-English movement has also had a salutary effect within the legal process. Jurors do not always understand fully the instructions given to them by judges. To get at the root of this problem, Robert and Veda Charrow, psycholinguists, conducted several experiments.[7] They had a group of subjects, who were Maryland citizens eligible for jury duty, listen to a tape-recording of jury instructions. The subjects were to paraphrase what they heard to the best of their abilities. Surprisingly, almost half of the information was missing from some of the paraphrases. What exactly was causing the incomprehensibility? The difficulty was due, not so much to vocabulary items, but mostly to particular types of grammatical constructions, such as the occurrence of multiple negatives and the excessive use of passive sentences and of nominalizations. The experimenters then simplified the instructions by eliminating these complex sentence types and presented the revised versions to a second group of comparable subjects. Although the rewritten instructions did result in some improvement in the comprehension scores, it was also clear that it was highly unlikely that there would ever be complete understanding. A subsequent group of researchers then conducted some experiments to determine what exactly ought to constitute an acceptable level of comprehension.[8] They proposed two standards: the lesser one stipulated that for eight out of ten juries at least eight members of a twelve-person jury ought to understand any given point of law; the stricter criterion required for nine out of ten juries a minimum of nine jurors.

The research into jurors' potentially poor comprehension alerted the legal community, and in an effort to tackle the problem some US states have been revising their instructions. Here is an example of an old California instruction and of the corresponding new one written in 'plain English'. Both attempt to explain the distinction between direct and circumstantial evidence:[9]

Old California instruction: BAJI 2.00
Evidence consists of testimony, writings, material objects or other things presented to the senses and offered to prove whether a fact exists or does not exist.

Evidence is either direct or circumstantial. Direct evidence is evidence that directly proves a fact. It is evidence which by itself, if found to be true, establishes that fact.

Circumstantial evidence is evidence that, if found to be true, proves a fact from which an inference of the existence of another fact may be drawn. A factual inference is a deduction that may logically and reasonably be drawn from one or more facts established by the evidence.

It is not necessary that facts be proved by direct evidence. They may be proved also by circumstantial evidence or by a combination of direct and circumstantial evidence. Both direct and circumstantial evidence are acceptable as a means of proof. Neither is entitled to any greater weight than the other.

New instruction: No. 202
Evidence can come in many forms. It can be testimony about what someone saw or heard or smelled. It can be an exhibit admitted into evidence. It can be someone's opinion.

Some evidence proves a fact directly, such as testimony of a witness who saw a jet plane flying across the sky. Some evidence proves a fact indirectly, such as testimony of a witness who saw only the white trail that jet planes often leave. This indirect evidence is sometimes referred to as 'circumstantial evidence'.

In either instance, the witness's testimony is evidence that a jet plane flew across the sky. As far as the law is concerned, it makes no difference whether evidence is direct or indirect. You may choose to believe or disbelieve either kind. Whether it is direct or indirect, you should give every piece of evidence whatever weight you think it deserves.

Nor should attorneys believe themselves to be immune from the plain-English movement. They too must rethink how they write. Richard Wydick, a professor of law and author of a popular manual on legal writing, maintains that the best legal English is plain English, and he condemns that abstruse style so typical of many legal practitioners. He notes:

> We lawyers do not write plain English. We use eight words to say what could be said in two. We use arcane phrases to express commonplace ideas. Seeking to be precise, we become redundant. Seeking to be cautious, we become verbose. Our sentences twist on, phrase within clause within clause, glazing the eyes and numbing the minds of our readers. The result is a writing style that has, according to one critic, four outstanding characteristics. It is '(1) wordy, (2) unclear, (3) pompous, and (4) dull'.[10]

The critic was none other than Mellinkoff, who was an early advocate of simplicity and clarity in legal expression and was highly critical of any lawyer's 'defense of "legalese" '.[11]

We have noted that both specialized vocabulary and unusual sentence structure contribute to the peculiarities of legal writing. These two elements, lexicon and grammar, are the fundamental building blocks of every human language. To know a language – to speak it, write it or understand it – requires control of both components. Imagine you were learning a foreign language and had memorized all of the common words with their various meanings but had studied no grammar. To create a sentence you wouldn't know in which order to place the words or what endings to attach to them. Conversely, if you were intimately acquainted with the grammar of a language (as many linguists are) but had no vocabulary items to plug into the slots where nouns, verbs and other parts of speech are supposed to occur, you would also be incompetent as a speaker, writer or hearer of that language. It is around this twofold nature of language that the four chapters of this book are structured. The first two deal primarily, although not exclusively, with word meaning; the last two with sentence meaning.

Ambiguity and misunderstanding

A word may have more than one meaning or dictionary definition, and if there is no context to suggest which of the possible senses is intended then the word will be ambiguous. In Chapter 1, we shall look at three court cases that the law describes as containing ambiguity. One of them deals with a contract for the sale of chickens. The buyer contends that a 'chicken' is a young bird suitable for broiling or frying, but definitely not a stewing fowl. The seller maintains that a 'chicken' is any suitable member of the genus regardless of age. Which definition will the court embrace? Another case deals with two different ships coincidentally having the same name, a fact apparently unknown to the protagonists of this dispute, also a buyer and a seller. The former expected the goods he had purchased to be placed aboard a ship called the *Peerless* leaving in October; the seller put the merchandise on a different *Peerless* departing in December. The buyer refused to accept the later shipment. Which *Peerless* should the court read into the contract? The third case once again is about chickens. The Interstate Commerce Commission, responsible for regulating the transportation of manufactured products among the states, asserts that 'frozen eviscerated chickens' fall into this category. The Department of Agriculture insists that the birds, although processed, nonetheless are still bona fide agricultural commodities of the type that do not fall under the shipping jurisdiction of the Interstate Commerce Commission (ICC). Will the court decide that frozen eviscerated chickens are manufactured products or agricultural commodities?

Within linguistics the term 'ambiguity' has a more restricted meaning than the one generally occurring in law and in popular usage, where it is not uncommon for the term to refer to a construction that is unclear, uncertain or vague. Although the three court cases do exemplify 'ambiguous words' in this general sense, the narrower linguistic signification will reveal how the cases are really quite different from one another, as each represents a different type of misunderstanding.

There is also *syntactic ambiguity*. In English, this kind is most often due either to the order of the words in a sentence or to grammatical properties, such as the relationship between a pronoun and possible words to which the pronoun may refer. In Chapter 1, we shall examine a court case where syntactic ambiguity has become a life-or-death issue. The Supreme Court of the United States must decide the constitutionality of a jury instruction that contains an adjective followed by several nouns. Does the adjective modify only the noun immediately after it or all of the nouns in the series? Even though the distinction may seem rather trivial, this instruction originally was given to a jury deliberating in a capital case. Now a man's life is to hinge on the court's resolution of the ambiguity!

Metaphor and legal fictions

One of the ways that words acquire new meanings is through metaphor. Consider, for example, the following expressions: *a broken vase, a broken leg, a broken heart, a broken promise*. The most basic, literal meaning of 'broken' would characterize a physical object, such as a vase, and it is easy enough to see the extension of this word to body parts containing bones. Although a human heart is also a concrete object, a heart that is broken has not been shattered physically into several pieces. And a promise would not be any kind of physical entity at all. The application of 'broken' to hearts and promises was doubtless metaphorical in origin, although today we no longer think of it as such. Because we view these expressions as natural ways for describing these situations, 'broken', for all intents and purposes, is a word with several different meanings, as any dictionary will reveal. We shall return to this important point in Chapter 2.

The law too has expressions that began as metaphors – for example, a *meeting* of the minds, a *ripening* of obligations, a *binding* agreement, a *broken* contract. However, the law has found the need for an even more intriguing kind of metaphor – the 'legal fiction'. Acknowledged not to be literally true, nonetheless fictions are treated as though they were. Lon Fuller, who was a law professor at Stanford University and whose book, *Legal Fictions*, is now a classic, introduced this topic to the English-speaking legal community.[12]

I shall examine in depth two of the more notorious fictions. One of them is the 'attractive nuisance' doctrine. A child wanders onto a stranger's property and is injured due to the presence of an unsafe condition on the premises. The dangerous object or condition is an attractive nuisance that has 'invited' the child onto the property, and consequently, the child is treated not as a trespasser but as an invitee. The other fiction is the well-known one of 'the corporation as a person', which was the topic of my first research project. Because corporations legally can engage in many of the same kinds of activities as people, such as owning property or entering into agreements, the law will often deal with corporations as though they were indeed persons.

Although fictions are not true, they are not lies either, for there is no malicious intent to deceive. Fuller observes:

> Anyone who has thought about the legal fiction must be aware that it presents an illustration of the all-pervading power of the word. That a statement which is disbelieved by both its author and his audience can have any significance at all is evidence enough that we are here in contact with the mysterious influence exercised by names and symbols. In that sense the fiction is a linguistic phenomenon.[13]

This linguistic phenomenon has its basis in metaphor. Now one tends to think of metaphor as belonging mostly to literary and rhetorical language. However, research in cognitive linguistics over the past twenty-five years has shown this perspective to be untenable. Rather, metaphor structures ordinary thinking and speaking. George Lakoff, a linguist, and Mark Johnson, a philosopher, with the publication of their book, *Metaphors We Live By*, ushered in a completely new way of studying the interrelation of thought and speech.[14] They note:

> The concepts that govern our thoughts are not just matters of the intellect. They also govern our everyday functioning, down to the most mundane details. Our concepts structure what we perceive, how we get around in the world, and how we relate to other people . . . If we are right in suggesting that our conceptual system is largely metaphorical, then the way we think, what we experience, and what we do every day is very much a matter of metaphor.[15]

I shall use this cognitive approach to metaphor in my analysis of legal fictions. Although at first they may appear to be clever inventions for the sole convenience of the law, the fictions actually have their origins in conceptualizations that have long been a part of normal language and thought.

Speech acts

In Chapters 3 and 4 we shall go beyond the meaning of individual words and turn to the interpretations of complete utterances. Both chapters will adopt speech-act theory as their linguistic foundation for legal analysis. The theory is concerned with how speakers intend to use language and how hearers comprehend what is said to them and how they respond. This approach owes its success to the pioneering work of two language philosophers, John Austin of Oxford University and John Searle of the University of California at Berkeley. Austin's *How to Do Things with Words* and Searle's *Speech Acts* have influenced all subsequent research in this field.[16]

The term 'speech act', due to Searle, is particularly appropriate for describing how speakers put language to use. When talking, one regularly does much more than just mouth words. One also engages in or performs some kind of act. In fact, Austin routinely employs the term 'performative' for this activity. Here are some examples: a minister who, under the proper circumstances, says, 'I now pronounce you husband and wife', by means of these words helps to bring about the marital state; when an umpire yells 'you're out!', a player thereby becomes 'out' at that very moment; if I inquire, 'what time is it?', I am engaging in an act of asking a question; if I say to you, 'leave the room!' I have issued a command; and if I sincerely tell you, 'I promise to take you to Paris next weekend', by uttering this sentence I have placed myself under a commitment to you. According to Searle, speech-act theory aims to find answers to the following sorts of questions:

> How do words relate to the world? How is it possible that when a speaker stands before a hearer and emits an acoustic blast such remarkable things occur as: the speaker means something; the sounds he emits mean something; the hearer understands what is meant; the speaker makes a statement, asks a question, or gives an order?[17]

Certain speech acts have legal import, such as *promising* to repay a loan or *accepting an offer* for a piece of property. Some take legal effect only under special conditions: during a marriage ceremony, two persons each *declaring* 'I do'; just before testifying in court, a witness *vowing* 'to tell the truth, the whole truth, and nothing but the truth'; or at the inauguration proceedings, the President *swearing* 'to uphold the Constitution of the United States of America'. Still other kinds of speech acts are unlawful and severe penalties may be attached to their performance: *asserting* knowingly a false statement when under oath; *threatening* to harm physically an ex-spouse; or *offering* a bribe to a public official.

For the latter class of speech acts, Roger Shuy has coined the term 'language crimes', which is also the title of his fascinating book where he discusses bribery, extortion, threatening speech and even solicitation to murder.[18] Shuy, a sociolinguist, has served as an expert witness and a consultant on a multitude of criminal cases where the prosecution presented taped evidence, much of which was surreptitiously recorded by government agents. Using the tools of discourse analysis and of speech acts, he examines chunks of text or conversation and demonstrates how dialogues are intricately structured – that is, which participant initiates a topic of conversation, which topics are dropped or recycled, and whether speech acts have actually occurred or only seemingly so. Shuy's book is a stunning account of the application of linguistic methodology for the investigation of crucial issues within the criminal law.

Lawrence Solan, a law professor with an advanced degree in linguistics, in his book, *The Language of Judges*, looks at the speech act of 'admitting' in relation to the 'self-incriminating' clause of the Fifth Amendment to the US Constitution. It states that 'no person . . . shall be compelled in any criminal case to be a witness against himself'.[19] Solan defines an 'admission' as an intentionally communicative act that goes against the speaker's interest and, as a consequence, may well be self-damaging and self-incriminating.

Peter Tiersma has written several legal articles making extensive use of speech-act theory. He has looked at the language of defamation and at the question of what constitutes perjury.[20] He finds that the speech act of 'accusing' is a fundamental aspect of a defamatory statement. Moreover, the accusation must concern an act that is considered reprehensible or blameworthy in the eyes of the community. Turning to perjury, Tiersma notes that it raises the interesting possibility of whether an assertion that is 'literally true', but is not 'the whole truth', counts as perjury. He provides the following example: Your boss asks, 'why weren't you at work?', and you respond, 'I was sick yesterday'. In actuality, you became ill only towards evening. Have you lied? Solan and Tiersma, in their book, *Speaking of Crime*, present an insightful analysis of the perjury allegation in the Clinton impeachment trial, where the president, when questioned about his relationship with Monica Lewinsky and the frequency of their encounters, adroitly engaged in the tactics of a 'literal truth' defence.[21]

Speech acts have found their way into other areas of the law. Dennis Kurzon analyses legislatures' promulgations of statutes as the speech act of 'enacting'.[22] For example, many laws, both in the UK and in the USA, begin with the formula: 'Be it *enacted*, That . . .'.

Hearsay

The rule against hearsay concerns those statements that may be admitted as evidence by a witness testifying in court. The law has carefully worked out a classification of the kinds of utterances that would *not* be hearsay and hence are admissible. Appended to this is a long list of exceptions, that is, statements that technically would be hearsay but nonetheless will be admitted into evidence. In Chapter 3, I shall apply speech-act theory to an analysis of hearsay data, and I shall show how the various speech-act components neatly accommodate all of the traditional legal categories. As for the exceptions, the main interest will centre on statements having to do with 'state of mind'. Legal scholars have argued whether such utterances indeed are exceptions or whether in reality they should be considered non-hearsay. Speech-act analysis offers an interesting perspective on this long-standing debate within the law of evidence.

Contract law

A valid legal agreement or contract has three essential requirements: an offer, an acceptance and consideration. Suppose, for example, that I make the following offer: 'I will sell you my car for $1,500'. You may accept my offer, reject it, make a counter-offer, or even do nothing. Let us assume that you accept it. Then there will be a binding contract if there is a valuable 'consideration' in return for the automobile. There indeed is – namely, the $1,500 that you will hand over to me. Thus, consideration involves a *quid pro quo*: my car in exchange for your $1,500.

Classical Anglo-American contract law considers the notion of 'promise' as essential to a valid agreement, although this view is by no means universal. Legal scholars have battled back and forth with this issue and, in Chapter 4, we shall look at some of the pros and cons. Nonetheless, the role of promise will be crucial for a speech-act analysis of offer and of consideration.

We noted that some speech acts, if they are to take effect, must be performed by particular individuals and under the appropriate circumstances – for example, only a properly empanelled jury can declare a defendant 'Guilty!'. Hence, in order for a speech act to be well formed, it must satisfy certain criteria known as 'felicity conditions'. Searle has proposed a set of such conditions for characterizing well-formed ordinary promises.[23] These criteria, with some minor tweaking, will suffice to accommodate the special requirements of legal offers. Moreover, the satisfaction of these conditions simultaneously will ensure valid consideration.

About this book

My own research agenda has been to look at areas of interest in linguistics and to find similar topics of concern in the law. Each of the four chapters of this book presents a major area where language and law intersect in this way. The linguistic topics include: ambiguity, metaphor, speech acts and promise. The corresponding legal themes cover: misunderstanding, legal fictions, hearsay and contract formation.

Each chapter in turn contains four sections. The first section is concerned with the law. It introduces the legal topic for the chapter, notes relevant court cases and furnishes necessary background information. The second section concentrates on language. It provides the linguistic notions and explains the theoretical concepts that will be required for analysing the legal material. The third section presents the analysis. It offers an insightful account and at times a novel treatment of the legal data. The fourth section deals with the language–law interface. It considers the relevance of linguistic analysis to the legal material presented in the chapter. In the Appendix, I have included excerpts of some of the court cases that I discuss. To facilitate the identification of these twelve cases, I cite them in the regular way (e.g. *California* v. *Brown*) within the main text. Other cases are not cited in this way, but proper reference to them can be found in the endnotes accompanying the discussion of those cases in the text.

Much of the material to be covered here began as lectures from a course on law and language that I have been teaching annually, for nearly twenty years, at the University of California at San Diego.[24] The class attracts a sizeable number of students contemplating lawschool, a handful of linguistics majors and a healthy group of the curious. Because of this diverse mix, there are no course prerequisites: I do not require any prior training in formal language analysis for the potential law students or any previous course work in legal studies for the linguists.

Throughout this book, I have taken a similar approach for the presentation of subject matter. I realize that some readers will have had prior exposure to legal studies, others will have had previous training in linguistics, and still others may have had little experience in either discipline. Therefore, I have not presupposed any particular background on the part of the readers. To accommodate the different interests and varying levels of preparation, I have tried throughout to explain clearly all necessary linguistic and legal concepts and, where possible, to do so in a non-technical manner. I have incorporated all of this material into the main body of each chapter. The endnotes contain reference information exclusively. I have endeavoured to make this book accessible to a wide audience: to legal scholars and language professionals interested in the intersection of law and linguistics; to students and academics encountering this interdisciplinary area for the first time; and to those general readers curious to know more about the intriguing connection between language and the law.

1 Ambiguity in Language and Misunderstanding in Law

> It depends upon what the meaning of the word 'is' is.
>
> *William Jefferson Clinton*[1]

In spite of all good intentions, the meanings of the words found in a legal document – whether a statute, a contract or a will – are not always clear and unequivocal. They may be capable of being understood in more ways than one, they may be doubtful or uncertain, and they may lend themselves to various interpretations by different individuals. When differences in understanding are irresolvable, the parties having an interest in what is meant may end up in litigation and ask the court to come up with its interpretation. In the eyes of the law, when this kind of misunderstanding arises, the disputed document contains 'ambiguity'.

Paradoxically enough, the word *ambiguity* itself has more than one interpretation. One of the senses, what I shall call the 'broad' or general meaning, has to do with how language is used by speakers or writers and how it is understood by listeners or readers. Ambiguity occurs where there is lack of clarity or when there is uncertainty about the application of a term. It is this sense of *ambiguity* that generally is meant within the law, as well as by speakers of the language. But there is another sense, what I shall call the 'narrow' or restricted meaning. This sense is concerned with certain lexical and grammatical properties that are part of the very fabric of language, irrespective of anyone's usage or understanding. A word may have multiple definitions or a group of words may partake of more than one grammatical parsing. Linguists and grammarians have extensively investigated these features of language.

We shall begin by looking in depth at three court cases claimed to contain 'ambiguity' or 'ambiguous words'.[2] (The texts of these cases can be found in the Appendix.) The claims of ambiguity are appropriate for the broad meaning of this term. On closer examination we shall see that the three cases are quite different from one another. Only one of them exemplifies the narrow sense of ambiguity, where a word has more than one meaning.

The other two cases present problems of *reference* and of *vagueness*, respectively. I shall discuss these differences of misunderstanding and show that they played a role in how the cases were decided. Then we shall turn to a fourth case, one concerned with a jury instruction preceding the sentencing phase of a capital crime.[3] This case will exemplify an entirely different kind of ambiguity, where not the meaning of a particular word is at issue, but instead its grammatical role within a sentence.

Three law cases of so-called 'ambiguity'

The first case, *Frigaliment Importing Co. v. BNS International Sales Corp.*, gets embroiled in the definition of 'chicken'. The buyer, a Swiss company, has ordered frozen eviscerated chickens from a New York wholesaler of poultry. The order called for chickens of two sizes: 1½ to 2 pounds, and 2½ to 3 pounds. When the shipment arrives in Europe, the buyer discovers that the larger birds are all stewing chickens. Expecting broilers and fryers, the buyer cries 'foul' and brings a suit against the seller for breach of contract.

The legal issue before the court is whether the seller supplied the buyer with the goods that the buyer had ordered. In order to resolve this issue the court must ask the question: 'what is chicken?' The plaintiff buyer contends that ' " chicken" means a young chicken, suitable for broiling and frying'. The defendant insists that a chicken is 'any bird of the genus that meets contract specifications on weight and quality, including what it calls "stewing chicken" '. Judge Friendly (that really is his name!), who heard the case, concedes that both meanings are possible. Consequently, he declares that 'the word "chicken" standing alone is *ambiguous*' (emphasis added), and he decides to look to the contract to see whether it offers any aid for the interpretation of this word.

The second case, *Raffles v. Wichelhaus*, is notoriously known to law students. The bizarre events of this English case took place in 1864, before there were telegraphs, telephones or email. The buyer purchased bales of cotton that were to be sent from Bombay, India to Liverpool, England on a ship called the *Peerless*. At the time of the making of the contract it was unknown to the parties that there were two different ships by the name of *Peerless*. One of them was to leave Bombay in October, the other in December. The buyer expected the goods to be on the October ship, whereas the seller planned to place them on the December vessel. When the October *Peerless* arrived in England, naturally there were no bales of cotton on it for the buyer. When the December *Peerless* sailed into port with the shipment, the buyer refused acceptance. The seller then brought a suit against the buyer. Counsel in support of the defendant buyer's plea noted that 'there is nothing on the face of the contract to shew [sic] that any particular ship called the *Peerless* was meant; but the moment it appears that two ships called the *Peerless* were about to sail from Bombay there is a latent *ambiguity* . . .' (emphasis added).

The third case, *Interstate Commerce Commission* v. *Allen E. Kroblin, Inc.,* once again deals with eviscerated chickens. This time we find the ICC against farmers in a heated dispute over whether dressed and eviscerated chickens are 'manufactured' products. One of the roles of the ICC is to certify trucking companies engaged in interstate commerce, and most goods that are transported between states must be carried by these certificated or regulated carriers. However, there is an exemption for certain agricultural commodities, such as fruits and vegetables, fish, livestock, and other kinds of agricultural commodities that are not manufactured products. Thanks to this exemption, farmers are able to use less costly uncertificated conveyances for moving agricultural goods from state to state.

The ICC claims that dressed and eviscerated poultry is a manufactured product, whereas the Department of Agriculture maintains that it is an agricultural commodity. The court notes that 'all parties are agreed that the words "agricultural commodities" and "manufactured products thereof" used in the agricultural exemption are *ambiguous words*' (emphasis added).

Here, then, are three cases claimed to contain ambiguous words. But exactly what is meant by 'ambiguity'?

The linguistics of ambiguity

The term *ambiguity* has more than one interpretation: a broad sense that pertains to language use, and a narrower meaning that deals with some fundamental properties about language itself. How has this term usually been defined within the law? A good place to start is the legal reference work, *Words and Phrases*.[4] This multivolume tome of legal terms and words, alphabetized much like a dictionary, contains definitions drawn from various US court cases. Here, for example, are three definitions found under the entries 'ambiguity' and 'ambiguous'.

> The words 'ambiguous' and 'ambiguity' are often used to denote simple lack of clarity in language.[5]

> 'Ambiguous' means doubtful and uncertain.[6]

> The word 'ambiguous' means capable of being understood in more senses than one; obscure in meaning through indefiniteness of expression; having a double meaning; doubtful and uncertain; meaning unascertainable within the four corners of the instrument; open to construction; reasonably susceptible to different constructions; uncertain because susceptible of more than one meaning; and synonyms are 'doubtful', 'equivocal', 'indefinite', 'indeterminate', 'indistinct', 'uncertain', and 'unsettled'.[7]

It is this general or broad usage of the word *ambiguity* that is common to the three court cases of interest to us. There is a contract for the sale of chickens but it is *unclear* what kinds of chickens are called for; there are two boats with the same name but it is *indeterminate* as to which one was to carry bales of cotton; and there are deplumed and eviscerated chickens but it is *uncertain* whether they are to be classified as manufactured products. The broad meaning attributed to the term *ambiguity* has to do with language use – with what is said and with how it is understood. Lawyers and legislatures, as well as ordinary citizens, ideally should use language that is clear, certain, unequivocal and to the point, and when it is unclear, uncertain, doubtful or equivocal, then language is considered to be 'ambiguous'.

Opposed to this general view of ambiguity is a more restricted meaning. It is this narrow sense that typically finds expression in grammatical treatises and in the field of linguistics, the discipline that studies the properties of human language. One of the truly fascinating aspects of language is the potential for ambiguity. Linguists recognize two principal types: lexical ambiguity and syntactic ambiguity. Both have relevance for misunderstandings that may arise in the interpretation of legal documents.[8]

Lexical ambiguity potentially occurs whenever a word has more than one objective or dictionary meaning. The ambiguity is potential because it is only in certain contexts that more than one of the meanings may be possible. A well-known example from the linguistics literature concerns the word *bank*. It can refer to a financial institution or to the edge of a river or stream. The sentence, 'I'll meet you at the bank at three o'clock', written or uttered in isolation, could be ambiguous between the two meanings. Yet, most of the time we are unaware of any ambiguity, and, in fact, we find none because other linguistic features from elsewhere in the discourse, or even non-linguistic clues, render only one of the readings as possible. Thus, if I had said, 'I'll meet you at the bank at three o'clock because I have to go there to make a deposit', the meaning to be attributed to the word *bank* is quite unambiguous. Or if we had planned to go fishing, and later you see me walking to my car with a fishing rod over my shoulder, and I say to you, 'I'll meet you at the bank at three o'clock', you probably would infer that our rendezvous is to take place at the riverbank. But when there are neither linguistic nor situational features to help out, the ambiguity could be very real.

A less common type of lexical ambiguity – for the spoken language only – is *homonymic ambiguity*. This involves words that are pronounced the same but are spelled differently – for example, 'In Las Vegas they can raze [raise] a building overnight,' or 'While traipsing through the garden, Harry tripped over the hoes [hose]'. Puns are frequently of this type. However, homonymic ambiguity has little relevance to the law, at least not for its written form, and so we will not be concerned with it.

Syntactic ambiguity is the other common linguistic type. It has to do with grammatical structure. Words occur in a particular order and grammatical relationships are established by those orderings. There is the potentiality for syntactic ambiguity whenever a given word order may allow for more than one grammatical relationship. This kind of ambiguity often involves what linguists refer to as *scope of modification*. Notice the scope of the word *skinny* in the sentence: 'The skinny president's daughter was the belle of the ball'. Who is skinny? The president or his daughter? The adjective *skinny* could modify either noun. Here is a more intricate example, where the adjective *small* potentially (although not necessarily realistically) could modify any of the three following nouns: 'The small claims court judge had difficulty making decisions'. Are we talking about a judge presiding over a court that deals with small claims? Or a judge presiding over a small court that deals with claims? Or a small judge presiding over a court that deals with claims?

Structural ambiguity also frequently results due to the placement of a prepositional phrase. Consider the sentence: 'John asked Bill to leave on Wednesday'. Did John do the asking on Wednesday, or was Bill to leave on that day? The phrase *on Wednesday* can modify either the main clause or else the contained infinitive clause. But if the prepositional phrase were to be moved to the front of the sentence, there would be no ambiguity: 'On Wednesday John asked Bill to leave'. Here the prepositional phrase can modify only the main clause (i.e. John's asking). Similarly, for the sentence: 'The president's skinny daughter was the belle of the ball', the placement of the adjective *skinny* before the second noun makes it refer unambiguously to the daughter.

A sentence may be even multiply ambiguous due to various combinations of lexical and syntactic factors. Consider the sentence: 'The chicken is too hot to eat'. This sentence is ambiguous in at least four ways. (There are even a few additional meanings that the reader is invited to discover.) The lexical ambiguities involve the interplay of the words *chicken* and *hot*. The different meanings for these two words are indicated in the top part of Figure 1.1, and paraphrases of the four ambiguities can be found in the lower part of the figure.

Meanings of the words *chicken* and *hot*

chicken	hot
1. live animal	a. sensation of internal heat (i.e. feeling hot) b. sexually aroused
2. a human food	c. heat emitted from an entity (i.e. hot to the touch) d. spicy (of food)

Ambiguous: 'The chicken is too hot to eat.'

1a. The live chicken is feeling excessively warm and doesn't want to eat.
1b. The live chicken is highly aroused sexually and not in the mood to eat.

2c. The chicken as food is just off the grill, is sizzling, and is unable to be eaten now.
2d. The chicken as food is excessively spicy and therefore unable to be eaten.

Figure 1.1   'The chicken is too hot to eat.'

Notice that two of the senses of *hot* are compatible only with the meaning of 'chicken as a live animal', and the other two senses only with 'chicken as food'. (In fact, the two senses of 'hot' pertaining to food are so frequently ambiguous in ordinary conversation, that for clarification one often asks: 'Do you mean "*hot*" hot or "*spicy*" hot?'.) There is also syntactic or grammatical ambiguity for the sentence, 'The chicken is too hot to eat'. It concerns whether the verb *eat* is interpreted actively (i.e. the chicken is doing the eating), or passively (i.e. the chickens are being eaten). The paraphrases in Figure 1.1 reflect this covert active–passive distinction.

Now, the law has by no means entirely overlooked the narrow sense of 'ambiguity' – that is, as a function of lexicon or grammar. Here is another definition from *Words and Phrases*:

> 'Ambiguity' can exist in a written document only in those cases where language is susceptible of more than one meaning.[9]

(It is paradoxical that this quote about ambiguity contains within itself a potential lexical ambiguity. Does the word *cases* mean 'instances' or 'legal suits'? Given the overall context, it is the former meaning that is doubtless intended.) Now the author of this quote specifically talks about *language in itself*. A document is not ambiguous merely because it is unclear or doubtful, but rather because within the language of the document there is something that creates more than one meaning. Moreover, this particular definition allows for both lexical and syntactic ambiguity. Language is like a coin with two faces – lexicon and grammar, and both of these essential features can be sources of ambiguity.

It is the broad sense of 'ambiguity' that is common to the three cases that we shall now review in greater detail. We shall see that only one of them actually exemplifies the narrow meaning of this term. The other two represent additional types of 'misunderstanding' – *referential indeterminacy* and *vagueness of categorization*. Let us then at the three cases.

Frigaliment: lexical ambiguity

A word with more than one meaning has the potentiality of being lexically ambiguous. Dictionaries are our obvious sources for discovering the multiple meanings of a word. These reference works employ two ways of displaying the various meanings: either as separate lexical entries, each with its own set of definitions, or else as a single entry with multiple definitions. For example, *Webster's Unabridged Dictionary*, 3rd edition, lists distinct entries for *bank* as a noun and as a verb. Moreover, the noun itself bears three separate lexical entries: (a) 'bank' of a river, (b) 'bank' designating a row or a tier and (c) 'bank' as a financial institution. Dictionaries typically provide separate entries for the same part of speech to reflect the fact that the words, although now identical in spelling and pronunciation, nonetheless have distinct etymologies or origins. The three entries for the noun *bank* are indicative of this procedure: (a) 'the bank pertaining to a river' comes from Middle English *bank*; (b) 'the bank designating a row or a tier' goes back to Middle English *banck* via Old French *banc*; and (c) 'the bank relating to finance' is derived from French *banque* or Italian *banca*.[10]

On the other hand, a word with multiple meanings but with a single etymology will generally have one entry with its various meanings enumerated as subentries. This situation obtains, for example, for the noun *chicken*, a word going all the way back to Anglo-Saxon (Old English) *cicen*, which was the diminutive form of *coc*, 'a cock'. If we look up the word *chicken* in *Webster's* 3rd edition, we find the following definitions under a single entry:[11]

1. a. the common domestic fowl (*Gallus gallus*); also now Brit: the young
      of this bird when less than one year old;
   b. the flesh, esp. of the young of such fowl used as food.
2. the young of any of various esp. gallinaceous birds whose young run
   about soon after hatching;
3. slang: a young person, esp. a woman;
4. coward, sissy.

We consider a word with more than one objective dictionary meaning, whether the different meanings occur as separate entries or as subentries of an entry, to be potentially lexically ambiguous.

The *Frigaliment* case provides a prime example of lexical ambiguity. As a handy way of distinguishing between the two meanings of *chicken* that are directly relevant to this case (i.e. the first two definitions cited from *Webster's*), Judge Friendly refers to a 'broad' sense – that is, any member of the genus *Gallus gallus*, and a 'narrow' sense – especially a young one of this genus. Now in most situations there would be no ambiguity, as the context would make it clear which sense was intended. For example, if I said 'Harry breeds and raises chickens', you would doubtless understand that I was using the word in the broad sense. On the other hand, if I were to ask you to go to the market to buy chicken to cook on the outdoor barbecue, I clearly desire a younger bird, such as a broiler or a fryer, that is suitable for grilling, which is probably what you would find anyway, as stewing chickens have become a rare commodity in most supermarkets.

What is furthermore interesting about this particular lexical ambiguity of *chicken* is that there is an inclusion relationship: Entities that satisfy membership in the narrow sense also constitute membership in the broad sense – that is, any fowl that is a 'broiler' or a 'fryer' is also a 'chicken'. We can find other examples of this kind of set inclusion. In the world of dog breeders, *dog* not only denotes the species but may also refer just to the male (the female is the *bitch*). *Man* can be a collective term for humans or designate only an adult male. In an analogous fashion, the word *gay* can refer to a homosexual person of either sex or exclusively to a male (as in the conjoined expression 'gay and lesbian'). Moreover, proper names that have become common nouns often have this relationship, where the proper

Meanings of *chicken* and *bank*

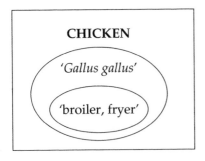
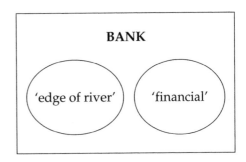

Figure 1.2   'Chicken' versus 'Bank'

name has become the subset or included member. This phenomenon is quite common for trade names that have turned generic – for example, *Kleenex®* (a specific brand/a tissue), *Jello®*, *Band-Aid®*, *Xerox®*, *Mace®*, *Velcro®*, *White-Out®*, *Rollerblade®* and *Hoover®*. And let us not forget that what I have been calling the broad and narrow senses of the word *ambiguity* belong here too: that which is lexically ambiguous (the narrow meaning) will be also uncertain or equivocal (the broad meaning). The fact that there is this kind of inclusion for the two meanings of *chicken* has importance for how the *Frigaliment* case would be decided. However, most instances of lexical ambiguity do not exemplify set inclusion. The two senses of *bank* – 'river bank' and 'financial bank' – are quite distinct and have few if any properties in common. The difference between the lexical ambiguity of *chicken* and that of *bank* is depicted in Figure 1.2.

Lexical ambiguity is not restricted solely to nouns. It can occur with all parts of speech. Consider the verb *to lease*, which has two distinct, but closely related, senses: (a) X leases land *to* Y (where X is the 'lessor') and (b) Y leases land *from* X (where Y is the 'lessee'). The following sentence then is potentially ambiguous: 'Anyone *leasing* property should consult Ordinance 613'. Is this advice intended for the lessor, for the lessee, or for both of them?

A similar ambiguity, where a word has almost opposite meanings, is possible for the verb *to sanction*, which can mean either (a) 'to approve' or (b) 'to punish' (in the legal sense). Again, the following sentence is potentially ambiguous: 'Such conduct is *sanctioned* by Statute 81B'.

Certain pronouns are particularly susceptible to misunderstanding. Consider the following sentence: 'The seller will convey the property to the buyer after *he* has paid the closing costs'. Who is supposed to pay these costs, the seller or the buyer? Now this particular 'ambiguity' of the pronoun *he* does not arise because of two distinct meanings, but because of its grammatical role. From a grammarian's perspective, the pronoun could have either noun (*seller* or *buyer*) as its antecedent – that is, the pronoun could *refer* back to either noun. The problem then is one of *reference*, and this brings us to our next topic.

Raffles: referential ambiguity

The case of *Raffles* deals with two vessels having the same name. Now, at first blush it may seem that the name *Peerless* is potentially ambiguous in a way analogous to the ambiguity of the word *chicken*: we have two different ships with the same name in the one case, and two different definitions of the same word in the other. Yet, linguistically, *Peerless* and *chicken* are quite different, most obviously because of their grammatical classifications. Although both are nouns, the former is a proper noun and the latter is a common noun. For this reason, it is more natural to refer to *Peerless* as a name, but to *chicken* as a word (as I have done throughout this text).

Let us consider some of the differences between these two classes of nouns. At a fairly superficial level they differ in their translatability from one language to another. Common nouns are readily translated, but proper names, aside from spelling variations, tend to be relatively stable from language to language, with the exception of certain fixed correspondences, such as Spanish *Julio* and English *Julius*. Yet, even here, it is unlikely that in an English-language newspaper the singer *Julio Iglesias* would ever be referred to as *Julius Iglesias* (or, even worse, *Julius Churches*). The exceptions to this generalization involve proper names, such as *the White House*, composed from words that occur freely as common nouns. These types of proper names are readily translated – for example, *la Casa Blanca* in Spanish or *la Maison Blanche* in French.

The different functions between proper names and common nouns have been of great interest to both philosophers and linguists. The British philosopher, John Stuart Mill, claimed that proper names are *denotative*, whereas common nouns are *connotative*.[12] According to Mill, proper names denote or point to the individuals or entities having that name, but they do not designate or imply any particular qualities or attributes of those entities. The purpose of a proper name is to enable one to talk about someone or something without relating anything specific about him, her, or it. On the other hand, a common noun like *chicken*, besides denoting an indefinite number of individuals of that type, connotes specific properties of an entity belonging to that class, such as a domesticated fowl, a producer of eggs, flightless, having feathers, used for food, etc. Whereas a proper name connotes nothing and therefore has no particular signification, other than it is a name and hence a means of referring to a specific person, place or thing, a common noun has meanings and it is precisely these meanings that dictionaries try to capture by means of their definitions.

Proper names are not the only class of words with a denotative function. Personal pronouns, such as *I, you, she,* etc. and the demonstrative pronouns – *this, that, these, those* – play a similar role: *I* refers uniquely to the speaker, *you* to the person or persons being addressed, and *she* to a feminine individual already established in the discourse. Moreover, a common noun that is preceded by a possessive article, a demonstrative article, or the definite article *the* also has this function. Suppose that I request that you go to *my* office and put *this* manuscript on *the* desk. I have referred to three unique entities – the office where I work, a particular manuscript that is before us, and a unique desk located in that office. Now, Mill does not deny that common nouns when preceded by certain articles have a denotative function in addition to their connotations or meanings. But he does claim the converse – that proper names can be only denotative and never have connotations. However, not everyone would agree with Mill.

The Danish linguist, Otto Jespersen, suggested that the relationship between proper names and common nouns is much more fluid than what appears from Mill's rigorous dichotomy.[13] Jespersen provides several cogent examples. Common nouns may be the source of proper names, as we noted with *the White House*. Other examples of this phenomenon include *the Blue Grotto* on the island of Capri, *the Black Forest* in Germany and *the Capitol* and *the Mall* in Washington. Note that the definite article *the* is often retained as part of the name.

Conversely, proper names can turn into common nouns and in the process they may lose their orthographic capitalization. Recall the examples of *xerox, jello, band-aid, kleenex, mace, velcro, white-out, rollerblade* and British *hoover*. As proper names these words were originally associated with new products. There may have been no common word for the product and so it became known by the proper name. Even where a common expression may have existed or been coined from the outset, either it never gained widespread currency, such as *tissue* for *kleenex* in the United States, or else it was awkward at best, such as *gelatin dessert* for *jello, adhesive bandage* for *band-aid, self-defense spray* for *mace, hook and loop fastener* for *velcro* or *in-line skates* for *rollerblades* (note the pluralization). On more than one occasion the transition from proper name to common noun has concerned the law. Proper names as well as the product names of commercial companies are registered or trade-marked. Hence, when a competitor with a similar product begins to use the trade-marked name in its advertising, inevitably a lawsuit will follow. Courts have had to decide whether what began as a proper name, such as *Band-Aid*® or *Kleenex*®, has become sufficiently integrated into the language as a general vocabulary item and should be available for ordinary use.[14] What the court must determine essentially is whether a new common noun has entered the language.

Mill's claim that a proper name is purely denotative meant, of course, that unlike a common noun, it lacks any connotation. Jespersen also argued against this position. He noted that proper nouns often take on connotations associated with specific properties attributed to the referent of the name. The proper noun with its implicit connotations is then available for describing a different but similar kind of entity. Consider the following two sentences: 'Prague has become *the new Paris* of Europe'; and 'Sadam Hussein was *another Hitler*'. For the first sentence, features of Paris, such as its wide boulevards, its outdoor cafés, and its sophisticated lifestyle are now associated with Prague, and in the second sentence, the cruelty and despotism of Hitler are traits characterizing Sadam. When proper names are used in this fashion they are generally accompanied by an article or other kind of modifier (i.e. *the new* Paris; *another* Hitler).

In spite of Jespersen's valid observations that proper names and common nouns are not so categorically separate as claimed by Mill, the latter's distinction between denotation and connotation – between *reference* and *sense* – still provides a useful starting point for understanding the crucial difference between a name like *Peerless* and a word like *chicken*.

One need only consult a dictionary of English to determine that the word *chicken* does indeed have the two senses that were under dispute in the *Frigaliment* case. The potential ambiguity is precisely what Judge Friendly discovered when he consulted his dictionary. But the protagonists in *Raffles* could have no such luck. Who would ever think to look up the name *Peerless*? But one might object that this example is unfair. What about less obscure names? To be sure, there are many dictionaries and other kinds of reference works that do include proper names. For example, one of those references might state that Paris is a city located in the north central region of France and that it is the capital and largest city of that country. A good gazetteer would also note that in Texas there is a much smaller city with the same name. These characterizations are not definitions in the strict sense of the word, but rather they represent an attempt to situate the various 'Parises' geographically or politically. The descriptions serve as verbal pointers indicating the location of these places. Is the name *Paris* then potentially ambiguous? Not according to the narrow sense of 'ambiguity', where a word is lexically ambiguous if there is more than one meaning. The name *Paris*, when designating more than one entity with that name, may present a problem of reference so that one may not be entirely sure to which city the name refers, but it is not a word exemplifying multiple meanings. When an uncertainty of reference arises, as it did in the *Raffles* case, the uncertainty engendered is distinct from that of lexical ambiguity. Rather the misunderstanding is due to *referential indeterminacy* or *referential ambiguity* (so long as the latter term is not confused with *lexical ambiguity*). Figure 1.3 depicts the various characteristics attributed to the two classes of nouns.

ICC: vagueness of categorization

Let us turn now to the case involving the Interstate Commerce Commission (ICC), where the issue is whether dressed and eviscerated chickens are manufactured products. The Department of Agriculture suggested that, for the purpose of the agricultural exemption, a definition of *manufacture* that had been approved in a separate case involving fruit growers was appropriate here for determining whether a commodity is a *manufactured product*.

'Manufacture,' as well defined by the *Century Dictionary*, is 'the production of articles for use from raw or prepared materials by giving to these materials new forms, qualities, properties, or combinations, whether by

Common versus proper nouns

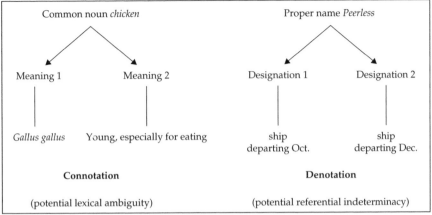

Figure 1.3   'Chicken' versus 'Peerless'

hand–labor or by machinery'; also 'anything made for use from raw or prepared materials'.[15]

It is the contention of the Department of Agriculture that dressed poultry is not a manufactured product according to this definition. The ICC, accepting the same definition, is just as adamant in its claim that dressed poultry is a manufactured product. Is the word *manufacture* (or *manufactured*) ambiguous? Clearly, there are *not* two distinct objective meanings of the word *manufacture*, one that accords precisely with the ICC position and the other with that of the farmers. Nor is there any dictionary that is ever likely to have anything to say about dressed poultry within its definitions of *manufacture*. How is it possible, then, for each side to maintain vehemently its position vis-à-vis a definition that both sides find acceptable?

This misunderstanding arises not in the definition itself but in the vagueness of its application to the classification of particular items. For the class of *manufactured products*, it is indisputable that my computer and the desk it sits on belong to this category, and that a live chicken and a head of lettuce do not. Now, if we were to set up a scale labelled *unmanufactured* at the left end and *manufactured* at the right end, we would have no difficulty in placing the chicken and the lettuce at the very left end of this scale and in situating the computer and the desk at the very right end. But in between these two clear end points there extends an intermediate area, where there is no longer complete certainty and where vagueness enters. Here entities will be classified differently by different individuals. Some persons may assign an entity closer to the left edge, whereas others may place the same entity closer to the right. As an exercise, consider the following list of items in Figure 1.4, all of which involve dead chickens in some form or another. At what point does an entity become a *manufactured product*?

Which items are *manufactured products*?

(a) a whole chicken with its feathers still on and with head, feet and innards intact

(b) a whole chicken that is plucked but still retaining head, feet and innards

(c) a whole chicken plucked (dressed) and eviscerated, but with head and feet

(d) a whole fresh chicken dressed, eviscerated, and without head or feet

(e) same as (d) but frozen

(f) a whole chicken cut into pieces, packaged and wrapped in cellophane (as sold in the typical supermarket)

(g) a dozen raw chicken wings, packaged and wrapped in cellophane

(h) a dozen precooked hot wings (with a spicy sauce) packaged and frozen

Figure 1.4 *Agricultural commodity* or *manufactured product?*

In the debate over the classification of dressed and eviscerated poultry (items (c) to (e) in Figure 1.4), the ICC had placed the entities towards the *manufactured* end of the scale, whereas the Department of Agriculture had put them closer to the *unmanufactured* end. Such impassioned disputes regarding classification and categorization are by no means unusual. Recall the infamous statement of former US President Clinton: 'I never had a sexual relationship with that woman'. Which of the following physical acts constitute 'having a sexual relationship' – 'holding hands', 'kissing on the lips', 'touching the genitals', 'oral sex', 'sexual intercourse'? Neither Clinton nor 'that woman' ever acknowledged engaging in intercourse. Would Clinton have been lying if he considered only the final item of this list to be a 'sexual relationship'? (Actually, though, his denial was based on a bizarre definition of 'sexual relationship' presented to him during his deposition in the *Jones* v. *Clinton* case: 'a person engages in "sexual relations" when the person knowingly engages in or causes contact with the [erogenous zones] of any person with an intent to arouse or gratify the sexual desire of any person'.)[16]

The problem of classification has captivated philosophers, psychologists and linguists. The classical notion of categorization goes back to early Greek philosophy. Aristotle made a distinction between the *essence* of a thing and its *accidents*. The essential properties are those that are *necessary* and *sufficient* for defining a category and they are the properties that all members of the category must share. For example, an entity belonging to the category *bird* has 'feathers, wings, a beak and scaly feet'. These particular properties are necessary for determining whether a creature belongs to this category, and they are sufficient for eliminating any entity not belonging to it. On the other hand, accidental properties – such as 'nest-building' and 'flight' – although characteristic of many birds, are not germane for determining whether a creature belongs to the category. Thus, penguins, which neither build nests nor fly, are classified as birds, but bats, although they fly, are not. The classical view assigns entities to one of two opposing sets: those entities belonging to a category and those excluded from it. Moreover, all members of a category are considered to be of equal status.

Since the 1970s, cognitive psychologists and linguists have been investigating the nature and structure of classificatory systems. These researchers claim that the classical approach is no longer tenable. They reject the view that a category is defined exclusively by its essential properties. Nor do they accept the idea that all members of a category have equal status. Rather there are *prototypes*.[17] The concept of 'prototype' has engendered an alternative theory bearing its name. According to prototype theory, some entities are judged as better exemplars of a category than others. Thus, wrens and robins are considered to be prototypical 'birds', but chickens, penguins and ostriches, being of larger size, flightless and non-arboreal, are regarded as poorer representatives of this category. Hence, a prototypical bird is small, is a nest-builder, sings, flies and is neither a raptor nor a fowl. In fact, the prototypical bird has some of the very properties that would be designated as accidental within the classical perspective. Eleanor Rosch, a cognitive psychologist noted for her pioneering work in prototype theory, has investigated the structure of various categories, including that of *bird*.[18] In an endeavour to validate the psychological reality of prototypes, she asked subjects to rate the degree to which an entity was a good exemplar of a category and she found a high degree of consistency between their responses. Furthermore, in experiments testing reaction time, it took subjects less time to verify that a robin is a bird than to confirm that a duck is one.

Let us see how the notion of prototype is applicable to the *ICC* case. We have the category of *manufactured product*. Now, computers and desks are prototypical manufactured products, but loose-cut diamonds and packaged peeled garlic are inferior examples, whereas pebbles, flowers and live chickens are clearly outside of the category. We wish to decide whether dressed and eviscerated chickens are members. Now the entities in question are by no means prototypical. Consequently, there are two alternatives: either they are nonprototypical but nonetheless still members of the category (like 'ostriches' vis-à-vis *birds*), which is the position maintained by the ICC, or else they are entirely outside of the category (like 'bats' vis-à-vis *birds*), which is the view of the agricultural people. The misunderstanding in the *ICC* case is due neither to lexical ambiguity nor to referential indeterminacy, but rather it has to do with *vagueness of categorization*.

It is even possible to regard the 'chicken' issue in *Frigaliment* as a problem of categorization. Assume that we set up a category of *chickens suitable for cooking*. Then broilers and fryers would be prototypical exemplars of this category, but day-old chicks, old roosters, and stewing hens would not be. Viewing the issue in this way provides an additonal perspective on the *Frigaliment* controversy. The buyer expected to receive exclusively 'prototypical' chickens, whereas the seller was convinced he was abiding by the contract so long as he provided legitimate members of the category. Although it is possible to analyse *Frigaliment* as a dispute about categorization, I prefer the analysis involving lexical ambiguity. It is the latter that the court adopts. From the outset Judge Friendly inquires into the definition of *chicken*, and clearly, as he discovered by consulting a dictionary, the word indeed has the two meanings that are in dispute.

Let us summarize the similarities and differences between the three cases that we have been examining. Although they have words or terms that are open to more than one interpretation, they illustrate 'ambiguity' only in the rather general or broad sense that where there is more than one interpretation, *ipso facto* there will be a certain indefiniteness or lack of clarity. On closer scrutiny, the nature of the misunderstanding is by no means of the same type: In *Frigaliment*, the equivocal meaning of the word *chicken* is attributed to lexical ambiguity; in *Raffles*, the uncertainty of the application of the name *Peerless* results from referential indeterminacy; and in the *ICC* case, the indecisiveness concerning the assignment of items to the class of *manufactured products* occurs because of vagueness of categorization.

Analysis of the misunderstandings

Although the three cases differ in regard to the nature of the misunder-standing, nonetheless there is still a common structure underlying them. They all deal with the relation of language to some real-world situation. At issue for each case is how or whether the definition or reference of a term applies to specific entities. Does the word *chicken*, appearing in a contract for the sale of poultry, include stewing fowl or not? Does the name *Peerless*, designating a ship sailing with goods from Bombay to Liverpool, refer to a vessel departing in October or to a different one leaving in December? Does the expression *manufactured product*, as used in an act governing the trans-portation of goods by certificated carriers, apply to dressed and eviscerated poultry? How did the courts answer these questions?

Frigaliment *and other similar cases*

Treatises discussing contract law frequently make reference to two oppos-ing theories: the *objective theory* of contracts and the *subjective theory*.[19] The objective theory takes the position that the words used in an agreement are sufficient for interpreting the contract and that the court need not and should not inquire into the subjective intentions of the parties – that is, the way they may have thought they were using those words. The legal scholar, Arthur Corbin, although himself not an advocate of the objective theory, summarized it beautifully in an article attacking this position:

> Contracting parties must be made to know that it is their written words that constitute their contract, not their intentions that they try to express in the words. They, not the court, have chosen the words; and they,

not the court, have made the contract. Its legal operation must be in accordance with the meaning that the words convey to the court, not the meaning that they intend to convey.[20]

A strict adherence to this position leads to adoption of the *plain-meaning rule*. For a contract that appears to be complete (i.e. an integration) and that is not ambiguous on its surface, the court must interpret the words with their ordinary meaning and must not resort to any extrinsic evidence for ascertaining the intent of one or both parties.[21] But there is an exception. Extrinsic evidence, or what the law calls *parol evidence*, will be admissible whenever the contract itself is unclear or ambiguous and the court is unable to arrive at an interpretation entirely from the language within the 'four corners' of the document. Extrinsic evidence can take various forms, such as previous agreements by the parties, written correspondence between them, opinions of experts, trade usage and even direct inquiries about the parties' intentions and their understanding of the meanings of terms. The purpose of parol evidence is not to alter a contract but to assist the judge in interpreting it.

The subjective theory of contract, on the other hand, requires that there be a *meeting of the minds* – that without an agreement of intention, properly expressed, a contract has never been created. Judges adhering to this doctrine have no qualms about admitting extrinsic evidence in order to ascertain each party's intent, even where the parties thought that they had created a final expression of their agreement. In any case, regardless of the theory to which one subscribes, it happens that the parties to a contract, when drawing it up, may think that they have reached agreement, and only subsequently do they learn that each has a different interpretation of some crucial term or terms. It is this discrepancy in belief, known in contract law as a *misunderstanding*, that ultimately brings the two disputants to court.

When the seller ships stewing fowl to the buyer in the *Frigaliment* case, there ensues a major misunderstanding: the plaintiff intends for the term *chicken* to refer to birds no larger than broilers or fryers, whereas the defendant believes that *chicken* includes stewing fowl as well. Judge Friendly begins his discussion of the case with a comment about the objective theory:

> Assuming that both parties were acting in good faith, the case nicely illustrates [Oliver Wendell] Holmes' remark 'that the making of a contract depends not on the agreement of two minds in one intention, but on the agreement of two sets of external signs – not on the parties' having *meant* the same thing but on their having *said* the same thing'. [empahases in the original][22]

Judge Friendly continues: 'Since the word "chicken" standing alone is ambiguous, I turn first to see whether the contract itself offers any aid to its interpretation'.[23] There were actually two separate contracts, differing only with respect to the amount of each kind of chicken and its price. However, the nature of the dispute and the legal issues remain the same. The contract stated that the New York firm would sell to the Swiss corporation:

> US Fresh Frozen Chicken, Grade A, Government Inspected, Eviscerated
> 2½–3 lbs. and 1½–2 lbs. each
> all chicken individually wrapped in cryovac, packed in secured fiber cartons or wooden boxes suitable for export
> 75,000 lbs. 2½–3 *lbs*........@$33.00
> 25,000 lbs. 1½–2 *lbs*........@$36.50
> per 100 lbs. FAS New York
> scheduled May 10, 1957 pursuant to instructions from Penson & Co., New York.[24]

After examining the 'four corners' of the contract, Judge Friendly could find nothing within the written lines indicating that the larger-size birds were to be broilers and fryers and not stewing chickens. Extrinsic evidence was then admissible.

The extrinsic evidence begins with an interesting linguistic quirk. The plaintiff asserts that preliminary communications were all in German, a language known by both parties. The plaintiff claims to have used intentionally within its German correspondence the English word *chicken* because of its understanding that the English word meant 'young chicken' and it was for that reason that the plaintiff had eschewed the German word *Huhn*, which includes both stewing chickens (*Suppenhuhn*) and broilers (*Brathuhn*). The defendant then pointed out that the plaintiff attempted to sell some of the larger birds as *poulets* (was this in French-speaking Switzerland?) and it was only after customers started complaining, that the plaintiff came forth with his contention that *chicken* meant 'young chicken'. The court did not attach much credence to this allegation by the defendant.

The plaintiff then called forth three witnesses to support its assertion that there was an established trade usage that favoured its interpretation of *chicken*. One of the witnesses, a resident buyer in New York for a chain of Swiss cooperatives, testified that for him *chicken* meant a 'broiler', but he admitted under oath that in his own dealings he was careful to specify 'broiler' when that was what he wanted. The other two witnesses were more consistent in their beliefs and stated that, within the trade, *chicken* did not include stewing fowl.

The defendant claimed to be new to the chicken business and at the time of making the contract was unaware of any particular trade usage. Nonetheless, it had no difficulty in finding witnesses in support of its interpretation. One of them, an operator of a chicken-eviscerating plant in New Jersey, testified that 'chicken is everything except a goose, a duck, and a turkey. Everything is a chicken, but then you have to say, you have to specify which category you want or that you are talking about'.[25] A second witness for the defendant maintained that in the trade *chicken* encompassed all classifications. The defendant's third witness held that he would consider a chicken to be anything categorized as *chicken* within the regulations of the Department of Agriculture, whose classification includes fowl along with broilers and fryers, although the contract made no reference to the Department's classification. Finally, the defendant argued that broilers and fryers were not available at the cheaper price charged for the larger birds and that the plaintiff should have been aware of market conditions and known that it would not be receiving younger birds at that price.

After considering all this extrinsic evidence, what did Judge Friendly conclude? The plaintiff's claim for the narrow sense of *chicken* certainly corresponded with one of the objective meanings found in dictionaries and there was even some support from trade usage, but one arrives at similar observations in regard to the broad meaning of *chicken* as claimed by the defendant. Hence, both positions are more or less equally tenable. But since the plaintiff was the one who had brought suit, it had the burden of showing that, in the contract, *chicken* was to be interpreted with a clear preference for the narrow meaning as opposed to the broad one. Having failed to do so, the plaintiff did not prevail.

Previously, I noted that there is an inclusion relationship between the narrow meaning of *chicken* and the broad one – that is, anything that is a member of the class of broilers or fryers is also a member of the class of chickens (*Gallus gallus*). The same inclusion relationship holds, of course, for the members of the class of stewing fowl. Nonetheless, although stewing chickens were sent to the plaintiff, it did not receive geese, ducks or turkeys instead of chickens (in the broad sense). To that extent, the terms of the contract were satisfied. I believe that the inclusion relationship is an important element in the decision of this case. There are other court cases where the inclusion element is also relevant.

Cows or heifers?

There is another case remarkably similar to *Frigaliment*.[26] The contract specified '134 head of Cows'. Buyer understood *cows* to mean mature female bovines that had produced calves. Seller meant any female bovine including heifers, which are young females that have never calved. The buyer's interpretation would be the narrow meaning, whereas the seller's would be the broad one. Raper (that's his name), the appeals judge that wrote the opinion, observed that 'the whole case revolves around what the parties intended by the use of the word "cow" in describing the subject matter of the contract. Taken by itself it has any number of meanings'. He then cited the meanings relevant to the case that he found in *Webster's Third New International Dictionary*, unabridged:

1a: the mature female of wild or domestic cattle of the genus *Bos*, or any of the various animals the male of which is called *bull*;
 b: a domestic bovine animal regardless of its sex or age . . .[27]

Finding that the term *cow* as it appeared in the contract was lexically ambiguous, the judge ordered that the case be remanded back to the lower court for retrial.

Carrying a firearm

Inclusion is not restricted solely to entities, such as chickens and cows, but it applies as well to activities. The US Supreme Court had to interpret the meaning of the expression, *carries a firearm*. This phrase appeared in a federal statute that imposed a mandatory prison term of five years on anyone who used or carried a firearm in the commission of a drug-trafficking crime. There were two cases. In one of them, the defendant was caught transporting marijuana in his truck and during a search of the vehicle the police found a handgun that had been locked in the glove box. In the other case, the defendants, who were engaged in the trafficking of cocaine, had placed several guns in the trunk of their car. In both trials the lower courts had found that the defendants had been carrying firearms in violation of the statute. Due to their similarity, the Supreme Court consolidated the two cases.[28]

The defendants in their appeals argued for a narrow interpretation, maintaining that the phrase *carries a firearm* is limited to the kind of carrying done with the hands or on the person. The lower courts, on the other hand, had arrived at the broad meaning, stating that the phrase covers the kind of carrying that encompasses personally transporting, whether on one's body or in a vehicle. The Supreme Court in its review of the cases remarked:

> Although the word 'carry' has many different meanings, only two are relevant here. When one uses the word in the first, or primary, meaning, one can, as a matter of ordinary English, 'carry firearms' in a wagon, car, truck, or other vehicle that one accompanies. When one uses the word in a different, rather special, way, to mean, for example, 'bearing' or (in slang) 'packing' (as in 'packing a gun'), the matter is less clear. But . . . we believe Congress intended to use the word in its primary sense and not in this latter, special way.[29]

The court, in support of the broad sense of *carry*, cites dictionaries, well-known authors and even the popular press. They note that the first meaning listed in the *Oxford English Dictionary* (OED) is 'convey, originally by cart or wagon, hence in any vehicle, by ship, on horseback, etc'. The etymology of the word explains this first citation. The *OED* traces its origin back to Old French *carier* and Late Latin *caricare*, which meant 'to convey in a cart'. Then the court looks to the use of this word by some famous authors. Defoe's *Robinson Crusoe* says: 'with my boat, I carry'd away every Thing'; and Melville, in *Moby Dick*, writes that the owners of Queequeg's ship 'had lent him a [wheelbarrow], in which to carry his heavy chest to the boarding-house'. Although these examples do not explicitly refer to the carrying of guns, there is nothing special about the use of the word *carry* by these authors that would exclude weapons as the objects to be carried. The court states: 'Robinson Crusoe might have carried a gun in his boat; [and] Queequeg might have borrowed a wheelbarrow in which to carry, not a chest, but a harpoon'.[30] The court also cites several usages from newspapers. For example, the *New York Times* had a story about an 'ex-con' who 'arrives home driving a stolen car and carrying a load of handguns'.

The court does not deny that there are probably just as many definitions and examples for the narrow meaning. As an illustration, they cite a definition for the phrase *carry arms or weapons* that is given in *Black's Law Dictionary*:

> [T]o wear, bear or carry them upon the person or in the clothing or in a pocket, for the purpose of use, or for the purpose of being armed and ready for offensive or defensive action in case of conflict with another person.[31]

But the court, regardless of competing definitions, does not believe that Congress in creating the statute had intended for *carry* to be circumscribed to its narrow sense of being carried on the person.

Because it is the function of the judicial branch to interpret the laws promulgated by the legislature, the question facing the court becomes: what meaning did Congress intend for the phrase *carrying a firearm*? To arrive at an answer the court considers the statute's purpose and its legislative history, a procedure reminiscent of the admission of extrinsic evidence in a contracts case. The purpose of the statute was to discourage the 'dangerous combination' of 'drugs and guns'. Anyone involved in drug dealing is encouraged to leave his or her firearms at home. Congress had no reason to treat more benevolently the trafficker driving to a drug sale with a gun in the trunk of his car than the trafficker going on foot with a gun in a holster strapped around her waist. After looking at the legislative history of this statute and other similar ones, the court concludes that Congress never intended for the expression *carry a firearm* to be interpreted in its narrow sense.

The cases that we have just reviewed all deal with the kind of lexical ambiguity where there is an inclusion relation – where entities encompassed under the narrow meaning are a subset of the broad meaning. The fact that many lawsuits exemplify inclusion is not surprising, due to the similarity beween the things having this kind of relationship and consequently the likelihood of one of the parties having in mind entities belonging exclusively to the subset. However, not all cases of lexical ambiguity are necessarily of this type.

A lost ring

Mr and Mrs Viviano were dining in a restaurant.[32] During the meal Mrs Viviano got up to go the ladies' room. She placed her handbag and her engagement ring on the sink. After washing her hands, she retrieved her handbag but failed to take her ring. It was only after leaving the restaurant that she realized that the ring was missing. The couple rushed back to the restaurant to look for the ring but could not find it. They subsequently placed a claim with their insurance company requesting compensation for accidental loss. The insurer denied coverage alluding to an exclusion clause in the policy that stated that 'there shall be no coverage under this policy if the article insured is lost, stolen or damaged in any way when not in the *care, custody and control* of the named insured . . .' (emphasis added). The insurance company took the position that Mrs Viviano had 'voluntarily parted with or mislaid' the ring; once it was no longer on her finger it ceased to be under her *care, custody and control*. The Vivianos insisted that the ring was lost (and not 'voluntarily parted with') and that at no time did Mrs Viviano relinquish *care, custody and control*, as they understood this phrase to mean. Based on the Vivianos' pleading, the court acknowledged that the language of the clause was ambiguous and that there was more than one conceivable interpretation.

Let us consider two of the several meanings of the noun *care*. One of them, advantageous to the insurance company, is 'caution; watchfullness; close attention' as in 'to take care when crossing a street'.[33] According to this sense, was Mrs Viviano 'careless' when she took off her ring and left it on the sink – hence, not taking proper care? Another meaning of *care*, one more favourable to Mrs Viviano, is 'watchful regard or attention; a liking or regard (for)' as in 'to take care of one's children'. Did Mrs Viviano care for her ring in this sense? After all, she had no intention of abandoning this piece of jewellery, and she took the ring off so as not to get it wet or soapy, or to mar its appearance.

In the end, the court did not actually delve into each of the parties' precise meanings of the phrase *care, custody, and control* because of two factors that made this semantic investigation unnecessary. The Vivianos had taken out a 'personal property floater policy', which is often used to cover the loss of jewellery. This type of policy reimburses the insured even where the loss is due to negligence, so long as no fraud is involved. Moreover, the maxim of *contra proferentem* was applicable to the language of this policy. The literal meaning of this Latin expression is: 'against the one proffering something'. The maxim favours a plaintiff suing an insurance company where ambiguity exists in the interpretation of the policy. Now, why should the insured benefit in this way? When two private individuals draw up a contract (as the two parties did in *Frigaliment*), they are free to state their own terms, so that both parties then have a share in the wording of the document. This give-and-take in reaching an agreement does not happen with insurance contracts. The insurance company has prepared the written policy with its own interests in view. The client has no input in the preparation and has no choice but to 'take it or leave it'. Now, because these giant companies have the financial means for hiring teams of lawyers (and even an occasional linguist), they are expected to create an impeccably tight document, one where the terms are absolutely clearly defined and where no ambiguity or misunderstanding ever arises. Subsequently, though, if an insured is able to demonstrate to the court that there is an alternative, but plausible, interpretation of some aspect of the wording relevant to his or her claim, then the court will settle the contract in favour of the insured and against the insurer. Putting all these various reasons together, the court was able to affirm:

> [I]t is clear . . . that the phrase [care, custody, and control] is one which is subject to various meanings depending upon the factual situation that may arise . . . Based upon the foregoing and upon the fact that this is a comprehensive all-risk policy for which coverage may arise even when the insured is negligent and also upon the public policy of this State to construe an insurance policy least favorably against the drafter if ambiguity is found, this court finds that the engagement ring in question was lost while in the care, custody, and control of the plaintiff . . .[34]

Raffles *and other similar cases*

Goods were to be transported on a ship called the *Peerless* sailing from India to the UK. When it arrived at Liverpool the defendants refused acceptance. The plaintiff sued. The contract stipulated:

> [T]hat the plaintiff should sell to the defendants, and the defendants buy of the plaintiff, certain goods, to wit, 125 bales of Surat cotton . . ., to arrive ex 'Peerless' from Bombay; . . . and that the defendants would pay the plaintiff for the same at a certain rate, to wit, 17¼ d. per pound, within a certain time then agreed upon after the arrival of the said goods in England.[35]

Why did the defendants refuse to accept the merchandise or to pay for it? After all, the proper goods did arrive in England from Bombay on a ship called the *Peerless*, exactly as the contract had specified, and, moreover, the plaintiff was prepared to deliver the merchandise. In their plea, the defendants averred that a ship called *Peerless* had left Bombay in October and they were ready and willing to accept the merchandise when that ship arrived in England. Instead, the goods arrived on a different ship, coincidentally bearing the same name, one that left in December. The plaintiff retorted that it had always intended to transport the goods on this other *Peerless* and so it had acted in good faith. The testimony revealed that each party had a different *Peerless* in mind, and, moreover, was unaware of the other's intention. As the counsel for the defendants pointed out to the court, 'the moment it appears that two ships called *Peerless* were about to sail from Bombay there is a latent ambiguity, and parol evidence may be given for the purpose of shewing [sic] that the defendant meant one *Peerless*, and the plaintiff another'.[36]

Judges sometimes make a distinction between *latent ambiguity* and *patent ambiguity*. The latter applies when words in an agreement have more than one objective meaning. The term *chicken*, as it occurs in the *Frigaliment* contract, is an excellent example of patent ambiguity. Judge Friendly was able to find in his dictionary the two contested definitions of *chicken*. In latent ambiguity, on the other hand, the disputed term is not potentially ambiguous on the face of the document, but the so-called 'ambiguity' arises only because of the particular facts of the situation. In *Raffles*, the fact that there were two ships called *Peerless* could not be ascertained from a perusal of the words in the contract but became known only when two different ships with the same name had left India and arrived in England on substantially different dates. In any case, once the court was willing to recognize the 'ambiguity', parol evidence would be admissible. The court subsequently concluded that there was 'no consensus ad idem, and therefore no binding contract' – that is, there was no *meeting of the minds* and so the contract was dissolved. Each party could walk away and anyone who had suffered damages had to bear the loss.

It is significant that the referential ambiguity in the *Raffles* case involves reference to two entities equally obscure. Had one of the ships been well known and the other not, the interpretation would surely have been in favour of the well-known vessel. Suppose I am selling raffle tickets for a voyage on the *Queen Mary II*. It just so happens that I own a rowing boat that I have named the *Queen Mary II*, but you are unaware of its existence. You win the raffle expecting a cruise on an ocean liner, but I inform you that you have won a trip on my rowing boat. The court would in all likelihood embrace your interpretation of the *Queen Mary II* or, even more likely, conclude that I have acted fraudulently.

We regarded the decision in *Frigaliment* as a prime example of the objective theory of contracts. Judge Friendly scrutinized the 'four corners' of the contract, and only after determining that the document itself gave no clue as to which meaning of *chicken* was meant did he then allow extrinsic evidence to enter the picture. The *Raffles* case, on the other hand, serves as a good example of the subjective theory. The court dissolved the contract precisely because of the subjectivity on the part of each side regarding its interpretation of the reference to the *Peerless*. However, Oliver Wendall Holmes, the jurist that was mentioned in our discussion of *Frigaliment*, was a staunch advocate of the objective theory. He in fact had a very different analysis of the *Raffles* case. Judge Friendly (in *Frigaliment*) had quoted Holmes as saying 'that the making of a contract depends not on the agreement of two minds in one intention, but on the agreement of two sets of external signs – not on the parties' having *meant* the same thing but on their having *said* the same thing'. It is this objective view (as opposed to the *Raffles* court's subjective one) that Holmes would advocate in his own analysis of *Raffles*. He maintained that the state of the parties' minds was of no consequence and that the import of the *Raffles* decision was 'not that the parties *meant* different things but that they *said* different things'.[37] Hence, according to Holmes, the contract was dissolved not because each party had a different *Peerless* 'in mind', but because the parties had different objective references for the name *Peerless*, as though they were actually employing 'two different words'. However, most legal scholars would probably not subscribe to Holmes' analysis of the *Raffles* case. The distinction between objective and subjective interpretations may look like nit-picking. After all, in spite of this philosophical controversy, the various analysts all reach the same conclusion – namely, that there is no contract. Yet these philosophical differences do influence how judges relate to the parties and to the nature of their dispute.

Two streets with the same name

Just a few short years after *Raffles*, but this time on the opposite side of the Atlantic, another case of referential indeterminacy transpired. It never acquired the notoriety of *Raffles*; yet this case is hauntingly similar.[38] The contract was for property situated on Prospect Street in Waltham, Massachusetts. The defendant expected to get land located on a different Prospect Street, coincidentally also in the town of Waltham. The defendant contended that the land that he had agreed to purchase was a long way off and was in no way connected with what was mentioned in the deed. The judge instructed the jury that, 'if the defendant was negotiating for one thing and the plaintiff was selling another thing, and if their minds did not agree as to the subject matter of the sale, they could not be said to have agreed and to have made a contract'. The jury, in a decision analogous to *Raffles*, returned a verdict for the defendant. Here, too, there was deemed to be no meeting of the minds.

The coins in a coin collection

Referential indeterminacy does not involve only proper nouns – such as ship names and street names. Recall that common nouns preceded by definite or demonstrative articles may also have this function. A fascinating case of this sort involved a coin collection.[39] Dr Oswald, the plaintiff, was a coin collector from Switzerland. Mrs Allen, the defendant, owned a valuable collection of Swiss coins. Dr Oswald was interested in the coins and arranged to meet with Mrs Allen to look over her collection. In actuality there were two different collections, which she referred to as '*the* Swiss Coin Collection' and '*the* Rarity Coin Collection'. They were kept in separate vault boxes at her bank. Both collections contained Swiss coins. After a round of negotiations, the two parties agreed on a price of $50,000 for the Swiss coins. When it came time to consummate the transaction there was a gross misunderstanding. Dr Oswald thought he would be getting the Swiss coins from both collections, whereas Mrs Allen had intended to sell him only those coins in the Swiss Coin collection. The court had no choice but to concede that there was referential ambiguity. Did the phrase *Swiss coins* refer only to those located in the Swiss Coin Collection or to those from both collections? Adopting the rule of *Raffles* v. *Wichelhaus*, the court concluded that there was no *consensus ad idem*, and hence no valid agreement. Again, it was the defendant who prevailed, if only by default.

One job site or multiple sites?

One should not jump to the conclusion that all cases involving referential ambiguity lead to situations where there is no 'meeting of the minds'. There may be parol evidence that will tip the scale in favour of one of the parties. One such case is concerned with the charge of an unfair labour practice.[40] Commonwealth Communication, Inc. (CCI), a Pennsylvania company providing telephone and telecommunications services, received a sub contract to perform telephone cabling work at the Philadelphia airport. The company that subcontracted to CCI had an agreement with Local 98, a union, to hire only union members and it encouraged CCI to work with the union on the airport project. Subsequently, Local 98 representatives claimed to have noticed CCI trucks at job sites other than at the airport and to have found non-union employees working at those sites. Local 98 then sent to CCI a written request for information on all jobs performed by CCI employees working anywhere within the union's jurisdiction. CCI responded by furnishing information relating only to the airport job and declined to honour the request pertaining to any of the other jobs. The union then filed a charge of unfair labour practice. Local 98 claimed that the collective-bargaining agreement with CCI referred to all job sites within the union's geographical jurisdiction, while CCI maintained that the agreement only applied to the airport site. An administrative law judge found that the agreement was ambiguous as to the 'scope of the unit' and consequently was willing to consider parol evidence. On the basis of that evidence, which comprised mostly oral agreements between the parties, the judge ruled that the contract was valid only for the airport jobs. The National Labor Relations Board subsequently reversed that decision and concluded that the union did indeed represent workers at all job sites within its jurisdiction. The case then landed before the appeals court.

The main issue before the court is to determine whether the agreement contained referential ambiguity. Does it refer to multiple job sites or uniquely to the airport site? The court finds that there is 'more than one reasonable reading of the parties' agreement', and consequently 'the agreement is ambiguous on the question of the scope of the unit. We must therefore look beyond the written agreement, and consider extrinsic evidence on the question'. It concludes: 'We find that this extrinsic evidence makes clear that the parties understood the scope of the agreement to be limited to the airport job. Therefore, we hold that the Board erred in concluding that the bargaining unit covered by the disputed agreement is multisite in scope'.[41]

ICC and other similar cases

Is a dressed eviscerated chicken a *manufactured product*? This question came before the federal district court in the state of Iowa.[42] The ICC was of the opinion that dressed chickens are manufactured products and must be transported by certificated trucks, whose licensing is under its jurisdiction. The Department of Agriculture and farm groups, on the other hand, maintained that dressed poultry is to be classified as an *agricultural commodity* (and not a *manufactured product*) and therefore can be transported by uncertificated carriers, because an Act of Congress had exempted agricultural commodities from the requirement of ICC certification. The relevant part of the Act, section 203(b)(6), exempts:

> [M]otor vehicles used in carrying property consisting of ordinary livestock, fish (including shell fish), or agricultural (including horticultural) commodities (*not including manufactured products thereof*) [emphasis added], if such motor vehicles are not used in carrying any other property, or passengers, for compensation.[43]

Previous to the lawsuit, the ICC had set up its own commission to find an answer to the question of whether a dressed eviscerated chicken is a *manufactured product*. A group of scientists stated that 'chickens and turkeys, New York dressed, drawn, eviscerated, cut up, or frozen [are] unmanufactured agricultural commodities . . . [But] such treatments as smoking, cooking, and canning . . . are said to cause the fowl to become a manufactured product'.[44] The issue is not whether an agricultural commodity has been subjected to some type of processing, but 'whether, as the result of processing, such "agricultural commodity" has been so changed that a new and distinctive commodity or article is produced'.[45] The ICC's own commissioner concurred with much of the report. He stated:

> The dressing and cutting into pieces of a chicken or a turkey does not result in the production of a distinctive article having any new characteristics or uses. It is still an agricultural commodity. Surely the Thanksgiving turkey which the farmer's wife so carefully stuffs and places in the oven is not a manufactured product.[46]

The commissioner made an astute linguistic observation: 'Chickens, ducks, geese, and guineas alive and after having been killed are still known by the same names'. On the other hand, in English, we have different names for some of the larger animals and the meat that is derived from them – for instance, *cow/beef, sheep/mutton, pig/pork*, where the names for the food items were borrowed from Norman French. (Apparently, William the Conqueror brought his French chefs along with him when he invaded England.) Interestingly, though, the meat products resulting from the slaughter of these mammals, such as steaks or chops, were not within the agricultural exemption to the ICC regulations and so were never part of the dispute between the ICC and the farmers. But then a steak hardly resembles the animal from which it comes in the same way that a drumstick does. From his statements it appears that the commissioner for the ICC favoured the agricultural people. Yet, it is amazing that in spite of this positive conclusion, the ICC reversed the very recommendation of its own commissioner. It is this reversal which brought the case to court.

The court laments the fact that the terms *agricultural commodities* and *manufactured products* were never defined in the Act. Although the word *manufactured* certainly has dictionary meanings and has been defined in other court cases, each party nonetheless contends that those definitions accord with its interpretation. The court takes the view that any attempt to deduce the meaning of *manufactured products* from general definitions is a futile endeavor that can only lead one into a 'semantic wilderness'. From a linguistic point of view the semantic enigma arises from *vagueness of categorization*. It is by no means obvious where one should place entities labelled as *dressed eviscerated poultry* along the bipolar scale of *unmanufactured/manufactured*. The Department of Agriculture veers towards the left end of this scale, whereas the ICC steers towards the right. The court seems situated somewhere in the middle, not knowing in which direction to turn, and so it must consider extrinsic evidence.

The court first looks for an administrative interpretation under the guise that a particular agency ought to have expertise in its field of specialization. The Department of Agriculture asserts that Congress has made it the expert in all things pertaining to agriculture and, therefore, it is the one that knows how poultry is to be classified. The ICC counters this assertion by claiming that because it is responsible for enforcing regulations pertaining to interstate trucking, its administrative interpretation of the provisions of section 203(b)(6) should be given greater weight. The court's hope of finding an acceptable administrative interpretation leads only to another standstill.

The court then turns to a different extrinsic aid – the legislative history. What was the intent of the legislature in enacting the various statutes? The parties were agreed that the purpose of the Act was to benefit the farmers. By using uncertificated trucks, the farmers are able to transport their goods more rapidly and at a much lower cost. Rapid transport and lowered cost also benefit consumers. Throughout the years a number of amendments had been proposed to restrict certain provisions of the Act, and each time Congress either rejected the amendments or else liberalized even further some of the provisions. After scrutinizing the legislative history, the court reached the decision that it was the 'intent on the part of Congress that the words "manufactured products" . . . are not to be given the restricted meaning contended for by the Interstate Commerce Commission herein'.[47] The farmers prevailed and so they could continue to make use of uncertificated carriers to transport their goods across state lines.

Let us look briefly at a few other cases where there has been an issue about categorization.

What is a dress?

The plaintiff operated a retail store selling 'ladies' dresses, coats and suits and ladies' sports clothes'.[48] His lease contained a restrictive covenant stating that the landlord agreed 'not to rent any other store in the same building for the retail sale of ladies' dresses, coats and suits'. Subsequently, the landlord, with the knowledge and consent of the plaintiff, leased a store to the defendant for the retail sale of 'ladies' hosiery, gloves, lingerie, brassieres, girdles, bathing suits, sweaters, bags and accessories, blouses, skirts and beachwear'. The plaintiff was aghast to discover that the defendant was displaying in his shop window and offering for sale matching skirts and blouses. Maintaining that these combinations were in reality two-piece dresses, the plaintiff brought suit asking the court to enjoin the defendant from selling such combinations. The defendant acknowledged that he did not have the right to sell either a one-piece dress or a conventional two-piece dress consisting of a lower garment with an upper vest or jacket. At issue was whether the restrictive covenant precluded the 'sale of a "blouse–skirt combination", also sometimes called a "dress" '. So, asked the court, when is a 'dress' not a *dress*?

From the perspective of prototype theory, this question can be formulated as follows: is a blouse–skirt combination a non-prototypical *dress*, but still a 'dress' because it belongs to the category, in which case there would be a violation of the restrictive clause? Or is a blouse–skirt combination outside of the category *dress*, in which case there would be no prohibition against its sale?

In order to resolve the issue, the court considered usages and practices within the ladies' garment trade. The industry recognizes a long-standing division between those houses that produce dresses and those that are sportswear-oriented and that manufacture skirts and blouses, and there are even separate collective-bargaining units within each of these divisions – a skirt union, a blouse union and a dress union. Moreover, at the retail level, large metropolitan department stores tend to sell regular dresses in the dress department but matching skirts and blouses in sportswear. In these stores two-piece dresses are sold at a single unit price and are generally worn together as a suit. On the other hand, matching skirts and blouses are priced separately and are frequently featured as 'mix-and-match' – that is, they can be worn together or in combination with other skirts and blouses. After taking into account this extrinsic evidence, the court decided that matching skirts and blouses were not *dresses* and that there had been no violation of the restrictive covenant. In deference to the plaintiff the court stipulated that the defendant could continue to sell matching skirts and blouses on condition that they were priced individually and that customers were not compelled to buy a matching set but were able to purchase each piece separately.

Is water a mineral?

Whether water is to be classified as a mineral was the subject matter of a case heard before the Supreme Court of the state of Oklahoma.[49] The estate of the defendant had originally brought suit against the Mack Oil Company, which had an oil and gas lease on the property. The oil company had drilled a well for water, at first for its own use, but subsequently it sold some of the water to third parties off the premises. Now Laurence, the defendant, had the 'surface rights only' to this particular piece of land, while the previous owners had retained the 'mineral rights', defined as 'all of the oil, petroleum, gas, coal, asphalt and all the other minerals of every kind or character, in and under and that may be produced from the above lands'. Laurence maintained that the water was part of the surface rights, which belonged exclusively to her, and therefore she was entitled to be reimbursed for the monies profited by Mack from the sale of the water. The original court did in fact decide in favour of Laurence, but Mack appealed to the Supreme Court of Oklahoma, claiming that water was embraced within that part of the clause that makes reference to 'all the other minerals of every kind and character'.

The court acknowledged that water is a substance that shares some properties common with minerals as it is found in the ground and can be sold for profit. Nonetheless, even though it might be technically a mineral, water is not a prototypical mineral. The court said: 'It is a fluid and mobile', and the rules governing its use 'must logically vary from those applicable to coal, ore, and the like . . . Although in large measure a commodity of commerce, [water] is essential to the natural use of land for agricultural and other purposes, and to the support of human life itself'. From all this, the court concluded that, within the terms of the contract, water was not a mineral. Consequently, Mack was permitted the use of water for its own operations but could no longer sell it to others.

Is gravel a mineral?

An analogous case before the US Supreme Court raised the issue of whether *gravel* is a mineral.[50] Although, at first blush, gravel appears to be more of a 'mineral' than water is, still gravel is not a prototypical mineral. The case dealt with a mining company that acquired interest in land originally belonging to the US Government. In the congressional Act authorizing the deeding of such land, Congress had stipulated that the US Government would continue to retain title to 'all the coal and other minerals' found on the land. The mining company began removing gravel from a pit on the property and was using it for paving streets and pavements in the company town where most of its workers resided.

The legal question before the court was whether gravel was a mineral and, if so, did its removal constitute a trespass against the US Government? The court noted a 'broad' meaning of the word mineral:

> In the broad sense of the word, there is no doubt that gravel is a mineral, for it is plainly not animal or vegetable . . . While it may be necessary that a substance be inorganic to qualify as a mineral . . . it cannot be sufficient. If all lands were considered 'minerals' [sic] . . . the owner of the surface estate would be left with nothing.[51]

The court then discussed some narrow meanings. Does the term *mineral* encompass every type of 'stone and rock deposit'? Does it apply only to substances that are metallic? The court found the various broad and narrow definitions to be inadequate for resolving the classification problem. Analogous to the *ICC* case, the court then proceeded to look to the intent of Congress. The justices finally concluded that gravel was to be classified as a mineral, a conclusion supported by the fact that there were other federal statutes where gravel had been categorized as such.

Syntactic ambiguity and the rule of lenity

The various cases of misunderstanding that we have examined thus far – whether lexical ambiguity, referential indeterminacy or vagueness of categorization – all had to do with the interpretation of particular words. But ambiguity can also arise from the grammatical relationships of the words within a sentence. This kind of ambiguity is often a function of the *scope of modification*. A common potential ambiguity of this type occurs when an adjective precedes a series of two or more nouns – such as, *old men and women*. Does *old* modify only the first noun of the series or both nouns? We can make use of bracketing to illustrate the two different parsings: [*(old men) and (women)*] versus [*old (men and women)*]. In linguistics, the adjective is said to have *narrow scope* when it modifies only the first conjunct but to have *wide scope* when it modifies the entire series. There are, of course, conventional ways of disambiguating this kind of utterance. One can reverse the order of the conjuncts to get the narrow reading – *women and old men*, or repeat the adjective to get the equivalent of the wide reading – *old men and old women*.

Now consider the following somewhat fanciful hypothetical situation. A state legislature has established a curfew. The law states that 'old men and women must not be out in public after 8 o'clock at night'. A young woman is arrested for violating the curfew. She claims that the law does not apply to her, that it affects only old women, and hence that she has been unlawfully arrested. The arresting officer maintains that the law does apply to her, that it is applicable to all women, and therefore the arrest of the young woman is valid. How must a court handle this situation?

Within the jurisprudence of Anglo-American law there is a common law principle that has come to be known as the *rule of lenity*. It states that 'penal statutes should be strictly construed against the government or parties seeking to enforce statutory penalties and in favor of the persons on whom penalties are sought to be imposed'.[52] The rule essentially says that where a criminal statute is ambiguous (as our hypothetical one clearly is), it should be interpreted in such a way as to favour the accused.

One rationale behind the principle of lenity is for laws to be clearly stated. Citizens should not have to guess whether a law applies to them or not. A second rationale behind the rule of lenity has to do with the separation of powers. The rule serves to prevent the judicial system from creating laws unintended by the legislature. Because the function of the courts is to interpret statutes and not to enact them, in the case of an ambiguous statute the courts do not necessarily know whether the legislature intended for it to apply broadly (affecting a greater number of individuals) or narrowly (affecting fewer). Because courts are loath to condemn those whom the legislature may not have intended to punish, they are inclined to adopt an interpretation that snares fewer individuals, even though the net thus created may not gather in all those that the legislature may have actually intended to designate as violators. However, once the courts determine that a statute is ambiguous, they will often suggest that the legislature undertake a rewording of it so as to eliminate the ambiguity.

For our hypothetical law, a narrow legal interpretation comes about through the wide-scope reading. A curfew that applies to old men and to old women deprives fewer citizens of the right to be out at night than one applying to old men and to all women, which would be interpreting the statute *broadly*. One must be careful to differentiate the use of *narrow* as a linguistic term applying to scope and its use as a legal term when applying to the interpretation of a law. Figure 1.5 should help to clarify this difference in terminology, where OM = old man, OW = old woman, YM = young man, YW = young woman, and the shaded area represents both the scope of the adjective *old* and those groups of individuals to whom the law is addressed.

Narrow versus wide scope

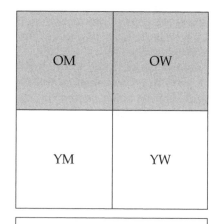

Figure 1.5 *Old men and women*

According to the rule of lenity, the young woman of our hypothetical example must be released from custody. We now examine a criminal case where a defendant's life-or-death sentence turned on the scope of an adjective preceding a series of coordinated nouns.

California v. Brown *and another case*

In *California* v. *Brown*, a jury convicted the defendant for the forcible rape and first-degree murder of a 15-year-old girl. These heinous crimes made the defendant Brown eligible for the death penalty. Under California law, which is consistent with US Supreme Court guidelines, there is a second trial after conviction to determine whether the death penalty should be imposed. The California penal code permits capital defendants to introduce during the penalty trial any mitigating evidence concerning 'the nature and circumstances of the present offense . . . and the defendant's character, background, history, mental condition and physical condition'. The purpose of the mitigating evidence is to enable the jury to recommend life in prison in lieu of the death penalty. In order for them to determine the appropriate penalty for Brown – death or life in prison – the trial court instructed the jurors to weigh both the aggravating and the mitigating circumstances. They were given the following jury instruction: 'You must not be swayed by mere sentiment, conjecture, sympathy, passion, prejudice, public opinion or public feeling'.

Brown was sentenced to death. On automatic appeal the case was referred to the California Supreme Court to consider whether the jury instruction violated the defendant's right to have the jury view his situation with compassion or sympathy.[53] The linguistic issue was whether in the instruction the adjective *mere* modified only the word *sentiment* or all of the words in the series. The main focus, however, was the relationship between the adjective and the noun *sympathy*. Depending on the scope of the adjective, there would be a crucial distinction between 'sympathy' and 'mere sympathy'. The California Supreme Court interpreted the instruction as informing the jury 'not to be swayed by . . . sympathy', and it found the instruction to be in violation of federal constitutional law, which recognizes the right of a capital defendant to have 'sympathy factors' taken into account during the determination of the penalty. As a consequence of its interpretation, the California Supreme Court reversed the lower court's sentencing decision. Eventually, though, the US Supreme Court agreed to review the constitutionality of the California jury instruction. In a 5:4 decision, it reversed the finding of the California High Court. Chief Justice Rehnquist, who delivered the Supreme Court's majority opinion, disagreed with the California court's assertion that the jury had been instructed not to be swayed by 'sympathy'; rather, according to Rehnquist, it had been told not to base its decision on 'mere sympathy', and for that reason the instruction passed constitutional muster.

What is the difference between 'sympathy' and 'mere sympathy'? Why is it that an instruction not to take 'sympathy' into consideration is deemed unconstitutional, but an instruction not to take 'mere sympathy' into account passes muster? 'Sympathy' comprises those sentiments pertaining to legitimate mitigating factors, such as the defendant's growing up under the domination of an abusive parent, being a victim of physical or sexual abuse, exhibiting severe mental or emotional problems, or showing sincere remorse for having committed the crime in question. Jurors are required to be sensitive to these kinds of mitigating circumstances and to take them into account in reaching a decision regarding the ultimate penalty. But jurors are strictly advised not to be moved by 'mere sympathy', those emotional responses not related to appropriate mitigating elements, such as their feeling sorry for the defendant's plight, upset by his forlorn demeanour throughout the trial, or moved by the distress of his family. In other words, the sentence that is to be imposed at the penalty stage should reflect a reasoned response to the defendant's character and background and to the nature of the crime rather than mere emotions or general feelings of sympathy unrelated to the defendant's character, background and crime.

It was Rehnquist's contention that the California Supreme Court had improperly focused *solely* on the word 'sympathy' in determining that the instruction interferes with the jury's consideration of mitigating evidence. He maintained that the crucial question was not how the state's Supreme Court had interpreted the instruction but rather how a 'reasonable juror' would have understood it. According to Rehnquist:

> [A] reasonable juror would be unlikely to single out the word 'sympathy' from the other nouns accompanying it, and would most likely interpret the admonition to avoid basing a decision on 'mere sympathy' as a directive to ignore only the sort of sympathy that was not rooted in the aggravating and mitigating evidence introduced during the penalty phase.

The opinion noted the various kinds of aggravating and mitigating evidence that had been presented during the penalty trial. The state prosecutor related that Brown had previously raped another young girl. But there was also a fair amount of compelling mitigating evidence. Family members testified on Brown's behalf, commenting on his 'peaceful nature' and disbelieving that he was capable of such a heinous crime. A psychiatrist that had examined him declared that Brown had killed the young girl because of humiliation and fear over sexual dysfunction. Brown himself took the stand. He asserted that he was ashamed of his prior criminal conduct and he asked the jury for mercy. The questionable instruction was given to the jury at the conclusion of the penalty phase. There had been three full days of testimony and thirteen witnesses had spoken in favour of the defendant. Rehnquist maintained that it was highly unlikely that the jurors understood the instruction to mean that they were completely to ignore and not to take into account the three days of mitigating evidence that had just been presented to them.

Four of the nine federal Supreme Court judges did not agree with the majority decision. Justice Brennan wrote the principal dissenting opinion. He began his critique by reviewing the issues: 'The State acknowledges that sympathy for the defendant is appropriate, but contends that the anti-sympathy instruction simply prevents the jury from relying on "untethered sympathy" unrelated to the circumstances of the offense or the defendant'. (*Untethered* sympathy is just another name for 'mere sympathy'; *tethered* sympathy, on the other hand, is the appropriate type of 'sympathy', that which is *tied to* the mitigating evidence.) Brennan observed, however, that 'the instruction gives no indication whatsoever that the jury is to distinguish between "tethered" and "untethered"'.

Brennan then engaged in a lengthy linguistic analysis of the jury instruction, commenting on its syntactic ambiguity. He began his analysis by addressing the interpretation where the adjective *mere* has narrow scope and modifies only the first noun of the series:

> The instruction . . . counsels the jury not to be swayed by 'mere sentiment, conjecture, sympathy . . .' A juror could logically conclude that 'mere' modified only 'sentiment,' so it is by no means clear that the instruction would likely be construed to preclude reliance on 'mere sympathy'.

An interpretation for 'mere sympathy', on the other hand, would require that the adjective have wide scope. Brennan astutely noted the linguistic consequences of such an interpretation: 'In order for "mere" to be regarded as modifying "sympathy," . . . "mere" must be read to modify all the other terms in the instruction as well: conjecture, passion, prejudice, public opinion, or public feeling'. However, a wide-scope reading leads to the following dilemma:

> [S]ince 'mere' serves to distinguish 'tethered' from 'untethered' sympathy, it also serves to distinguish 'tethered' from 'untethered' versions of all the other emotions listed. Yet surely no one could maintain, for instance, that some 'tethered' form of prejudice relating to the case at hand could ever be appropriate in capital sentencing deliberations.

That is, it would be absurd for jurors to assume that they were being admonished not to entertain 'mere conjecture', 'mere passion' or 'mere prejudice' toward a defendant, but permitted to take into consideration some *appropriate* form of these sentiments. Since any form of 'conjecture', 'passion' or 'prejudice' is unacceptable in a capital case, it makes no sense to instruct the jurors not to be swayed by 'mere conjecture' 'mere passion' or 'mere prejudice'.

Brennan has effectively demonstrated the syntactic ambiguity inherent in the California jury instruction. Because a wide-scope reading would entail contextual incongruity between the adjective and several of the nouns of the series, he clearly favours a narrow-scope reading where the adjective *mere* modifies only the first conjunct of the series. Although both narrow- and wide-scope readings are technically possible (because of the potential ambiguity that occurs when an adjective precedes a series of nouns), nonetheless it seems to me that Brennan's interpretation is preferred given the contextual problems of a wide-scope reading.

In view of Brennan's rather insightful analysis, are we to assume, then, that judges make good linguists? Lawrence Solan raises this question in his discussion of the *Brown* case.[54] Did Rehnquist really subscribe to the wide-scope reading for the adjective *mere*, and did Brennan truly prefer the narrow one? Solan maintains that a judge's particular interpretation at times may be politically motivated. Solan examined the record of these justices in regard to capital punishment. Chief Justice Rehnquist was an avid supporter of the death penalty. In over thirty capital cases, only rarely did he vote to overturn a death sentence and, on occasion, his was the only vote favouring the death penalty. On the other hand, it is well known that Brennan was vehemently opposed to capital punishment. In fact, even before launching into his linguistic analysis in the *Brown* case, at the very outset of his minority opinion he expressed his opposition to the death penalty, labelling it as 'cruel and unusual punishment forbidden by the Eighth and Fourteenth Amendments'. According to Solan, judges at times are guilty of employing linguistic analysis idiosyncratically and of using linguistic argumentation for justifying their own sociopolitical agendas.

Justice O'Connor, who sided with the majority, wrote her own concurring opinion in *Brown*. She recommended that the California Supreme Court take a fresh look at the state's jury instructions to determine whether they appropriately apprised jurors of their duty to take into account relevant sympathy factors in capital decisions. This revision, in fact, is taking place. Peter Tiersma has been a member of a task force charged with rewriting California jury instructions.[55] In the section of the report dealing with aggravating and mitigating conditions to be considered in the determination of the death sentence, jurors are explicitly informed to take 'sympathy' into account and furthermore are given substantial leeway in deciding what is a mitigating factor. Jurors will be told: 'In reaching your decision, you may consider *sympathy* or compassion for the defendant or anything you consider to be a mitigating factor, whether or not I have specifically mentioned it here' (emphasis added).

Earlier in our discussion of syntactic ambiguity, we referred to the *rule of lenity*, which requires that an ambiguous criminal statute be interpreted to the benefit of the defendant. Had it been applied in the *Brown* decision, the jury instruction might have been found to be unconstitutional (according to the narrow-scope reading), and Brown could have escaped the death penalty. Why was lenity not applicable here? The principle was nowhere mentioned in the *Brown* decision, so we can only guess at some possible answers. First, the rule of lenity is typically concerned with the legality of a criminal statute, whereas the *Brown* case deals with the constitutionality of a jury instruction. Is such a distinction justified? Next, although Justice Brennan recognized the syntactic ambiguity of the jury instruction, Chief

Justice Rehnquist did not. His majority report assumes only one reasonable interpretation of the 'sympathy' factor. Hence, without syntactic ambiguity, the rule of lenity becomes irrelevant. But this view concerning the majority decision does not explain why Brennan, in his minority report, failed to raise the issue of lenity, since his report explicitly focused on the syntactic ambiguity of the jury instruction. Finally, it may not have occurred to any of the justices to invoke the rule of lenity during their consideration of the case. In any event, the question of lenity for *Brown* remains with no satisfying answer. Lenity does surface, though, in a case where the syntactic ambiguity of a federal statute was at issue.

Food-stamp fraud

The defendant, Liparota, and his brother were co-owners of Moon's Sandwich Shop in Chicago, Illinois.[56] On three different occasions, Liparota had purchased food stamps from an undercover agent for substantially less than the face value. Subsequently, he was indicted for illegally acquiring and possessing food stamps. The federal statute dealing with food-stamp fraud states that 'whoever *knowingly* uses, transfers, acquires, alters, or possesses coupons or authorization cards in any manner not authorized by [the statute] or the regulations', is subject to a fine and imprisonment (emphasis added).

The case was tried in a federal district court. The defendant wanted the jury to be instructed that the government must prove that the 'defendant *knowingly* did an act which the law forbids, purposely intending to violate the law'. The District Court rejected this proposal and instead instructed the jury that the government had to prove that 'the defendant acquired and possessed food stamp coupons for cash in a manner not authorized by federal statute or regulations' and that 'the defendant knowingly and willfully acquired the food stamps'. These instructions did not include the 'specific intent' feature proposed by the defendant: that he had knowingly engaged in an unlawful act. The jury found him guilty. He appealed. The Court of Appeals rejected his argument that the District Court had erred by failing to include 'specific intent' in the jury instructions. The US Supreme Court then agreed to hear the case.

The controversy between the parties concerns the defendant's mental state, if any, that the government must show if it is to prove that Liparota acted in any unauthorized fashion. Each side, of course, had a different interpretation in regard to the 'state of mind' requirement of the statute – in particular, what the defendant must 'know'. Without a doubt, the statute contained syntactic ambiguity in regard to the scope of the adverb *knowingly*. For a narrow-scope reading, the adverb would modify only the sequence of verbs – i.e. [(knowingly uses, transfers, acquires . . .) in any manner not authorized]. For a wide-scope reading, the modification by the adverb would extend also to the following prepositional phrase – i.e. [knowingly (uses, transfers, acquires . . . in any manner not authorized)].

Let us be clear how each side has parsed this sentence. The government, advocating narrow scope, maintains that the defendant has violated the statute if he knew that he had acquired or possessed food stamps and if those stamps had been acquired or possessed in an unauthorized manner. In other words, the government has taken as given that the stamps were obtained unlawfully and that the only knowledge required of the defendant is his knowing that he has obtained and possessed them. The defendant, espousing wide scope, claims that he would have violated the statute not only if he knew that he had acquired or possessed food stamps but also if he knew that those stamps had been acquired or possessed in an unauthorized manner. Although he admits knowing that he has obtained and possessed food stamps, the defendant does not admit knowing that he has done so unlawfully.

The Supreme Court, in an opinion delivered by Justice Brennan, acknowledged:

> Congress has not explicitly spelled out the mental state required. Although Congress certainly intended by use of the word 'knowingly' to require some mental state . . . the interpretations proffered by both parties accord with congressional intent to this extent. Beyond this, the words themselves provide little guidance. Either interpretation would accord with ordinary usage.

The court surmises, however, that because Anglo-American law generally requires that a criminal act be accompanied by a particular mental state or *mens rea* (literally, 'guilty mind'), it would have been highly unusual, although not completely ruled out, for the legislature to promulgate a law requiring no knowledge of wrongdoing on the part of the perpetrator. The failure of Congress to indicate explicitly whether *mens rea* was required did not mean that this legislative body had departed from this traditional assumption of criminal law. Adopting this assumption, the court felt that the statute dealing with food-stamp fraud necessitated 'a showing that the defendant knew his conduct to be unauthorized by statute or regulations'. However, at the trial the government had failed to prove this element of the crime. The Supreme Court went on to aver that a requirement of *mens rea* was 'in keeping with our longstanding recognition of the principle that "ambiguity concerning the ambit of criminal statutes should be resolved in favor of lenity" '.[57] The verdict of the lower court was then reversed.

Understanding legal misunderstandings

In this chapter we have examined various court cases where there was misunderstanding or ambiguity. The latter term is broadly used in the law to mean that the language of a document – whether a contract or a statute – is uncertain, unclear or doubtful. We showed that a linguistic analysis of these various instances of so-called 'ambiguity' reveals different kinds of misunderstanding. At the level of the word, we explored some of the subtle differences among lexical ambiguity, referential indeterminacy and vagueness of categorization. At the sentence level, we delved into syntactic ambiguity, looking at some of the problems of meaning that are due to the scope of a modifier. But does the linguistic perspective provide more than just an alternative analysis of legal data? I believe it does. This kind of knowledge can be beneficial in enabling lawyers to see the contours of language issues and in aiding judges to explicate the linguistic aspects of such issues in their decisions. Moreover, it can help us understand why mistakes arise in the first place. Let us consider some of these problems.

The objective theory of contract contends that the words used in an agreement concretely represent the intentions of the drafters. This perspective requires that a court must look exclusively to the 'four corners' of a document and should not inquire into what the drafters thought they meant. Such a view puts the responsibility for a correct formulation squarely on the creators. But are language users always at fault? There are features inherent to language that can contribute to misunderstanding, such as the multiple meanings or references of words and expressions. Speakers may not know all the nuances, and even if they do, they may believe that some of these are not at all applicable to their legal situation and so they do not feel compelled to specify which meaning or reference is intended.

In *Frigaliment*, the buyer of chickens believed that it was common knowledge that only broilers and fryers were suitable for a family meal, and it may never have occurred to him to have to inform the seller that old chickens would not do. Conversely, the seller had the obligation of providing chickens at a certain price and weight and he probably believed that the contract specification for the larger ones could be satisfied only by supplying older birds, since younger ones were not available at the contract price, and hence there was no need to indicate that the larger birds were not going to be broilers or fryers. What I am suggesting is that even though both parties were probably acquainted with both meanings of *chicken*, nonetheless their perceptions of the external context were such as to render in their minds only one of the meanings as likely, so that neither party was cognizant of a potential ambiguity. If this series of events is what occurred, does this scenario suggest that *Frigaliment* was decided wrongly? In fact, the *Restatement of the Law of Contracts*, a compendium of the principles of American contract law, proposes a possible conclusion for *Frigaliment* similar to that of *Raffles* – that is, where there was no 'meeting of the minds' and hence no contract.[58] But that is not the decision that actually occurred. Why, in *Frigaliment*, was the plaintiff forced to accept goods (i.e. stewing fowl) that he claimed not to have ordered, but in *Raffles*, the contract was dissolved?

As mentioned previously, an important legal element in the *Frigaliment* decision was the nature of the parol evidence. Both sides referred to earlier negotiations and brought forth witnesses in support of their respective interpretations. The plaintiff's evidence was no stronger than the defendant's. Since it was the plaintiff that had brought suit, he had the obligation of convincing the court of the validity of his interpretation of 'chicken'. He failed to do so. Consequently, the defendant's meaning was then imputed to the contract. In *Raffles*, the only parol evidence that apparently came forth was that there were different vessels, equally obscure, named *Peerless*, departing from India on different dates. Moreover, the parties to the contract were unaware of this fact, they had not intended the same ship, and neither knew of the other's intention. The case, as reported, gives no indication that there was any testimony from witnesses or any other evidence to suggest that more weight should be given to one of the interpretations over the other. The only logical conclusion was that there was a gross misunderstanding, no possible *consensus ad idem*.

However, we must not overlook the linguistic element in the *Frigaliment* decision. There are two objective meanings of *chicken* and they correspond precisely to the respective meanings claimed by the disputants. Moreover, the fact that there is an inclusion relationship between the narrow sense of *chicken* and the broad one also played a crucial role. Even though the seller did not send exclusively younger birds, nonetheless he still supplied chickens. Hence, the terms of the contract were not egregiously violated. Let us contrast this actual situation with a hypothetical one where a relationship between the two meanings is tenuous at best. Suppose that one of the objective meanings of *chicken* were 'a certain kind of child's toy animal resembling a mother hen' and that the plaintiff had ordered the toy animals but instead had received frozen eviscerated stewing hens. I doubt whether such a case would ever be decided in the same way as *Frigaliment*. For this hypothetical scenario there is no longer a question of which *meaning* of a term should be imputed to the contract. Although the parties had used the same words, the meanings are so diametrically opposed to each other that it would appear near impossible to claim even a remote 'meeting of the minds'. But where there is an inherent connection between the two disputed meanings of a lexically ambiguous word (as in *Frigaliment*), courts are inclined to try to find a solution that favours one of the interpretations.

If *Frigaliment* illustrates the inadvertent failure to recognize the two meanings of a word, then *Raffles* presents an analogous failure in regard to the reference of a name. Recall the view of John Stuart Mill that proper nouns serve to denote or point to specific entities. Frequently, though, more than one person or thing bears the same name. Suppose, for example, that you and I have a friend, John Smith, and he is the only acquaintance of ours with that first name. Then it is perfectly normal for me to begin a conversation by saying that I saw John yesterday. However, if John Smith and John Jones are our friends, it would not be appropriate – with no other context for reference – for me to say that I saw John yesterday. I would need to specify, either by adding a last name or by supplying additional information, to which John I was referring. Now let us apply this protocol for the use of proper names to *Raffles*. If both parties knew that there were two different ships named *Peerless*, we would expect them to have stipulated either the *October Peerless* or the *December Peerless*. In fact, if one of the protagonists had reason to know which *Peerless* the other had in mind, then the court would have decided the case in favour of the other. But that is not the situation before us. From all that can be determined, the contract stated simply that the goods were to leave India on a ship called *Peerless*, and one is led to assume that at the time of making the agreement each party was aware of only one ship bearing this name and moreover believed that the other party had the same ship in mind. At the time of drawing up their agreement, should the parties have been expected to know all of the ships named *Peerless*? If not, then their mistake was undoubtedly inadvertent, and the claim that there was no 'meeting of the minds' provides a reasonable resolution.

Recognizing lexical ambiguity or referential indeterminacy is relatively straightforward once one is aware of the different meanings of a word or expression or of the various entities designated by a name. Vagueness of categorization, however, is more problematic. A dictionary or a legislative definition of a category may not be precise enough for determining whether a particular item is supposed to belong to the classification. Moreover, if one is dealing with an ordinance or an administrative act, it is helpful to know the purpose of the ordinance or act, as was necessary in the *ICC* case. Consider the well-known legal example of a hypothetical ordinance that prohibits 'vehicles in the park'.[59] If we assume that the intent of the statute is to allow people to stroll casually in the park and for children to play safely there, it should be fairly evident that trucks, automobiles and motorcycles are prohibited from entry and that the ordinance does not bar little kids on tricycles or mothers pushing prams or pushchairs. But what about skateboards, rollerblades, bicycles or scooters with motors? Do any of these items belong to the class of prohibited *vehicles*? Prototype theory, although not resolving the dilemma, at least helps us to understand its dimensions. Trucks, automobiles and even motorcycles qualify as prototypical *vehicles*, but skateboards, rollerblades, bicycles and some types of scooters are either outside the category or, at best, on the fringes. Tiersma, as a way of resolving this kind of problem, has proposed a twofold solution – one that comprises both lists and definitions.[60] In relation to our hypothetical ordinance, the legislature could provide a list of specific prohibited items, particularly where there are disparate types (like trucks and rollerblades), as well as some general definitions where applicable (such as, 'any kind of motorized vehicle'). But even this approach may not completely accommodate all situations. Might it be permissible for younger kids to ride bicycles and to use skateboards, but not teenagers or adults? Although a combination of lists and definitions would reasonably account for a majority of the entities to be classified, there could be some residual items whose classification remained uncertain. One might still need to inquire into the intention of the legislature vis-à-vis the purpose of the ordinance: in a public park, do teenagers on skateboards interfere or endanger children and strollers?

In the *ICC* case, the court noted that the legislature had failed to provide definitions for the two crucial terms mentioned in the act: *agricultural commodity* and *manufactured product*. Nor had the legislature provided a list of the kinds of processing that convert poultry from an agricultural commodity into a manufactured product. Yet the scientists, in their report to the commissioner of the ICC, did provide a listing of the kinds of processes relevant for classifying poultry as either an *unmanufactured agricultural commodity* or a *manufactured product*: 'Chickens and turkeys, New York dressed, drawn, eviscerated, cut up, or frozen [are] unmanufactured agricultural commodities . . . [But] such treatments as smoking, cooking, and canning . . . are said to cause the fowl to become a manufactured product'.[61] It is not entirely clear to me why the court, in spite of having this report before it, chose not to adopt these definitions in reaching its decision. Perhaps the justices felt compelled to pay homage to the intentions of the lawmakers, and therefore there was an overarching necessity on their part to look to the legislative history of the act.

Inadvertent mistakes can happen not only in the interpretation of individual words and phrases but also with entire sentences. Various factors determine whether an actual syntactic ambiguity will surface. A potential ambiguity may never be actualized due to the broader linguistic context or to accompanying situational clues. As an example, consider the scope of the adjective *fried* within the coordinate construction 'fried eggs and potatoes'. There is a potential syntactic ambiguity between a narrow-scope reading, where only the eggs are fried, and a wide-scope reading, where both food items are fried. A more extended linguistic context might very well eliminate the ambiguity. Suppose in a cookbook you were to read: 'Here is a recipe for fried eggs and potatoes, cooked together in the same pan'. The normal interpretation would be that the potatoes too are fried. Sometimes the external context may serve to disambiguate a potentially ambiguous expression. If you were passing through a buffet line and were asked if you wanted fried eggs and potatoes, and you could see that the potatoes were mashed or au gratin, you would realize (not necessarily consciously) that only the eggs are fried. Semantic or pragmatic factors may also help to eliminate ambiguity, as only one of the potential readings may make sense semantically or seem logical. For example, the expression 'fried eggs and salad' is unlikely to be interpreted with wide scope, since salad is not the kind of food that is typically fried. On the other hand, 'fried eggs and green tomatoes' would probably entail a wide-scope reading only for anyone familiar with the dish *fried green tomatoes*, popular throughout the south of the USA.

It is this kind of pragmatic or cultural knowledge which, in the *Brown* case, is at the heart of the potentially ambiguous phrase, 'mere sentiment, conjecture, sympathy, passion, prejudice . . .'. Both a narrow-scope reading and a wide-scope one are feasible. Note that for the wide-scope reading there is no semantic incongruity between the adjective and the nouns for the expressions 'mere conjecture', 'mere sympathy' and 'mere prejudice', provided these nouns have their ordinary dictionary meanings. It is only when we consider the pragmatic intent of these terms – that is, their distinctive legal significance – that an anomaly arises. A wide-scope reading of 'mere sympathy' would pass constitutional muster, so an admonition to the jury regarding 'mere sympathy' would be appropriate, but a warning against 'mere conjecture' or 'mere prejudice' would not. As Justice Brennan pointed out, a jury must not show any amount of 'conjecture' or 'prejudice', whether 'mere' or full-blown. The adoption of the narrow-scope reading fares no better. Although the jurors would be properly apprised now not to be influenced by any kind of 'conjecture' or 'prejudice', they would also be told not to consider any 'sympathy', a violation of the defendant's constitutional right.

The paradox in this jury instruction is the desire for a wide-scope reading extending only to the noun 'sympathy', but not to any of the other nouns of the series, an impossible syntactic feat. Whoever drafted this California jury instruction might have had in mind something such as: 'You must not be swayed by passion, prejudice, public opinion, public feeling, mere sentiment or mere sympathy'. But only a reordering of the constituents and a repetition of the adjective 'mere', where appropriate, can lead to this totally unambiguous, albeit clumsy, instruction. In fact, it is this meaning that Justice Rehnquist attempted to impute to the actual jury instruction. Although his wide-scope reading of the instruction allowed 'mere' to extend appropriately to 'sympathy', he failed to see or to acknowledge the incongruity of its extension to the other nouns of the series. The legislature that had composed this jury instruction was apparently equally unaware of the syntactic, semantic and pragmatic consequences. It took a Justice Brennan to bring this threefold anomaly to the fore.

2 Linguistic Metaphor and Legal Fiction

A fiction is frequently a metaphorical way of expressing a truth.

Lon Fuller[1]

What do fiction and metaphor have to do with the law? Do they not belong rather to the realm of literature? A fiction is an account known not to be true. Yet when reading a novel or a short story, we are asked to suspend our disbelief and to pretend that the characters are real and that the events indeed take place. A metaphor too is fictional. It is a rhetorical device that depicts one thing as though it were another. Thus, both fiction and metaphor share a similar pretence of asking the reader to envision something that is not literally true as though it were so. The law, on the other hand, is not supposed to deal with pretence but with 'real' facts. However, it may come as a surprise to learn that the law has its fictions too, which require one to assume as true principles and doctrines known to be false. Moreover, many of these fictions are grounded in metaphor – that is, jurists and lawyers think about them and talk about them using vocabulary drawn from the domains to which they are compared.[2]

Two famous legal fictions

We begin by looking at two well-known legal fictions. The first one is the doctrine of the 'attractive nuisance'. It presumes that children who wander onto premises where there is a dangerous condition are not trespassers but rather invitees. The second one is the fiction of 'the corporation as a person'. Because corporations have some of the same legal rights as people, this fiction sanctions treating corporations as persons for certain purposes within the law. Then we turn to metaphor – as a literary device, as an aspect of everyday language and as a legal phenomenon. We will explore not just the linguistic manifestations of metaphor but, more importantly, its conceptual bases. Having a proper understanding of the purpose of legal fictions and of the operation of metaphor, we will be equipped with the necessary tools for a linguistic analysis of the conceptual metaphors underlying the two fictions.

The attractive nuisance doctrine

Three young boys are playing along the railroad tracks. They enter a railroad yard and come across a turntable, which is a revolving platform that has a track on it and that is used to turn locomotives. No one from the railroad company is around to chase the youngsters away. The turntable looks very inviting and one of the boys suggests that they play with it. Much to their delight, they discover that it is neither bolted down nor locked. Two of them begin turning it. The youngest, who is around 6 years of age, while attempting to climb up on it, gets his foot jammed between the rail on the turntable and the rail of the main track. The child's foot is severely crushed, resulting in a serious and permanent injury.

The scene just described actually took place in the state of Nebraska back in 1873 in the case of *Sioux City & Pennsylvania Railroad Co.* v. *Stout*.[3] Now, this incident was not an isolated event. The late nineteenth century in America was an era of the expansion of railroads and so there were many accidents and injuries resulting from kids playing on tracks or in railroad yards. Most of these young victims came from the lower economic classes, living in those parts of town where trains typically passed through. The proliferation of accidents led to public outcry and pressure for the government to deal with this social problem. In fact, there were so many of these incidents confronting the courts that they became known as the 'turntable cases'.

Were judges to hold railroads liable for injuries sustained by children who had wandered onto the premises out of curiosity or for amusement? The courts faced the following dilemma: the children were technically trespassers. They had entered onto private property without the permission of the owners. Traditionally, the only duty that a landowner owes to a trespasser is not wilfully to inflict harm once the former discovers the presence of the latter, but the landowner is not required to look out for the intruder's welfare and safety. Contrast this limited duty with the much higher standard of care afforded to those who are invitees. For example, if you invite guests to your home, it is your responsibility to see that while they are on your premises they are not exposed to dangerous conditions that would cause them injury, such as a slippery pavement or broken steps.

The courts had no intention of throwing to the wind the traditional laws of trespass and so they needed to find some way to get these children 'invited' onto the property. The principle that evolved ultimately became known as the 'attractive nuisance' doctrine. According to this theory, an owner is liable for injuries to trespassing children if the harm was caused by conditions or objects on premises where children were likely to wander, and the owner failed to take reasonable precautions to protect the children against injury. This doctrine is based on a *legal fiction* – that of 'allurement' or 'enticement'. A turntable, a swimming pool, an open well or shaft, or any other similar hazardous condition that is *attractive* to a young child becomes an *invitation* that *allures* him or her towards the danger, and because of this *enticement*, the landowner owes to that child the duties and obligations reserved for an invitee. This view was cogently articulated by a court in one of these cases: 'What an express invitation would be to an adult, the temptation of an attractive plaything is to a child of tender years'.[4]

It is important to realize, though, that a legal fiction is not a lie. Although it is false, its intent is not to deceive or to fool anyone. No one believes that an attractive nuisance *literally* extends an invitation onto the property. So what is the purpose of a legal fiction? It is a way of adapting 'old' rules to 'new' uses, a way of making sense of a change in the law that is taking place, while at the same time preserving the authority of the older rule. Fictions are 'the growing pains of the language of the law'.[5] The alternatives to a legal fiction would be much more disruptive. For example, the legislature could retain the original law regarding trespassing, but declare that it no longer applies to children who wander onto premises where there are dangerous conditions and where the landowner has made no attempt to deter the intruders. Or the legislature could decide to do away completely with the traditional rule and to replace it with a new law that tries to preserve the intent of the original, while at the same time recognizing the need for protecting wandering children. Both the exception to a law and the creation of a new one raise other issues. What duties does a landowner owe to these wandering children? In what situations, though, are they to be regarded as trespassers? Are there other exceptions to the traditional rule that need to be recognized? The virtue of the legal fiction is that it keeps the original law intact. There is no need for exceptions or for creating additional rules. Children are automatically excluded as trespassers, due to the fact that, thanks to the fiction, the attractive nuisance has invited them onto the property. Hence, the landowner now owes these children the same duty of care that he must exercise towards any of his other guests.

Elsewhere in the law we find the fiction of an invitation by someone or something other than the actual owner. In the commercial domain, customers of a business are considered invitees. They enter a place of business either by the owner's request or else by 'inducement'. Some of the ways utilized by owner-merchants to 'entice' customers may include a hawker standing on the pavement, an advertisement in the newspaper or an 'attractive' window display. Whether through a person or an object, the intent is to 'invite' the public to come in. The words in quotes demonstrate that the vocabulary for the attractive nuisance doctrine is just as valid here.

In agency law, a *principal* is responsible for the acts of his *agent*, such as the relationship between an employer and an employee. The law of agency is based on the Latin maxim, '*Qui facit per alium facit per se*' – he who acts through another, acts through himself. This notion of transferred responsibility doubtless began as a legal fiction. Similarly, the doctrine of vicarious liability is based on the idea that the master should be 'deemed negligent' for hiring a careless servant. An extended form of this view is that a corporation, as a legal entity, can act only through its agents. Since it is almost impossible to distinguish between the corporate entity and its employees, 'the act of the agent is the act of the corporation'.[6]

The corporation as a person

The law allows corporations to do some of the things that people do. They may enter into contracts, buy and sell land, commit torts, sue and be sued. Other rights and liabilities are denied. Corporations cannot hold public office, vote in elections, or spend the night in jail. In spite of evident differences between a corporation and a flesh-and-blood human being, there are sufficient similarities for the law to treat the corporation as a person. The word 'person' as used in a statute will usually be construed to include corporations, so long as such an interpretation fits within the general design and intent of the act. The edification of the corporation to the status of person is one of the most enduring institutions of the law and one of the most widely accepted legal fictions.

The personification of the corporation is by no means a recent innovation. As early as 1444, it was asserted in the Rolls of Parliament that 'they [the Master and Brethren of the Hospital] by that same name mowe be persones able to purchase Londez and Tenementz of all manere persones'.[7] Three centuries later, Sir William Blackstone, the well-known English jurist, gave the following definition of legal persons: 'Natural persons are such as the God of nature formed us; artificial are such as are created and devised by human laws for the purposes of society and government, which are called corporations or bodies politic'.[8] In the nineteenth century, particularly in France and in Germany, there was a flourish of interest in the nature of corporate personality – what the French call *la personnalité morale*.

Three theories of corporate personality

The word 'corporation,' derived from the Latin *corporatus*, 'made into a body', designates a body of individuals joined together for a common purpose. Does this body have rights distinct from those of the individuals composing it? The philosophical implications of this question that occupied German and French jurists throughout the nineteenth century led to three different theories of corporate personality: the creature theory, the group theory and the person theory.

THE CREATURE THEORY

Savigny, in Germany, was the principal proponent of the *creature theory*.[9] His ideas stem from a belief in the individualistic nature of the person. According to Savigny, a human being, as a conscious and willing entity, by his or her very existence, possesses certain inalienable rights. The law must confirm this unique status of the individual. Legal relations, at the most fundamental level, take place between one person and another. Now, individuals may enter into an association, but the resulting group has no independent existence on its own, and unlike a natural person, it has no pre-existing rights. Only in contemplation of the law does it become a legal entity – a *persona ficta*, an artificial, moral or juristic person. John Marshall, Chief Justice of the United States Supreme Court from 1801 to 1835, described the corporation as an 'artificial being, invisible, intangible, and existing only in contemplation of law. Being the mere creature of law, it possesses only those properties which the charter of its creation confers upon it'.[10] Marshall's characterization has become one of the classic definitions of the corporation as a 'creature'.

The assumption that the corporation as a legal person is an artificial entity – a creature that emanates uniquely from the state – conflicts with two other notions: first, man as an independent being has the natural right to join freely with other persons and to form associations; and second, these associations take on a cohesion and an existence of their own. The first objection constitutes the main argument behind the group theory. The second forms the foundation for the person theory.

THE GROUP THEORY

The *group theory* had as its chief advocates Ihering in Germany and Vareilles-Sommières in France.[11] Like the creature theory, it recognizes human beings as the original bearers of rights. Among them is the right to join together and to do business under an assumed name. But the ensuing business enterprise thereby does not become a separate entity to be treated as a legal person. The group theory holds that although it may be convenient to speak of the rights of a corporation and therefore to think of it as a legal unit, corporate rights, in actuality, are nothing other than those of the component members. Persons conducting business under a corporate name are entitled to the same protection of the law that is guaranteed to them as individuals. Consequently, a corporate name can never be the name of any artificial being; it is simply a useful label for identifying the members of the group, in much the same way that a family name serves as a cover term for the members of a family.

THE PERSON THEORY

Gierke, in Germany, was the main spokesman for the *person theory*.[12] He advocated that groups are as 'real' as the persons who form them. He pointed out that it is an undeniable aspect of human nature for persons to join together to form groups. Families, clans, guilds, unions, corporations, nations – these are just a few of the kinds of associations that occur. Both individuals and groups are natural entities within all societies, and in societal interactions there must be a trade-off between the wishes of individuals and the endeavours of groups. Furthermore, the group is more than just an expression of the sum of its members. It acquires a common will and pursues its own goals, and its life continues regardless of changes in membership. The law may or may not recognize the group, but that endorsement in no way affects its reality, for it exists in its own right. Within the framework of the person theory, one may still refer to corporations as artificial persons, particularly whenever one needs to distinguish them explicitly from natural persons. Such reference, however, should not be confused with the similar terminology of the creature theory. Under the creature theory, the corporation is a legal person *created by law*. Under the person theory, the corporation is a legal person *naturally*, as much as any human being.

Corporate personality and corporate interests

At the beginning of the nineteenth century in America, it was the creature theory that dominated thinking on corporate personality.[13] This perspective was to change with the spectacular rise of private corporations in the latter half of the nineteenth century and the first part of the twentieth. The new economic needs clashed with the premises of the creature theory. There developed an increasing mistrust in the efficacy of special charters granted by the state. They restricted the creation of new companies and interfered with corporate growth. Worse yet, they led to corruption, political favouritism and monopolies. Consequently, there arose a movement for free incorporation – for making the corporate form available universally as a regular and normal feature of business activity. Although free incorporation turned out to be incompatible with the creature theory, for a while it appeared that the group theory could accommodate the new economic structure.

The group theory treated corporations in terms familiar to partnership law. After all, the corporate members had freely decided to come together to enter into agreement. Yet there were basic conceptual problems in attempting to adjust the partnership model to corporations. Whereas the composition of a true partnership tends to remain stable, a corporation has no such rigidity, and its membership may fluctuate constantly. Furthermore, unlike a partnership, where the members are individually and severally responsible for the debts of the company, a corporation brings limited liability to its members. Finally, in a partnership the members share in decision-making; however, with the growth of large corporations and with the advent of stock exchanges for trading shares, shareholders have become mere investors and decision-making has shifted to an elite corps of officers and directors.

The group theory, by treating the corporation as a partnership, did not effectively accommodate the special features of corporate immortality, limited liability and distribution of power. The person theory ultimately emerged as the most amenable to the evolving needs of US corporations. This theory conceived of the corporation as a real entity that existed independently of its members. Hence, the precise make-up of the membership became immaterial. A corporation could have its own property and incur its own debts. It was understandable, then, that the liabilities of the members were not coextensive with those of the company. Finally, as a person, a corporation had the power to delegate responsibilities to its agents – the officers and directors. The person theory, in its treatment of the corporation as a bearer of rights and duties, freed corporations from those restrictive notions that were built into the creature and group theories.

The three theories of corporate personality recognize different interests of society. The creature theory emphasizes the ultimate power of the sovereign; the group theory the contractual rights of individual persons; and the person theory the economic freedom of enterprises and organizations. These philosophical and historical developments provide the necessary background for approaching and appreciating a series of judicial events that occurred in America beginning in the nineteenth century. Although British and American jurists showed little enthusiasm for the metaphysical discussions that were taking place on the Continent, US law did not entirely escape the effects of the philosophical issues. On more than one occasion, the Supreme Court had to determine whether, within the meaning of the US Constitution, the terms 'person' and 'citizen' apply to corporations, and in order to resolve this issue the court could not totally ignore the nature of corporate personality.

Supreme Court views on corporate personality
The highest court of the land was compelled to take an interest in the nature of corporate personality and in the *language* for discussing it. One set of cases concerns federal jurisdiction. The issue is whether national courts, empowered by article III of the US Constitution to handle controversies between citizens of different states, can entertain suits by or against corporations. We shall see that in treating the jurisdictional question, the Supreme Court, from the outset, rejected the creature theory of corporate personality. At first, it would adopt the group theory. When this conception of the corporation proved impractical, the court would shift to the person theory. However, this move turned out to be prematurely radical, and the court would recant by adopting an interesting compromise position, one which embraces elements of both theories.

To state, in the analysis of a case, that the Supreme Court was operating within a particular theory is not to imply that the justices explicitly and knowingly reached decisions by applying well-defined sets of principles. In fact, at the time of most of the cases, the theories had not yet been articulated in the forms that we know them today. Nor did the discussions that were taking place in Europe seem to find their way into the opinions written by the court. The different theories must be understood as explanatory models useful for interpreting the court's decisions. They bring coherence and structure to what otherwise might be disparate events, and they provide a conceptual background against which to trace the evolution of American corporate personality. Here is the story of the jurisdictional issue.

ARTICLE III: DIVERSITY OF CITIZENSHIP
The USA has a dual judiciary structure. There are both federal and state courts. The Constitution envisages that the state courts will handle most

disputes. A federal court may become the forum of adjudication either because of subject matter – such as cases arising under the Constitution or from federal laws – or because of the character of the litigants. Article III recognizes seven classes of parties that may bring suit within a federal court. It is the fifth class that will be our focus of interest.

1. Cases affecting Ambassadors, other public Ministers and Consuls;
2. Controversies to which the United States shall be a Party;
3. Controversies between two or more States;
4. [Controversies] between a State and Citizens of another State;
5. *[Controversies] between Citizens of different States*; [emphasis added]
6. [Controversies] between Citizens of the same State claiming Lands under Grants of different States;
7. [Controversies] between a State, or the Citizens thereof, and foreign States, Citizens or Subjects.

When two persons are citizens of the same state and they have a dispute that concerns a matter of state law, they must appear in a court of that state. However, if they are citizens of different states, then a federal court may hear their case, even though the subject matter deals uniquely with state law. The rationale behind diversity of citizenship is to enable an out-of-state litigant, who feels that he might not receive equal treatment in a state court located in the territory of his adversary, to bring the suit into the more neutral domain of a federal court. Chief Justice Marshall aptly stated the rationale for federal jurisdiction:

> However true the fact may be, that the tribunals of the states will administer justice as impartially as those of the nation, to parties of every description, it is not less true that the constitution itself either entertains apprehensions on this subject, or views with such indulgence the possible fears and apprehensions of suitors, that it has established national tribunals for the decision of controversies . . . between citizens of different states.[14]

In allowing federal jurisdiction where there is diversity of citizenship, the Constitution expressly speaks of 'Controversies . . . between *Citizens* of different States' (emphasis added).[15] It does not mention corporations. The drafters of the Constitution were not unaware of corporate entities. Although not so common or extensive as they are today, nonetheless they were fairly numerous. At that time there were trading companies, banks, railroads and canal and toll bridge companies.[16] Because article III does not expressly single out corporations, is litigation involving them to be restricted entirely to state courts? If an individual of one state suing a citizen of another state can turn to the impartial umbrella of the federal courts, might this same individual not be equally desirous of this protection where he, as an outsider, sues a corporation in its home state? The Supreme Court definitely thought that the litigants in such cases were entitled to its beneficence. Under the guise of 'Controversies between

Citizens of different states', the court has managed to bring corporations through the doors of federal courtrooms.

THE DEVEAUX CASE

The question of federal jurisdiction in regard to corporations first came before the Supreme Court in 1809, in the celebrated case of *Bank of the United States* v. *Deveaux*.[17] The plaintiff bank, chartered in Pennsylvania, was suing Deveaux, a tax collector for the state of Georgia, for physically removing funds from the bank in payment of taxes that the bank claimed it did not owe. The defendant tax collector was quite happy to have the suit heard in a Georgia court. The plaintiff, of course, had reason to prefer a federal tribunal and brought an action of trespass in the Circuit Court of the United States for the District of Georgia. The defendant tax collector maintained that there could be no federal jurisdiction because the corporation was not a citizen of Pennsylvania – nor, for that matter, could it be a citizen at all. Yet the clause of article III that refers to 'controversies between citizens of different states' is the only one applicable to questions of diversity of citizenship. Whether corporations have access to national courts must hinge ultimately on the interpretation of this clause. Does the meaning of the term 'citizen', as used in article III, apply to corporations? The court began its inquiry by looking into the nature of a corporation:

> As our ideas of a corporation, its privileges and its disabilities, are derived entirely from the English books, we resort to them for aid, in ascertaining its character. It is defined as a mere *creature* of the law, invisible, intangible, and incorporeal . . . [emphasis added].[18]

Through its choice of adjectives and in its direct reference to the corporation as a creature, the court's definition fits squarely within the conceptual framework of the creature theory. Had the court adopted such a perspective of the corporation, then indeed, it would be difficult to see how such a lifeless, formless entity – a creation of a state – could ever be construed as a citizen. The court itself affirms this viewpoint:

> That invisible, intangible, and artificial being, that mere legal entity, a corporation aggregate, is certainly not a citizen; and, consequently, cannot sue or be sued in the courts of the United States.[19]

Had the court gone no further, the issue might have been permanently settled, and corporations would have been barred forever from the national courts. The Supreme Court did comment on a few English cases, where for taxation purposes corporations were considered as 'occupiers' of land. However, the court rejected these as precedents for treatment as citizens. Nonetheless, the Supreme Court had no intention of depriving corporations of entry to a federal courtroom.

The creature theory, in treating the corporation as a *non persona* and in denying that it could ever be a citizen, was totally inadequate for sustaining any argument for the admission of corporations into federal courts. The Supreme Court needed to find support for jurisdiction in some other conception of the corporation. The court shifted its view from the corporation itself, and instead focused on its constituent members: 'If the corporation be considered as a mere faculty, and not as a company of individuals, who, in transacting their joint concerns, may use a legal name, they must be excluded from the courts of the union'.[20] The court went on to develop the group perspective:

[A corporate] name, indeed, cannot be an alien or a citizen; but the persons whom it represents may be the one or the other; and the controversy is, in fact and in law, between those persons suing in their corporate character . . . and the individual against whom the suit may be instituted.[21]

By looking beyond the corporate name, one lifts the corporate veil and sees beneath it the true members of the corporation. It is they who are entitled to the court's protection.

The group theory was sufficient to bring corporations within the diversity of citizenship requirement of article III: the members, who are real persons – and not the corporation – qualify as citizens. The interests of the corporation become instead the interests of its members. Consequently, the latter cannot be deprived of their constitutional right of access to federal courts simply because they choose to band together to conduct their business under a corporate name. At this point in history, the court had no need to go further, and certainly it was not yet prepared to embrace the person theory – to recognize any claim that the corporation itself might qualify as a bona fide citizen. Citizens, after all, could only be real persons. This view appears among the summary statements: 'For the term citizen ought to be understood as it is used in the constitution, and as it is used in other laws. That is, to describe the real persons who come into court, in this case, under their corporate name'.[22]

The *Deveaux* ruling effectively treated a suit involving a corporation as though it were by or against the shareholders as partners. The decision also established a diversity procedure for corporations. One would look to the shareholders or members of the corporation. If their state citizenship was different from that of the other party to the suit, then the requisite diversity was met. This procedure had to be applied in conjunction with a rule established in a case heard three years earlier, in 1806.[23] The *Strawbridge* rule – still valid today – governs diversity whenever either party consists of several persons. It requires that there be no overlap of citizenship. None of the essential parties on one side of the suit may have the same state citizenship as anyone on the other side. In other words, the citizenships of the members of the groups must constitute disjoint sets. Such a requirement, when applied to corporations, would work well enough for local companies where the shareholders are either all residents of the same state, or if not, then at least of just a few states. It would work against any large national corporation having shareholders from virtually every state. In the latter situation, the corporation would in effect be barred from the federal courts, for whenever just one of its multitude of stockholders happened to share state citizenship with anyone from the opposing side, diversity would be defeated. This dilemma was bound to occur.

THE *LETSON* CASE

The Supreme Court confronted the special situation of overlapping citizenship in 1844.[24] Letson, a citizen of New York, brought suit for breach of contract against the railroad company in the federal circuit court for the district of South Carolina. The defendant railroad, in an endeavour to extricate itself from federal jurisdiction, contended that not all of its shareholders were citizens of South Carolina. Two of them were citizens of North Carolina. Worse yet, one of the shareholders was a banking corporation and two of its shareholders were from New York, Letson's home state. As a consequence of the *Deveaux* ruling, it appeared that the plaintiff and two of the true defendants were citizens of New York. According to the *Strawbridge* principle, this situation produced overlap of citizenship, and *ipso facto*, lack of complete diversity. The dilemma here is that some of the shareholders had citizenship that warranted the exercise of federal jurisdiction because of diversity of citizenship, while others had citizenship that militated against it. The court clearly favoured the former group: '[I]f it be right to look to the members to ascertain whether there be jurisdiction or not, the want of appropriate citizenship in some of them to sustain jurisdiction, cannot take it away, when there are other members who are citizens, with the necessary residence to maintain it'.[25] Once again, the court was anxious to allow diversity of citizenship for corporations.

The group theory of the corporation, as embodied in *Deveaux*, was decidedly unsuitable for admitting federal jurisdiction in cases such as *Letson*. Corporate citizenship would need to be established on an entirely different basis. The Supreme Court, in an astonishing act of verbal legerdemain, conjured up a new ruling, one which accords with the person theory:

> A corporation created by a state . . . though it may have members out of the state, seems to us to be a person, though an artificial one, inhabiting and belonging to that state, and therefore entitled, for the purpose of suing and being sued, to be *deemed* a citizen of that state. [emphasis added][26]

Further along in the opinion, the court reiterated this view:

> [A] corporation created by and doing business in a particular state, is to be deemed to all intents and purposes as a person, although an artificial person . . . capable of being treated as a citizen of that state, as much as a natural person.[27]

The language here is remarkably different from that in *Deveaux*, where the Supreme Court, in rejecting the creature theory, at first had characterized the corporation in terms drawn from that theory. The corporation had been referred to as an 'artificial being', as a 'mere legal entity', as a 'creature of the law', and as 'invisible', 'intangible' and 'incorporeal'. In *Letson*, the corporate description was quite different. The corporation was explicitly called a person. To be exact, it was an 'artificial' person, distinguishable from a 'natural' person, a human being. Such a distinction, of course, is acknowledged within the person theory. Yet, in spite of this contrast between artificial and natural, it is essential to note that the court has referred to both entities – the corporation and the human being – as persons. By means of a common label, corporations and people are made similar to each other. This linguistic ploy enables one to speak of the former but to treat it as though it were the latter.

In what way, then, is a corporation like a person? The court's reason for establishing corporate personhood rests on a somewhat curious notion of residency. A corporation that has been created and is doing business in a state resembles an individual born and living there. It seems to be a person simply by virtue of residency. Because place of residence is generally an important criterion for establishing state citizenship in persons, that notion constitutes a crucial link in the court's argument. From the premises that a corporation is a kind of person, that it is a resident of a state, and that residency governs citizenship for persons, the conclusion about citizenship for corporations must follow. But the court in *Letson* did not merely suggest that a corporation can be or should be a citizen. It took a more aggressive stance. The court decreed that a corporation *shall* be a citizen.

It is the 'magical' word *deem* that effects this transformation, a word drawn from the special class of verbs known as 'performative'. Under special circumstances (to be discussed in Chapter 3), a speaker, by using a performative verb, creates the condition denoted by that word. For instance, in asserting 'I *promise* to send you the money', I commit myself now to a future obligation of payment; my utterance of the performative verb 'promise' constitutes, at that moment, an act of promising. In a like manner, the Supreme Court, in declaring that it 'deemed' a corporation to be a citizen, by its use of that word, brought to fruition the new legal status so described.

This linguistic act on the part of the Supreme Court simultaneously bestowed on corporations both personhood and citizenship. Note that both attributes are essential. It would have accomplished nothing had the court declared corporations to be persons, but not citizens. Article III of the Constitution explicitly mentions 'controversies between citizens of different states', not persons from different states. But in order for a corporation to be a citizen, it must first be considered a person, for the notions of person and of resident are necessary conditions for the court's interpretation of 'citizen'. Moreover, the common term 'person' conveniently blurs some of the differences between corporations and human beings. Once the corporation, through residency, has been recognized as a person, albeit an artificial one, it is then 'capable of being treated as a citizen . . . as much as a natural person'. This indeed is language indicative of the person theory.

Even though the *Letson* case, decided nearly forty years after *Deveaux*, was a triumph for the person theory, the notion that a corporation is a citizen did not sit comfortably with all the brethren of the Supreme Court. Some of the justices questioned how it was possible for a corporation to be deemed a citizen when the meaning of the word 'citizen' had always been understood quite differently in the Constitution. Justice Peter Daniel attacked the very premise that had led to corporate citizenship in the *Letson* decision.

> [A]lthough citizenship implies the right of residence, the latter by no means implies citizenship. . . . [T]he Constitution does not provide that those who may be treated as citizens, may sue or be sued, but that the jurisdiction shall be limited to citizens only; citizens in right and in fact.[28]

Daniel, like a good semanticist, pointed out that residence and citizenship were not reciprocal relations: from the presence of the former one could not deduce the existence of the latter. To do so would be both bad logic and a juristic sham. He went on to suggest that if the court were indeed serious in treating a corporation as a citizen, then it must be so treated to all intents and purposes. As a citizen, it should be able to hold public office and even to 'aspire to the Office of President of the United States'.[29] Daniel had no doubt about the identity of citizens. They were, above all else, flesh-and-blood human beings.

The *Letson* decision turned out to be an embarrassment for the Supreme Court. So brazen an application of the person theory was unduly premature. Its method for establishing diversity of citizenship was to have a life-span of just ten years. In 1853, the court repudiated the idea of the corporation as a citizen, and in its stead put forward an odd compromise position. If the decision of *Letson* had been bold, the newer one was, in some sense, more radical yet.

THE *MARSHALL* CASE

The case of *Marshall v. Baltimore & Ohio Railroad Company* is interesting not only because it established an unusual procedure for diversity of citizenship, but also because it portrays one of the court's rare philosophical forays into the nature of corporate personality.[30] The court's amusing observations concerning the creature theory and the power of words are worthy of note:

> 'A corporation, it is said, is an artificial person, a mere legal entity, invisible and intangible.' This is no doubt metaphysically true in a certain sense. The inference, also, that such an artificial entity 'cannot be a citizen' is a logical conclusion from the premise which cannot be denied.[31]

The court was wary, though, of dealings with artificial entities.

> But a citizen who has made a contract, and has a 'controversy' with a corporation . . . did not deal with a mere metaphysical abstraction, but with natural persons . . . It is not reasonable that those who deal with such

persons should be deprived of a valuable privilege by a syllogism or rather sophism, which deals subtly with words and names, without regard to the things or persons they are used to represent.[32]

The court made it abundantly clear that it intended to play no metaphysical word games. Yet it expressed no doubt that corporations came under the provisions of article III, and in order to ensure them continuing access to the federal forum, the court found a new method for determining citizenship. The court's hybrid proposal, encompassing elements of both the group theory and the person theory, turned out to be not only the strangest twist in this story of diversity of citizenship, but also one of the most bizarre legal fictions in the history of the court.

The *Marshall* case involved a Virginian who was suing the railroad, a Maryland corporation, for fees allegedly owed him for services in obtaining a right of way through Virginia. He brought suit in a US Circuit Court in Maryland. The defendant railroad was described as a 'body corporate by an act of the General Assembly of Maryland'.[33] It had been objected that this declaration was insufficient to show jurisdiction in the federal courts. The Supreme Court, however, found it to be adequate, in spite of the fact that similar ones previously had been declared insufficient. In *Marshall*, the *place of incorporation* – and not the citizenship of the corporate members – became paramount. It was from this information that the court, in a most curious manner, was to deduce the citizenship of the shareholders:

> The persons who act . . . and use [the] corporate name, may be justly presumed to be resident in the State which is the necessary habitat of the corporation . . . and should be estopped . . . from averring a different domicil . . .[34]

It is true that in an ideal world where all of the shareholders are citizens of the state in which the corporation is incorporated, one would not need to look into the citizenship of each individual shareholder in order to see whether there was diversity of citizenship. It would suffice merely to ascertain the place of incorporation, for example, by a declaration to that effect. Then one could infer that all of the shareholders were citizens of that place. However, such a presumption about the citizenship of shareholders can withstand rigid scrutiny only in this ideal situation, where all of them are in actuality citizens of the state of incorporation. What about the not-so-ideal cases? What happens where there are shareholders from states other than the incorporating one? The Supreme Court dauntlessly proclaimed that, even in those cases, the presumption was not to be challenged.

The law has two kinds of presumptions – *rebuttable* and *conclusive*. A rebuttable presumption in law is like a hypothesis in science; it is a proposal that either finds support or else may be rejected, in accordance with the facts or the data. However, there is a significant flaw in the analogy between legal presumptions and scientific hypotheses. The law, unlike science, allows for conclusive presumptions – those that are not rebuttable, irrespective of the 'true' nature of the facts. The conclusive presumption enunciated in the *Marshall* case has as its consequence that shareholders will be estopped or prevented from ever averring that they are citizens of a different state. A conclusive presumption, of course, could very well be true. For example, all of the shareholders might, in reality, be citizens of the state of incorporation. It is important to note, though, that the law tends to resort to conclusive presumptions precisely in those cases where the facts are known to be false. The notion of 'conclusive presumption' counts among the most blatantly notorious legal fictions.

The court's embracing of a fiction in order to establish corporate citizenship expresses both its conviction that corporations indeed have the rights of citizens and, at the same time, its reluctance to attribute citizenship directly to them. Notice why the *Marshall* approach to citizenship represents a hybrid of the person and group theories of the corporation. First, one looks to the place of incorporation, thereby obtaining (although the Supreme Court does not admit to this) the citizenship of the corporation. In this way the corporation is treated as a person. However, because it is an artificial person, it lacks certain rights guaranteed to real citizens, such as the right to appear in a federal court in cases involving diversity. Nonetheless, from the corporate citizenship, one is able to deduce by conclusive presumption the citizenship of its members, which will be presumed the same as that of the corporation. As natural persons, the group of individuals is entitled to the constitutional protection that could not be given directly to the corporate citizen and hence they acquire admittance into a federal courtroom.

The *Letson* and *Marshall* cases share an important feature: the place of incorporation has become the decisive determinant of citizenship. In the former case, the corporation itself was deemed a citizen of the state of incorporation; in the latter, all the shareholders were presumed to be citizens of that state. In both instances, one looks to the place of incorporation, and if it is different from that of the other party, there is diversity. This ruling is admirably suited for a corporation chartered in a single state, where it has its principal place of business and conducts most of its operations. But many corporations do not fit this prototype. A company may be incorporated in more than one state. Nor is it uncommon for a company incorporated in one state to maintain its headquarters, factories and plants in some other state. Such companies essentially reside in the other state. Should citizens of that state be able to bring suit in a national court against what ought to be a 'home' corporation? Are citizens of the chartering state, in dealing with a corporation that, for all intents and purposes, resides elsewhere, to be denied access to federal courts? These questions suggest that, perhaps for diversity purposes, one should look to the principal place of business of a corporation rather than to the state of its incorporation. Or should corporations have dual citizenship, reflecting both place of incorporation and place of business activity?

In 1958, a little more than one hundred years after the *Marshall* decision, these problems were resolved by statute. Section 1332, under 'Diversity of

Citizenship', stipulates: '[A] corporation shall be deemed a citizen of any State by which it has been incorporated and of the State where it has its principal place of business . . .'.[35] According to the interpretation of this statute, a company may be incorporated in one or more states, but it can have its main place of business in only one. To be sure, the more states in which a corporation qualifies as a citizen, the more limited becomes its access to the federal courts.

Although the ruling in the *Marshall* case – that the shareholders are presumed to be citizens of the state of incorporation – still remains the official Supreme Court version for determining diversity of citizenship, nonetheless, the person theory, as it was articulated in the *Letson* case, in the end has triumphed. The very language of section 1332 attests to this vindication. In words reminiscent of *Letson*, the corporation, once again, has been *deemed* a citizen. Although this view has never received the official sanction of the Supreme Court, in the minds of most legal writers, jurists and corporate attorneys, the corporation itself is a citizen of a state, and for diversity purposes one compares directly its citizenship to that of the opposing party.

Yet there was a time lag of 114 years between *Letson* and the statute in reference. If a person theory had been rejected almost immediately after *Letson*, what events transpired in the interim so that this theory became more palatable? After all, the Supreme Court, on more than one occasion, had affirmed that corporations were *not* citizens. The support for a person view was buttressed from other areas of the Constitution, and it is this acceptability elsewhere that facilitated its penetration into the jurisdictional arena. One of these other areas concerned the rights of foreign corporations, those that had not received their charter from a particular state. Here is a brief survey of what happened.[36]

The Fourteenth Amendment: rights of foreign corporations

In 1839, the Supreme Court decided that a corporation created in one state does not have the unrestricted right to conduct business in another state.[37] The foreign or out-of-state corporation needs the host's consent. In other words, states were free to favour local business interests. This ruling by the Supreme Court laid the foundation for a series of decisions concerning the imposition by states of special fees and taxes on foreign corporations. The constitutional issues would turn on provisions within the Fourteenth Amendment to the US Constitution.

It was in 1868 that Congress ratified the Fourteenth Amendment. Section one begins by defining citizenship: 'All persons born or naturalized in the United States . . . are citizens of the United States and of the State wherein they reside'.[38] The remaining provisions of section one, in setting limits on state power, create an interesting dichotomy between citizens and persons:

No State shall make or enforce any law which shall abridge the privileges or immunities of *citizens* of the United States; nor shall any State deprive

any *person* of life, liberty, or property, without due process of law; nor
deny to any *person* within its jurisdiction the equal protection of the laws.
[emphases added]

The 'privileges and immunities clause' refers specifically to citizens,
whereas the 'due process and equal protection clause' mentions persons.
This dichotomy affects the treatment of aliens, for example. They are entitled to due process and equal protection, but not necessarily to all the
privileges accorded citizens. The distinction also had consequences for
corporations.

In a case heard twenty years after the ratification of the Fourteenth
Amendment, the court affirmed that, so far as the Constitution was concerned, corporations were not citizens: '[T]he term citizens . . . applies
only to natural persons, members of the body politic owing allegiance to
the State, not to artificial persons created by the legislature, and possessing only such attributes as the legislature had prescribed . . .'.[39] It is difficult, though, to see what else the court could have concluded in view of
the definition of citizenship at the outset of the Fourteenth Amendment.
The 'born or naturalized' qualification narrowly restricts citizenship to
natural persons. Corporations were not citizens, and so the privileges and
immunities clause could not apply to them. Nonetheless, the court was
unwilling to leave the fate of corporations completely at the whim of the
states. Corporations already residing within a state warranted fair treatment, and the court found a way to extend protection to them. Because the
equal protection and due process clause refers to persons, and not to citizens, the court was prepared to include corporations within the category
of persons. It accomplished this move in 1888, announcing: 'Under the
designation of person there is no doubt that a private corporation is
included'.[40]

The court had still recognized that a state had the right to regulate corporate entry within its boundaries, but once the corporation had complied
with requirements for admission there, such as obtaining any necessary
licences, then the state must afford it treatment equal to that of similar
domestic corporations. Why? Because to treat the foreign corporation
worse would be to single out for discriminating and hostile legislation a
class of persons – that is, the corporate members. The latter, once they have
been admitted to a state and are conducting business there, have vested
interests – property, franchises, agents, employees. Those interests, because
they are the interests of *real persons*, merit equal protection of the laws. In
this way a corporation came to be included under the rubric of 'person'
within the Fourteenth Amendment. To reach this decision the court essentially was working within the group theory.

The next stage was for the corporation itself to become a person. This
momentous step occurred in 1910, in a decision once again involving a railroad company.[41] Although chartered in Virginia, the railroad had acquired an
extensive network of lines in Alabama. Subsequently, Alabama imposed on

all foreign corporations a franchise tax. Naturally, a similar burden had not been levied on domestic corporations. The railroad claimed that because of this discriminatory treatment, it was not receiving the equal protection of the laws, and therefore Alabama's actions violated the Fourteenth Amendment. The court reached its decision with little fanfare: 'That a corporation is a person, within the meaning of the Fourteenth Amendment, is no longer open to discussion'.[42] Moreover, throughout the opinion, the court referred to the railroad as the 'corporation plaintiff'. Nowhere was there any reference to the members of the corporation. Nor did the court propose that the corporation was an artificial being. In proclaiming that the corporation was now a person, the court was clearly speaking from the perspective of the person theory.

Other constitutional rights
The Supreme Court has also considered whether corporations have other constitutional rights. It decided that the provision of the Fifth Amendment protecting individuals against self-incrimination does not apply to corporations, so that agents of a corporation must testify on corporate matters.[43] On the other hand, the provision of the Fourth Amendment against unreasonable search and seizure does apply to protect the papers and records of corporations. The court has ruled that corporations have the right to expend funds in order to influence the vote on referenda, even on issues not materially affecting their business.[44] The court refused to examine whether corporations have First Amendment rights of freedom of speech, rights that are coextensive with those of natural persons. The court cleverly sidestepped this issue by focusing, instead, on the question of the 'inherent worth of the speech', deciding that certain speech per se comes under the protection of the First Amendment.

We have reviewed the philosophical underpinnings and some of the judicial decisions concerning one of the most widely accepted legal fictions. The creature, group and person theories dominated the lively debates by European jurists throughout the nineteenth century. Even though the Americans were not actively engaging in these philosophical polemics, nonetheless the problem of corporate personality was indirectly thrust before the Supreme Court. At issue was the applicability to corporations of the provisions of article III regarding diversity of citizenship and of the Fourteenth Amendment concerning equal protection. In both arenas, it was the person theory of corporate personality that would ultimately triumph. The corporation was deemed a citizen for the question of diversity and declared a person for the issue of equal protection.

The law did not invent entirely on its own the language for talking about the corporation as a person. As we shall see, ordinary speakers – even those who are not lawyers – talk about institutions in language appropriate for persons. The basis for this manner of speech lies in a *conceptual metaphor*: THE CORPORATION IS A PERSON. (We follow standard practice of using exclusively capital letters for stating conceptual metaphors.) We need to investigate the nature of this metaphor, for it not only provides a vocabulary for talking about corporations but it also structures our ideas concerning them. However, first we need to make clear what metaphor is and, in particular, what we mean by a conceptual metaphor.

Metaphor in thought and language

One may be inclined to think of metaphor as belonging exclusively to the language of poetry and imagination, to rhetorical flourish and figures of speech, but certainly not to the stuffy, objective, verbose prose so often associated with legal discourse. However, research in cognitive linguistics over the past 20 years has shown this commonplace idea of metaphor to be untenable. The cognitive research has revealed that metaphor is not the sole province of literary language, but rather its images permeate everyday speech and it is a major component of conceptual thinking. Lakoff and Johnson, pioneers in this area, have expressed eloquently this novel view: '[Metaphors] are among our principal vehicles for understanding. And they play a central role in the construction of social and political reality'.[45]

Metaphorical conceptualization extends into all areas of discourse – from the humanities through to the sciences. For example, a traditional scientific view of the atom posits a nucleus of protons and neutrons that is surrounded by one or more rings of orbiting electrons. The structure of the atom has been compared to a miniature 'solar system', where the nucleus of the atom corresponds to the sun, and the revolving electrons to orbiting planets. We can state the essence of this imaginative correspondence as a conceptual metaphor: AN ATOM IS A MINIATURE SOLAR SYSTEM.

Advocates of superstring theory claim that the ultimate constituents of matter are nothing other than submicroscopic one-dimensional vibrating strings. A new metaphor has evolved:

> With the discovery of superstring theory, musical metaphors take on a startling reality, for the theory suggests that the microscopic landscape is suffused with tiny strings whose vibrational patterns orchestrate the evolution of the cosmos ... What appear to be different elementary particles are actually different 'notes' on a fundamental string. The universe – being composed of an enormous number of these vibrating strings – is akin to a cosmic symphony.[46]

What is the purpose of these various metaphors? They provide a way of understanding an unfamiliar concept – such as the structure and motion of an 'invisible' atom within the older theory or the behaviour of atomic sub-constituents according to the newer theory – in terms of more familiar conceptions: the sun with its revolving planets and vibrating musical strings. As Lakoff and Johnson remark: 'The essence of metaphor is understanding and experiencing one kind of thing in terms of another'.[47] A conceptual metaphor not only enables one mentally to structure experience across two different domains, but it also is often the source for the vocabulary that one uses in talking about the experience. Hence, the term 'metaphor' applies both to thought and to language. Whenever it is important to differentiate between the two types, we will refer to 'thought' metaphors as *conceptual* and to 'language' ones as *linguistic*.

Because the reader is likely already to be familiar with literary metaphors, this genre provides a useful entry to the general topic of metaphor and, in particular, to the important distinction between *conceptual* and *linguistic* metaphors. We shall begin by examining two different types of literary metaphors. One of them strictly belongs to the realm of poetry, while the other one resembles the kinds of metaphors that are part of everyday usage. We shall then look at some additional metaphors from ordinary language. With this preparation in tow, we will be ready to consider the conceptual metaphors that underlie the legal fictions of the attractive nuisance and of the corporation as a person.

The conceptual metaphor: LIFE IS THEATRE

Webster's dictionary defines *metaphor* as: 'A figure of speech in which one thing is likened to another, different thing by being spoken of as if it were that other'.[48] The *Oxford English Dictionary's* definition is similar: '[A] figure of speech in which a name or descriptive term is transferred to some object different from, but analogous to, that to which it is properly applicable'.[49] According to these definitions, metaphor is a property of language – 'a figure of speech'. As an example, let us look at the following celebrated lines from Shakespeare's play, *As You Like It.*[50]

> All the world's a stage,
>   And all the men and women merely players;
> They have their exits and their entrances,
>   And one man in his time plays many parts,
> His acts being seven ages.

Shakespeare depicts the human condition as a theatre performance – perhaps a not unexpected metaphor from a playwright. The world is a stage and we are mere actors. We make our exits and our entrances as the various events of our lives unfold, and there are many roles to be played in a lifetime – exemplifying our various personalities or identities, such as student, parent, worker. Each major period of life comprises an act in this evolving drama – from infancy, when the babe is 'mewling and puking in the nurse's arms', through youth, then adulthood, and right up to senility, when one is 'sans teeth, sans eyes, sans taste, sans everything'.

These five lines from Shakespeare, taken together, comprise one grand *conceptual metaphor*: LIFE IS THEATRE. Each line, in turn, contains its own 'figure of speech', a *linguistic metaphor* that reinforces this major theme. The

Source and target for LIFE IS THEATRE

Source (Y): THEATRE		Target (X): LIFE
the stage	⇒	the world
the players	⇒	men and women
the exits and entrances	⇒	the events of one's life
the parts (roles) played	⇒	various personality types
the acts of a play	⇒	the periods during one's lifetime

Figure 2.1 The conceptual metaphor: LIFE IS THEATRE

conceptual metaphor is not something that anyone – whether a playwright or a person on the street – actually says; it is the linguistic metaphors that encompass what is actually heard. Rather, the conceptual metaphor functions as a representation – a succinct description of the structural relationship between an abstract notion, such as 'life', and a more concrete one, such as 'theatre'. A conceptual metaphor generally has a structure represented as: X IS Y, where X stands for the more abstract concept and Y for the lesser one. We shall view this structuring as a mapping of the terms from the Y domain back onto the corresponding elements of the X domain – from *source* to *target*. This mapping for the conceptual metaphor LIFE IS THEATRE is shown in Figure 2.1, where THEATRE functions as the source and LIFE as the target, and the arrows indicate the direction of the mapping.

The genesis of this metaphor resides in a natural link between theatre and life: theatre imitates life. Theatre has always been an effective medium for portraying the human condition, and dynamic playwrights are masters at bringing to the stage a 'slice of life'. If powerful theatre is a reflection of life, it is not surprising that one way of comprehending the complexity of life would be to imagine it, in turn, unfolding as though it were a theatre production. Then life comes to imitate theatre.

The conceptual metaphor: A TREE IS A PERSON

In the lines cited above from *As You Like It*, Shakespeare explicitly mentions the source and the target for three of his correspondences – i.e. *stage* ⇒ *world*; *players* ⇒ *men and women*; *acts* ⇒ *ages*. The remaining two were left implicit, but from their sources – i.e. *exits/entrances* and *parts*, one is able to deduce the sorts of entities that ought to be the targets, as I have suggested in Figure 2.1. It is more the exception than the rule for a poet to provide an explicit indication of the connections between domains. In fact, much of the charm of poetry comes from discovering the associations. As an example, let us look at the poem, *Trees*, by Joyce Kilmer.

I think that I shall never see
A poem lovely as a tree;

A tree whose hungry mouth is prest
Against the earth's sweet flowing breast;

A tree that looks at God all day,
And lifts her leafy arms to pray;

A tree that may in summer wear
A nest of robins in her hair;

Upon whose bosom snow has lain;
Who intimately lives with rain.

Poems are made by fools like me,
But only God can make a tree.

Although our main concern is to explicate the nature of metaphor, it is of course not the only ingredient of a poem. Every poem has both *form* and *content*, an outer structure and an inner meaning, and metaphor is only one of the devices for expressing meaning. Often both form and content interact to reinforce the theme of a poem. Such is the case here. It is worthwhile, then, to look at these two elements of Kilmer's poem.

Let us begin with the form. Rhythm and rhyme stand out as its most obvious features. Looking at the rhythmic or metrical structure of this short, but pithy, poem, we note that it is composed of twelve lines that are divided into six rhyming couplets. Each couplet is self-contained; it expresses a unique idea. The independence of the couplets is further strengthened and formally expressed by the spaces separating them. Furthermore, each line of the poem contains exactly eight syllables, and except for the second from the last line, the syllables are grouped into four iambic feet. An iambic foot comprises an unaccented syllable followed by

Metrical analysis of 'Trees'

I think | that Í | shall név- | er sée
A pó- | em lóve- | ly ás | a trée

A trée | whose hún- | gry móuth | is prést
A-gáinst | the eárth's | sweet flów- | ing bréast;

A trée | that lóoks | at Gód | all dáy,
And lífts | her léaf- | y árms | to práy;

A trée | that máy | in súm- | mer wéar
A nést | of rób- | ins ín | her háir;

Up-ón | whose bós- | om snów | has láin;
Who ín | ti-máte- | ly líves | with ráin.

Pó-ems | are máde | by fóols | like mé,
But ón- | ly Gód | can máke | a tree.

Figure 2.2   'Trees' by Joyce Kilmer

an accented one. (See Figure 2.2 for a metrical analysis of the poem: acute marks over vowels denote accented syllables, vertical strokes separate feet, and hyphens divide words into syllables.) The exceptional penultimate line begins with a trochaic foot – that is, an accented syllable followed by an unaccented one, but then the final line reverts to the normal iambic rhythm. Why has the poet created one deviant line? We turn to the content of the poem for a possible explanation.

The poem starts and ends on a similar theme. It begins by informing us that even the most splendid poem pales next to the gracefulness of a tree. The conclusion to the poem presents a striking variant on this same theme. Whereas the opening couplet draws a contrast between the beauty of a poem and that of a tree, the closing couplet focuses on the creators of those products. The poet asserts that artists' creations can never be as magnificent as the Deity's handiwork. An interplay of metrics and grammar further contributes to the contrast. The final stanza begins with the word 'poems' and ends with the word 'tree'. Linguistically, the beginnings and ends of sentences often function as sites for emphasis. Moreover, the placing of these two key words in positions of prominence has introduced metrical tension. Because the two-syllable word 'poems' has its main accent on its first syllable, its position at the start of a line causes it to begin in an unexpected manner. As already noted, this is the only line of the poem to have an inverted or trochaic foot. Now we know why.

The positioning of the two critical elements, 'poems' and 'tree', also produces a striking grammatical effect, one having to do with syntactic prominence. The word 'poems' functions grammatically as the subject of a passive construction – i.e. 'Poems are made by fools like me'; whereas the contrasting word 'tree' functions as the direct object of an active utterance – i.e. 'But only God can make a tree'. Now, passive sentences are generally judged less dynamic than active ones. In fact, the very terms 'active' and 'passive' suggest this distinction. Thus, the syntactic structure of the couplet, along with the previously observed metrical effect, contributes to the idea that what is created by a poet is inferior to what God can do.

The opening and closing couplets make use of literal language. There are no metaphors here. It is in the four couplets sandwiched between the opening and the closing stanzas that metaphor blossoms. By means of *personification*, the poet describes the ways that a tree is so special. It has some of the physical characteristics of a person. Figure 2.3 shows the mapping of attributes from the source domain PERSON to the target domain TREE for the conceptual metaphor: A TREE IS A PERSON.

The human body is an ideal source domain if only because we are so familiar with it. In the poem the similarities between the anatomy of a person and the physical structures of a tree are quite obvious, even though the poet *never* makes explicit mention of 'roots', 'branches', 'leaves', or 'trunk'. Yet the reader has no difficulty in ascertaining the intended targets. The associations are apparent because of the way that Kilmer has juxtaposed human anatomical structures to specific properties and events relating to trees: a mouth

Source and target for A TREE IS A PERSON

Source : PERSON	Target: TREE
Body parts	Tree structures
mouth $\Rightarrow$ roots	
arms $\Rightarrow$ branches	
hair $\Rightarrow$ leaves	
bosom $\Rightarrow$ trunk	

Figure 2.3   The conceptual metaphor: A TREE IS A PERSON

pressed against the nourishing earth; arms *that are leafy*; hair *harbouring a nest of robins*; a bosom *overlain with snow*. The personification extends even to stature and movement. Both a tree and a person occupy upright postures. Because of this vertical orientation, the poet has imputed human-like behaviour to the tree: *looking up* towards the heavens; *lifting* appendages to *pray*; *wearing* a head-covering. The tree herself is womanly: she has a *bosom*; she lifts *her* arms in prayer and wears a nest in *her* hair. The personification extends even further – to the image of 'mother earth', through whose metaphorical *breast* flows life-giving sustenance.

Kilmer's poem illustrates how metaphor enables us to acquire familiarity with one set of concepts in terms of another. We know all too well what it means to look and to act and to feel human, but we have less immediate knowledge of what it means to be a tree. By endowing the tree with personal features, the poet invites us to relate to it more intimately and suggests that we envision it as never seen before.

Conventional metaphors

For a long time the idea had existed that metaphors belonged exclusively to poetry and other literary genres or else to rhetorical and persuasive speech. In fact, the phrase, 'figure of speech', which appears in dictionary definitions of 'metaphor', seems to strengthen this assumption. However, a significant body of research within the field of cognitive linguistics has persuasively demonstrated that in ordinary discourse speakers regularly use linguistic metaphors, and those expressions in turn reveal the conceptual metaphors of the underlying thought processes. A *conventional* metaphor is one that has found its way into normal, everyday language. It just so happens that the conceptual metaphor, LIFE IS THEATRE, has become conventionalized in this way. Note the following examples.

Someone who is not sincere is often described as 'putting on an *act*'.
Such an individual may even be facetiously referred to as 'a good *actor*'.
A person that has made a significant accomplishment may rightly 'take a *bow*'.

A job well done becomes 'a hard *act* to follow'.
One wonders whether rock stars are appropriate *'role* models' for young people.
One day each one of us will have to make that 'final *curtain call'*.

These linguistic expressions, part of ordinary discourse, demonstrate that the conceptual metaphor, LIFE IS THEATRE, is one of the ways that English speakers conceive of and talk about life. I suspect that this conventional metaphor also existed in Shakespeare's day. Playwrights and poets are quite skilful at taking a conventional metaphor and rendering it in completely unconventional ways. The lines from *As You Like It,* which we looked at earlier (see pp. 73–4) are so memorable because of Shakespeare's knack at creating novel linguistic expressions for this existing conceptual metaphor. For instance, 'all the world's a stage', was not in Shakespeare's time, nor is it for us, an ordinary language realization of the conceptual metaphor. Hence, a conceptual metaphor, such as LIFE IS THEATRE, may have as its realizations both conventional linguistic metaphors, such as 'a hard act to follow', and unconventional ones, such as 'all the world's a stage'.

The conceptual metaphor, A TREE IS A PERSON, is not a conventional one and therefore it has solely unconventional linguistic metaphors as its realizations. It is not part of our usual experience to conceive of trees and to talk about them as though they were human. However, precisely by employing this unconventional metaphor, Kilmer has presented us with an unforgettable image of what a tree could be. It is the uniqueness of this conceptual metaphor that makes this poem so unusual.

Some target concepts may be sufficiently abstract so that more than one conventional metaphor exists for characterizing them. The conceptual metaphor, LIFE IS THEATRE, is not the only way of talking about the complexities of living. Another powerful conventional metaphor for getting a hold on life is: LIFE IS A JOURNEY, where JOURNEY becomes the source and LIFE again is the target. The following examples have been adapted from Kövecses.[51]

He seems *lost,* and his life has *no direction.*
I've *reached a crossroads* in my career, but I'm not sure which *way to turn.*
She's clever and will *go far* in life.
I've finally *arrived* at *where I want to be* in my work.
He knows *where he's headed* and will never let anyone *get in his way.*
She's *gone through* a lot in her marriage.
A good education will give one a *head start* in a career.

How did the conceptual metaphor, LIFE IS A JOURNEY, evolve? Kövecses does not assume a direct correlation between life and journeys.[52] Rather, he sees this metaphor as a special instance of a more basic one: PURPOSES ARE DESTINATIONS. Attaining a goal or purpose is synonymous with reaching a destination. One can also imagine life as a series of goals. And the reason for taking a trip or journey is to arrive at a destination. The result of all of this is a complex conceptual equation composed of sources and their targets – DESTINATION : JOURNEY ⇒ PURPOSE : LIFE.

Let us look at one more conceptual metaphor for understanding life: LIFE IS A GAMBLING GAME. This time GAMBLING functions as the source. Here are some examples adapted from Lakoff and Johnson.[53]

> Even though the *odds are against me*, I'll still *take my chances*.
> If you *play your cards* right, you can do it.
> It's not a *toss-up*. Unfortunately, he *holds all the aces*.
> Don't believe a word she says; she's just *bluffing*.
> He *won big*, but he's still *a loser*.
> I think we should *stand pat* and wait to see what happens next.
> Sometimes you have to *take a chance* in life. The *stakes are too high* not to.
> What can I do? That's just *the luck of the draw*.

Without question, these expressions are drawn from the world of gaming. Nonetheless, as the examples illustrate, they constitute normal ways of talking about life, and not about gambling. Lakoff and Johnson make the point that this is *literal language* with *metaphorical structuring*. It is to be literal because anyone using these expressions would not be considered to be engaging in metaphor, simply because this is one of the *natural* ways of talking about life. Yet the fact that speakers are able to portray life as a gambling game makes this particular kind of talk metaphorically structured.

We have examined the conventional metaphors – LIFE IS THEATRE, LIFE IS A JOURNEY and LIFE IS A GAMBLING GAME – all three of which have LIFE, an abstract concept as the target and various concrete notions as sources for comparison. These three are not the only ones for representing 'life', but they illustrate that a single source domain may not always suffice for portraying a complex concept and additional concrete sources may come to the fore in order to depict other facets of a rich abstract domain. This unidirectionality – from concrete to abstract – is typical of the metaphorical process. It would be rare indeed for a more abstract concept to function as a source.

Analysis of the two legal fictions

We are now ready to examine the conceptual metaphors underlying the two legal fictions previously presented.

The conceptual metaphor: AN ATTRACTIVE NUISANCE IS AN INVITER

Previously, we noted that the 'attractive nuisance' fiction is grounded in the notion of 'allurement' or 'enticement'. That is, some hazardous condition, *attractive* to a young child, *allures* him or her onto the property. Moreover, the fiction gains further strength from a completely different one having to do with 'agency'. Because the attractive nuisance is located on and belongs to the property, it seems reasonable to view it as the impersonal 'agent' doing the *inviting*.

The two key words of this fiction – 'attractive' and 'invite', of course, are not strictly legal terms. They occur as ordinary words of the language and with meanings little different from the legal ones. For example, *Webster's New Universal Unabridged Dictionary* gives as one of its definitions for *attractive*: 'pleasing; alluring; inviting'.[54] For the verb, *to invite*, this dictionary has as its first definition: 'to ask (a person) to come to some place', but lists as one of the other meanings: 'to allure; to attract; to tempt'. The *Oxford American Dictionary and Thesaurus* has as synonyms for: (1) *attractive*: 'alluring' and 'inviting'; (2) *inviting*: 'attractive', 'enticing', 'tempting' and 'alluring'; (3) *to entice*: 'to allure' and 'to attract'; and (4) *to allure*: 'to attract'.[55] We see, then, that there is an inextricable connection among these four words. Not only in law, but also in everyday parlance, something that is 'attractive' has the linguistic aura of being capable of 'inviting'.

The conceptual metaphor that captures the essence of the doctrine is: AN ATTRACTIVE NUISANCE IS AN INVITER. Although the individual words, 'attractive', 'nuisance' and 'invite(r)', have ordinary meanings, the phrase 'attractive nuisance' is uniquely a legal term. *Black's Law Dictionary* defines it as 'a condition, instrumentality, machine or other agency, which is dangerous to young children because of their inability to appreciate peril and may reasonably be expected to attract them to premises'.[56] It is the legal notion of 'attractive nuisance' that makes this conceptual metaphor peculiar to the law. As a result, it is *not* a conventional metaphor and, therefore, it belongs to the same category as A TREE IS A PERSON. Yet, the 'attractive nuisance' metaphor does not strike us as unusual due to its closeness to another one that is quite familiar: AN ENTITY IS AN INVITER. Here are some ordinary language examples:

> On a hot summer day a swimming pool is very *inviting*.
> A good book can *entice* me to spend the weekend at home.
> The winding narrow street *pulled* him into investigating where it led.
> She is *attracted* to flashy jewellery and brightly coloured clothes.
> The idea of visiting Rome is quite *seductive*.
> An exquisite gown in the window *lured* her into the store.
> When one is low on cash, it is *tempting* to use a credit card.

The unconventional metaphor, AN ATTRACTIVE NUISANCE IS AN INVITER, although peculiar to the law, nonetheless is just a specialized version of the common conventional one, AN ENTITY IS AN INVITER.

The conceptual metaphor: THE CORPORATION IS A PERSON

The unconventional metaphor, A TREE IS A PERSON, has PERSON as its source. Of particular interest, because of its relevance to the law, is a conceptual metaphor with this same source: THE CORPORATION IS A PERSON. Unlike the former, though, this metaphor happens to be a conventional one.

What makes the thesis of the corporation as a person so attractive, in spite of the fact that everyone knows that corporations are not people? It is an interesting lexical curiosity that 'people', as one of the plural forms of 'person', refers uniquely to real persons. Although corporations are never people, they can be persons within the law. Is this personification no more than a convenient legal fiction that enables the law, for particular purposes, to treat corporations in ways similar to persons? If the law has need of a class that includes both humans and corporations, is 'person' the appropriate term? We shall show that, linguistically, it indeed is.

To demonstrate the affinity between persons and corporations, we shall look at the way language categorizes words for human and non-human entities. Nouns, of course, are the kinds of words that represent entities. The particular nouns that will be of interest to us will be divided among four classes – mythical nouns, which refer to individual imaginary beings; human nouns, which refer to individual human beings; collective nouns, which refer to aggregates of persons; and institutional nouns, which refer to associations. Table 2.1 contains examples of each of the types.

Our objective is to determine how language deals with nouns such as *corporation*. Does it treat them as artificial entities, similar to mythical nouns? In fact, one legal scholar has pondered over this very question: 'Nobody has ever seen a corporation. What right have we to believe in corporations if we don't believe in angels? To be sure, some of us have seen corporate funds, corporate transactions, etc. (just as some of us have seen angelic deeds, angelic countenances, etc.)'.[57] Are corporations more like real persons, resembling human or collective nouns, or do they belong instead to a class by themselves? If corporations can be described in ways appropriate to persons, is the language of such description necessarily metaphorical or might some of it be literal? In order to answer these questions, we need to look at the kinds of relations in which the different types of nouns can participate.

In language, relational phenomena are expressed primarily by means of verbs and verbal expressions. The analysis, therefore, must take into account the types of predicates that occur with the various nouns. We shall consider two sorts of relations between nouns, as subjects of sentences, and

Table 2.1 Noun categorization

Types of Nouns			
Mythical	*Human*	*Collective*	*Institutional*
mermaid	chairperson	committee	corporation
robot	teacher	faculty	Harvard University
pegasus	juror	jury	Supreme Court
angel	priest	clergy	Catholic Church
centaur	player	team	sporting industry

their verbs: *number agreement* (or singular/plural marking) and *semantic compatibility*. The examples of (1) illustrate number agreement, while those of (2) portray semantic compatibility. Examples preceded by an asterisk are ungrammatical or semantically anomalous; those preceded by a question mark are acceptable in special contexts only.

(1)   a.   The judge *has* reached a decision.
      b.   * The judge *have* reached a decision.
(2)   a.   * The president *took place* at twelve noon.
      b.   ? The cows *dined* in the pasture.
      c.   ? The dish *ran away* with the spoon.

The error in (1b) is an agreement violation, whereas the dubious examples in (2) are semantically incongruous. Thus, in (2a), a verb for expressing time occurs with a noun that does not describe an event; in (2b), a verb for a human activity has been attributed to a non-human; and in (2c), an animate activity has been assigned to an inanimate noun. However, sentences (2b) and (2c) would be acceptable in stories or nursery rhymes where animals or even inanimate objects can engage in human behaviour. The semantic incongruities of (2b) and (2c) make sense only in these special contexts.

Let us see how an analysis of the agreement phenomena and the semantic properties affecting nouns and verbs sheds light on the linguistic treatment of institutional nouns and of their relationship to persons. We turn to the class of human nouns, those depicted in column 2 of Table 2.1. Human nouns occur in either the singular or the plural referring to one individual or to more than one; and, in the singular, they govern gender (a masculine/feminine selection) in certain pronouns. These grammatical properties are so well known that there is no need to exemplify them. The semantic restrictions are of more immediate interest. The verbs that go with human nouns fall into three broad semantic groups – *physiological*, *cognitive* and *activity*. This division reflects some basic characteristics about humans: they are physiological beings; they have particular states of mind; and they engage in social activities. Figure 2.4 contains examples of the three classes of verbs.

The physiological set relates to the physical organism. Certain verbs (for example, *eat*, *sleep*, *run*) describe biological functions that humans share with other species. Other verbs (for example, *dine*, *take a siesta*, *jog*), although referring to similar physiological acts, normally apply to humans only. Some of these could be included in the third group – for example, dining also qualifies as a social activity. Because the categories represent broad classifications, we shall not be concerned with overlap. The cognitive group comprises verbs expressing mental states (*think*, *know*), perceptual characteristics (*hear*, *feel*) and communicative functions (*say*, *announce*). The activity class is the most comprehensive of the three. It encompasses the myriad social practices in which humans engage.

Thus far, we have set up four categories of nouns (Table 2.1) and three general verb classes that relate *specifically to human nouns* (Figure 2.4). Are

Some verbs for 'human' nouns

Physiological:
• eat, sleep, run; • dine, take a siesta, jog
Cognitive:
• think, know, realize, doubt, hear, see, feel; • announce, say, claim, ask
Activity:
• read, watch TV, build a house, make a phone call; • play chess, cook, vote

Figure 2.4 Types of verbs

any of these verb classes also compatible with mythical, collective or institutional nouns? This approach will enable us to determine the ways that language treats artificial beings, groups and corporate bodies as conceptually similar to real persons. Because we are most interested in the classification of institutional nouns, we shall also compare them to mythical nouns and to collectives. This excursion into the various similarities and differences will become an exploration into literal language, metaphor and personification.

MYTHICAL NOUNS

Mythical nouns refer to imaginary, artificial, fictitious and metaphysical beings, to creatures inhabiting other realms and other worlds, and to creations of the mind. These entities have whatever properties are bestowed on them through the imagination of their creators. For example, mermaids are females and they swim. Angels are asexual and they fly. Naturally, the more closely – physiologically, mentally and socially – mythical beings resemble humans, the more easily one can attribute human characteristics to them. Note that whenever verbs expressing such traits occur with mythical nouns, the verbs have literal interpretations, not metaphorical ones. This is because mythical nouns generally do not denote inanimate entities, with the exception of robots and dishes that run away with spoons. Compare the mythical nouns of (3) with the inanimate ones of (4):

(3) a. The dragon *gobbled up* the knight in shining armour.
    b. The mermaid *thought* she would *marry* the drunken sailor.
    c. The angels were *misbehaving* all morning.
(4) a. The automatic teller machine *gobbled up* my credit card.
    b. My PC *thinks* that it's a Mac®.
    c. My car has been *misbehaving* all morning.

In (3), the mythical entities, in the imaginary realms that they inhabit, can literally engage in the activities ascribed to them. To put this another way, if they were to exist in our world, they could also perform those same actions. In (4), the nouns refer to real objects of our world, but the entities denoted are inanimate. Because the verbs in (4) belong to the type that normally occur only with animate or human nouns, the entities there have become personified; consequently, the verbs of (4) have only metaphorical interpretations.

COLLECTIVE NOUNS

A collective noun denotes a group of persons (*faculty, jury, clergy*) sharing similar characteristics. One of the interesting grammatical properties of these nouns is a peculiar kind of number agreement. Earlier, we noted that singular nouns, as subjects, require singular forms of verbs, and plural nouns take plural forms. There is one important caveat to this fundamental rule of English grammar. A singular collective noun can refer either to the group as a unit, or else to the separate individuals composing it, and the number of the verb will vary accordingly. The verb shows singular number in the group sense, but plural number with the distributive meaning. This use is reminiscent of the 'joint' and 'several' distinction found within the law. Consider the examples of (5).

(5) a. The faculty *is* having a meeting at one o'clock. (joint or group sense)
     b. The faculty *are* having a meeting at one o'clock. (several or distributive sense)

As a further illustration of this variable number agreement, imagine a situation where each academic department of a university is entitled to a single vote on a certain administrative issue. In order to obtain that vote, each of the faculty members of that department casts his or her vote and sends it to the chair. The way the majority votes then becomes the departmental vote to be transmitted to the administration. The sentences of (6) characterize this two-step process.

(6) a. The law faculty *have* sent *their* votes to the chair.
     b. The law faculty *has* sent *its* vote to the administration.

There are other grammatical features that demonstrate the dual reference of collective nouns. The choice between a singular or a plural verb also affects the selection of a pronoun. Note, in (6), 'their' for the distributive sense and 'its' for the group sense. The sentences of (7) are of a different sort. They illustrate some adverbial expressions that are typically found with plural nouns. Yet the examples of (8) show these same adverbials occurring with singular collectives.

(7) a. There was little agreement *among* the senators.
    b. All of the ministers from the six churches met *together*.
    c. The jurors voted *unanimously* for acquittal.
(8) a. There was little agreement *among* the committee.
    b. All of the clergy from the six churches met *together*.
    c. The jury voted *unanimously* for acquittal.

The sentences of (9) and (10) indicate further that these adverbials when occurring with collectives are grammatical only for the distributive sense – that is, the collective noun must refer to the individual members of the group, not to the group entity itself. This restriction is not surprising in view of the fact that these adverbials carry plural references.

(9) a. The committee *are* unable to reach agreement *among themselves*.
    b. *All* of the clergy from the six churches *are* meeting *together* today.
    c. The jury *have* voted *unanimously* for acquittal.
(10) a. * The committee *is* unable to reach agreement *among itself*.
    b. * *All* of the clergy from the six churches *is* meeting *together* today.
    c. ? The jury *has* voted *unanimously* for acquittal.

Because collective nouns denote groups of like individuals – a faculty is composed of teachers, a jury of jurors and a clergy of clerics – we might expect such nouns to have the same semantic restrictions as the corresponding human nouns. This expectation, in fact, is borne out: as the examples of (11) show, a collective noun, even taken in its group sense, is compatible with any verb (physiological, mental or activity) that expresses a relation that can be attributed appropriately to the individual members of the group, as shown in (12).

(11) a. The faculty *ate* lunch.
    b. The jury *believed* that the defendant was lying
    c. The team *signed* a contract with the union.
(12) a. The teachers *ate* lunch.
    b. The jurors *believed* that the defendant was lying.
    c. The players *signed* a contract with the union.

INSTITUTIONAL NOUNS

An institutional noun denotes a formal organization of persons generally joined together for a common purpose. We are most interested in seeing how language deals with words such as 'corporation.' Does the grammatical behaviour of institutional nouns resemble that of collectives, which also refer to groups of individuals? The examples of (13) illustrate that singular institutional nouns are generally incompatible with plural verbs, pronouns or adverbials. These linguistic facts demonstrate that a singular institutional noun refers to the institutional body alone and – unlike a collective noun – not to its constituent members.

(13) a. The corporation *has* aligned *itself* with Labour.
    b. ? The corporation *have* aligned *themselves* with Labour.
    c. ? There is dissension *among* IBM.

(Some British colleagues have informed me that they find (13b) and (13c) acceptable.)

Consider now sentences, such as (14), where a plural pronoun refers back to a singular indefinite pronoun or to a singular noun (including an institutional noun) that is not a collective.

(14) a. Does *everyone* have *their* work finished?
    b. *A friend of mine* would like to know whether *they* can get permission to visit the rare book room.
    c. **My friend Harry* would like to know whether *they* can get permission to visit the rare book room.
    d. *IBM* announced that *they* were coming out with a new computer.

These peculiarities of usage, common in colloquial English, occur in contexts where the sex of the person is either not known, as in (14a), or else purposely concealed, as in (14b). Where the sex of the person is evident, as in (14c), the plural pronoun is ungrammatical. Because institutional nouns are neuter in gender, the appearance of 'they' in (14d) is similar to the other instances of unknown gender. This usage of a plural pronoun with a singular antecedent is found principally with nouns and pronouns referring to persons and with institutional nouns. Here is our first piece of evidence that grammar attributes person characteristics to institutions.

Let us turn now to the semantic restrictions between institutional nouns and the three classes of verbs – physiological, cognitive and activity. We begin by comparing in (15) and (16) the occurrence of physiological verbs with collective nouns and with institutional ones. Whereas the sentences of (15), with collective nouns, are perfectly natural, those of (16), with institutional nouns, are decidedly bizarre.

(15) a. The team *ate lunch*.
    b. The jury *took a walk*.
    c. The faculty *slept* through the meeting.
(16) a. ? Air France *ate lunch*.
    b. ? Harvard *took a walk*.
    c. ? Microsoft *slept* through the meeting.

Note that although the examples of (16) are anomalous in any literal interpretation – after all, institutions, as entities, simply do not have the physiology of humans – the readings become acceptable whenever they can be construed metonymically. Metonymy, a special type of metaphor, provides a way of referring to people through their institutional or professional affiliations. For example, (16a) would be an appropriate sentence in the following context. Imagine a meeting with representatives from several different airlines. Due to limited eating facilities, not all of the participants are able to go to lunch at the same time. An announcement is made that Air France will eat at 12 noon, British Airways at half past 12 and Iberia at 1 o'clock. The institutional names are being used here metonymically. That is, the act of eating is not imputed to the airlines per se, but rather to the persons representing those different companies. We could construct analogous situations for the other examples of (16). What is significant for metonymy is that the activity denoted by the verb has a literal interpretation, because the understood subject in reality is not the institution but rather persons representing it.

Metaphorical interpretations are also possible when a physiological verb occurs with an institutional noun. Compare the literal interpretation of (17a) with the metaphorical reading of (17b), where the institution has been personified. Note that (17b) is not an example of metonymy. It is not the persons representing the institution that are doing the 'gobbling up', but rather the corporation itself. Hence, the corporation as an entity has been metaphorically personified, exactly analogous to the 'automatic teller machine' of example (4a).

(17)   a.   The hungry teenagers *gobbled up* all the food in sight.
       b.   The giant corporation *gobbled up* the smaller companies.

Metonymy and metaphor, with institutional nouns, affect different parts of a sentence. In metonymy, it is the institutional noun that has a special sense; for example, in (16a), *Air France* stands for certain individuals that are associated with that institution. In metaphor, the noun is personified, and it is the verb that acquires a figurative meaning. For example, in (17b), the noun *corporation* still refers to the institution itself, but it has become personified due to its interaction with the physiological verb 'gobble up', and the verb then takes on a figurative sense that is compatible with the personification. Examples (15) to (17) are intended to establish that physiological verbs do not occur naturally with institutional nouns. When they do occur, the meanings are contrived – the interpretations can be only metonymic or metaphorical.

However, when we turn to cognitive verbs, we find a very different story. Note the examples of (18).

(18)   a.   Ford *denied* that the Pinto® was a deathtrap.
       b.   British Petroleum *announced* that it would need to raise oil prices.
       c.   Toyota *learned* that Nissan *was thinking* of coming out with a new hybrid car.
       d.   The sporting industry *believes* that Italians do not buy very many hockey sticks.

Cognitive verbs occur freely and naturally with institutional nouns. The verbs have their literal interpretations; hence, the sentences do not require special readings. Nor do there seem to be restrictions on the particular cognitive verbs that are allowed. All of them are likely candidates. At first, it might seem surprising that cognitive verbs occur so readily with institutional nouns. After all, the verbs do depict mental states, and there is no question that such states are in the domain of human capacity. One might contend that the verbs of (18) are being used metonymically analogous to those of (16) or metaphorically analogous to (17b). We can reject such an analysis. Recall that the sentences of (16), by themselves, are abnormal. They require special contexts in order to be acceptable. The sentences of (18), on the other hand, need no special settings for their intelligibility. In isolation, they appear as perfectly normal sentences. To treat them as metonymic would leave unexplained this important difference between these sentences and those of (16). One can make an analogous argument concerning the sentences of (18) and (17b). Sentence (17b) requires 'gobble up' – an activity typically associated with animate beings – to have a metaphorical interpretation when an institutional noun is its subject. In contrast, the sentences of (18), whose verbs describe human cognitive states, do not require any modification in the meaning of the verbs when occurring with institutional nouns. Their senses are identical to those used with human or group nouns.

Finally, let us compare the semantic restrictions of activity verbs with both collective and institutional nouns. The examples of (19) and (20) show activity verbs that are compatible with both types of nouns.

(19) a. The team *signed a contract* with the union.
      b. The clergy *sold* its tobacco shares.
      c. The faculty *sent* a representative to lobby Congress.
(20) a. Philips Electric *signed a contract* with the union.
      b. Fiat *sold* sports cars to China.
      c. General Motors *sent* a representative to Washington.

The sentences of (21) and (22) indicate that other activity verbs are acceptable with collective nouns, but abnormal with institutional ones.

(21) a. The faculty *played chess*.
      b. The committee *made phone calls* to new members.
      c. The clergy *voted* for Bush in the 2004 election.
(22) a. ? Philips Electric *played chess*.
      b. ? Fiat *made phone calls* to its clients.
      c. ? General Motors *voted* for Bush in the 2004 election.

The difference, of course, is that the activities depicted in (20) are those that the institutions in question are competent to perform, whereas those of (22) are outside of this range. However, the sentences of (22) do admit of metonymic interpretations. For example, (22a) can mean only that an individual representing Philips Electric or a team from there played in a chess tournament. However, the sentences of (20), like those of (18), have literal interpretations: British Petroleum of (18b) announces in the same manner that any live person announces, and the Fiat corporation of (20b) engages in selling just as any individual would. As a counter-analysis, one might wish to claim that the institutional nouns of (20) should be interpreted metonymically – that is, the nouns refer to representatives from the institutions. According to that analysis, the meanings of the verbs would still be literal because they denote activities being performed by the metonymic persons. However, compare once again the sentences of (22), which, if they are to be interpretable at all, must have metonymic readings, with the sentences of (20), which do not require any kind of specialized interpretation. To treat all the examples as metonymy simply misses this crucial distinction.

Another convincing way to show that the examples of (20) are very different from those of (22) is to find a sentence with both literal and metonymic interpretations. As a potential candidate, consider (22c). In its metonymic reading, it might mean that most of the employees of General Motors, as individual citizens, had voted for Bush. Suppose, though, that the Supreme Court were to decide – now that corporations are persons within the provisions of the Fourteenth Amendment and citizens for jurisdictional purposes – to make corporations fully-fledged citizens, entitled to vote in national elections. Thus, General Motors would have a single vote. If this state of affairs were to have transpired, sentence (22c) would acquire a straightforward, literal meaning analogous to the sentences of (20). Note that, in this hypothetical situation, the members of the corporation would still retain their individual votes. Hence, the corporate vote is not the vote of the members but the vote of the corporate body itself, and it is for this reason that (22c) would acquire a literal reading.

The relationship between corporate personality and noun categorization

In our earlier discussion about legal personality, we noted that basic legal relationships take place between one person and another. The natural person then becomes a barometer against which other kinds of legal persons are defined and measured. A similar situation obtains for our linguistic classification. Human nouns are basic, so that they too provided a point of departure for the analysis of the other noun classes. A surprising result of this comparison is that some of the features of the mythical, collective and institutional categories turn out to be uncannily similar to attributes from the creature, group and person theories, respectively. Let us consider some of the similarities that emerge between notions of corporate personality and properties of noun categorization.

The *creature theory* treats the corporation as an artificial entity whose legal rights arise through the act of incorporation. In language, mythical nouns are similar. They too refer to artificial entities, whose physical, mental and social traits are bestowed on them in their creation. As for nouns such as 'corporation', there are linguistic arguments demonstrating that they do not belong to this class. First, mythical nouns, because they generally depict animate entities, can have physical characteristics literally attributed to them, but institutional nouns cannot. Whenever verbs expressing physiological processes occur with institutional nouns, the sentences must be interpreted metaphorically or metonymically. Second, the entities denoted by mythical nouns may have restricted mental capacity, so that the nouns referring to such entities would not occur with all cognitive verbs. Institutional nouns, on the other hand, take the full gamut of cognitive verbs.

The *group theory* treats the corporation as a group of persons joined together for a common purpose. In language, collective nouns denote aggregates of similar individuals. Nouns such as 'corporation' are not in this category either. First, a singular collective noun can trigger either singular or plural number agreement depending on whether it refers to the group or to its members, but a singular institutional noun typically does not allow for a choice in number. Second, because collectives designate persons, any physiological, cognitive or activity verb that can be applied appropriately to an individual of a group can also refer to the group as a unit. Institutional nouns, on the other hand, do not exhibit literal interpretations with physiological verbs, nor with the full range of activity verbs that occur with collective nouns.

The *person theory* treats the corporation, an independent formal organization, as a legal person analogous to a human being. In language, institutional nouns refer to organizations. These nouns have some unique properties. First, although physiological verbs, in their literal senses, are inappropriate with institutional nouns, cognitive verbs reign supreme. As far as language is concerned, institutions do not have bodies – they indeed are incorporeal and intangible – but they certainly do have minds. They think and they feel and they say. Next, many activity verbs are compatible with, and literally applicable to, institutional nouns, so that, linguistically, the institutions are viewed as competent to perform the designated acts. To be sure, language does not regard institutions as fully human, but it does impute significant human characteristics to them – mentalities and the ability to pursue social activities. Therefore, language treats the ensuing thoughts and actions as belonging to the institutions themselves and not to the hidden members. This perspective from language turns out to be most congenial to the person theory of corporate personality.

Why the law needs fictions and metaphors

What is the purpose of a legal fiction? As Lon Fuller aptly noted: '[It] is frequently a metaphorical way of expressing a truth'.[58] Pierre Olivier, in his treatise on legal fictions, supports this theme:

> The basic reason for the employment of fictions, not only in law but in almost all sciences, is that they facilitate the thought process . . . The fiction is based on an analogy or similarity between two objects or situations, and enables us to equate the two so that they can be treated alike . . . and yet at the same time warns us that the analogy . . . is not true in all respects . . .[59]

A legal fiction literally is a false statement. As an illustration of how a false statement may have an air of truth, Fuller provides a whimsical scenario of the dilemma facing the judge who first came up with the 'attractive nuisance' doctrine.[60] Recall the facts. A child from an industrial area of town has been seriously injured while playing on a turntable in an open railroad yard. The plaintiff child brings suit against the defendant railroad. Issue: is the railroad responsible for the injury? In attempting to find an answer to this inquiry, Fuller imagines various solutions that might have gone through the judge's head. He knows that the current law asserts that a landowner owes a duty of care to 'invitees', but not to 'trespassers'. However, deep down inside, the judge feels that this unfortunate child should be treated more like an invitee and less as a common trespasser. The judge is reluctant to base a decision on his personal feelings; after all, the child really was trespassing. Perhaps the judge could state that the rule of trespass does *not* apply to children. Such a ruling would raise further problems: the types of children to be exempted, their ages and whether children entering the property were aware of the danger there. Or perhaps landowners should be held responsible for injuries sustained by anyone who enters upon their land. But the judge realizes that such a proposal would be much too broad (and brash); it would essentially do away entirely with the law of trespass. Finally, he could decide in favour of the plaintiff child without giving any particular reason, but the judge is very uncomfortable with that prospect, as it would not sit well with those seeking a rationale for the decision.

Our judge, faced with this dilemma and finding no real viable solution, feels compelled to go back to his original hunch – to treat the child as an invitee rather than as an ordinary trespasser. He announces before the court that the defendant railroad must be 'deemed to have invited' the child onto the land. This bold assertion by our hypothetical judge 'brings the case within the cover of existing doctrine and puts an end to these troublesome attempts to state a new principle'.[61] The law has adopted a fictional statement because of its *utility*. Although the statement is false, nonetheless it has expressed a truth – namely, that the child's status is more like that of an invitee than of a trespasser, and the only way to express this 'truth' is metaphorically – by claiming that the landowner (or his agent, the attractive nuisance) must be 'deemed to have invited' the child onto the premises. Once so 'invited', the landowner then owes the child the same duty of care that would be extended to any other guest. This scenario gives some idea, albeit fanciful, of the genesis of the 'attractive nuisance' doctrine, which, according to Fuller, is 'probably the boldest fiction to be found in modern law'.[62]

The law bases the fiction of the 'attractive nuisance' on the notion of 'allurement' or 'enticement'. We proposed for this fiction the conceptual metaphor: AN ATTRACTIVE NUISANCE IS AN INVITER. This metaphor in turn was just a special instance of a more general conventional one: AN ENTITY IS AN INVITER. Although the fiction of the attractive nuisance may be rather 'bold', its conceptualization already lies within a conventional metaphor, thereby making the legal metaphor more accessible and acceptable.

Not all legal fictions have corresponding conceptual metaphors. For example, the attractive nuisance doctrine finds additional support in that aspect of agency law that attributes to a principal, such as an employer, the acts of his agent, or employee. According to an 'agency' interpretation of the attractive nuisance doctrine, an invitation extended by the agent (i.e. the attractive nuisance) becomes the invitation of the principal (i.e. the landowner), who then has a responsibility towards the child 'invitee'. We can state succinctly the 'agency' fiction as: AN AGENT'S ACT IS THE PRINCIPAL'S ACT. However, this equation does not qualify as a conceptual metaphor. First, I am unaware of linguistic metaphors expressing this idea. More importantly, the two entities of the comparison do not satisfy the requirements for 'target' and 'source'. Is *agent* a more abstract notion than *principal*? Rather, both are technical legal terms having a reciprocal relationship. Furthermore, a conceptual metaphor requires source properties corresponding to target properties (such as, *stage* : *world* for Shakespeare or *arms* : *branches* for Kilmer). We find no such correspondence between the properties of the principal's act and those of the agent. This succinct formula simply asserts that whatever act the agent does is an act done by the principal. It clearly qualifies as a legal fiction, if only because it is not literally true, but it is not a metaphor, at least not in the sense developed throughout this chapter.

There are still other legal fictions not based on metaphor. One of these deals with 'implied conditions' in contract law. They are terms that the parties to an agreement never expressly stated, but nonetheless the terms are significant enough in order for the law to infer that they must be part of the contract. The fiction resides in a presumption that the conditions have emanated from a 'meeting of the minds'. In reality, the parties, when drawing up their contract, may have been completely unaware of the conditions or even not in accord with them. Another non-metaphorical fiction concerns the 'conclusive presumption', a fiction mentioned in the discussion of the *Marshall* case, where the shareholders were *presumed* to be residents of the state where incorporation took place. Now, a conclusive presumption is not an out-and-out lie, for it may well be true that some shareholders hold residence coinciding with the state of incorporation. The legal fiction, however, assumes coincidence even where the residence is actually elsewhere. Furthermore, a conclusive presumption is not rebuttable – that is, no one may offer evidence about the 'true' residence of shareholders where it differs from that of the corporation.

Literal language versus metaphor

The literature on metaphor sometimes distinguishes between 'live' metaphors and 'dead' ones. A live metaphor is one whose figurative meaning is patently transparent, such as: 'The giant corporation *gobbled up* the smaller companies'. A dead metaphor, historically, was once live, but is no longer perceived as such. Present-day speakers take its meaning to be one of the literal senses of the word, and standard dictionaries usually cite the meaning in this way. As an example of this linguistic process, consider the word 'leg' in the expressions 'leg of a triangle' and 'leg of a table'. Here, an anatomical term has been extended to concepts pertaining to mathematics and to furniture, respectively. Although there is doubtless a metaphorical origin in these other senses of 'leg' – after all, there is vertical extension and support of some structure – nonetheless, the new meanings filled previous gaps in vocabulary. The independence of the meanings is confirmed through language use. Thus, a hosiery manufacturer, aiming his advertising campaign at an audience interested in legs, is not directing his message to mathematicians or to furniture dealers. The circumstances under which there would be overlap between the different senses of 'leg' would be rare indeed.

Many words from everyday language have had their meanings extended in this fashion. In fact, this is one of the commonest ways of introducing new meanings into language. The eminent linguist, Edward Sapir, noted: 'The birth of a new concept is inevitably foreshadowed by a more or less strained or extended use of old linguistic material'.[63] This kind of metaphorical innovation is evident in computer talk. Consider such terms as: *address, bookmark, browse, chat, cookie, firewall, icon, information highway, link, mouse, password, search engine, server, site, surf, virus, web, worm*. Are these words still live metaphors or have many already become dead?

The law, too, is no stranger to this brand of linguistic evolution. One speaks of a contract that is 'binding', but that nonetheless may be 'broken'. Today, no one thinks of these words as particularly metaphorical. How else would one talk about these aspects of contracts? Of course, the legal senses are different from the meanings that these words have when they refer to physical objects. The binding of a contract is not the same kind of event as the binding of a stack of newspapers, and the breaking of a contract is a radically different activity from the breaking of a physical object like a dish. (To break a contract does not mean to rip up the sheets of paper on which the terms of an agreement are written, although someone breaking a contract might choose to engage in that symbolic act as well.)

Comprehensive dictionaries, of course, provide separate listings for the different meanings of a word. For example, *Webster's* among its various entries for *break*, has the following two that are relevant to our discussion. Notice that they have little in common, which seems to strengthen the idea that there is no longer a metaphorical connection.

1. to cause to part or to divide by force, as a solid substance; to separate into pieces by shattering; to crack; to smash; to burst; as to *break* a dish; to *break* a thread or a cable.
[. . .]
9. to fail to follow the terms of; to violate; as, he *broke* his agreement.[64]

Cognitive linguistic research, however, does not support the traditional view about live and dead metaphors, although the distinction does serve as a useful heuristic for differentiating between expressions whose meanings are unconventional – and hence metaphorical – from those whose meanings have now become completely conventionalized. Yet – and here is where the cognitive view goes beyond the traditional one – there remains a conceptual connection or commonality between the original concrete sense of a word and its various extensions, so that from a conceptual perspective the metaphor has never really died.

We can illustrate this claim from cognitive linguistics by providing for the transitive verb *break* a basic meaning that runs through its variants: 'to break a dish' is to shatter it into pieces; 'to break an engagement of marriage' is to alter radically the course of a personal relationship; 'to break a horse' is to make it suddenly tractable; 'to break prison' is to be at once free; 'to break a strike' is to end it by force; 'to break a fall' is to stop a rapid downward descent; and 'to break a contract' is to render its terms worthless so that it ceases to function as a document expressing the will of the parties. What notion is common to these different senses of *break*? *To break something is to change its form or function often dramatically, such that it may not always be possible to go back to the way it was once before.* Something like this concept constitutes the metaphorical structuring that continues to tie together the various concrete and abstract senses of *break*, which dictionaries now record as conventionalized, literal meanings.

To appreciate better the cognitive view, we can draw a useful analogy between: (a) the relation of a family of linguistic metaphors to their underlying conceptual metaphor; and (b) the relation of the various literal meanings of a word to the metaphorical underpinning around which those meanings cluster. We demonstrated for the former relationship how we talk about corporations using verbs of cognition and activity and how that discourse is expressed by means of literal language. However, beneath these surface manifestations lies the conceptual metaphor: THE CORPORATION IS A PERSON. In other words, although we may talk about corporations using literal language, our ideas about them still are structured metaphorically. In an analogous fashion, whether we talk about breaking a dish, breaking a relationship or breaking a contract, in each case we are using literal language. Yet, there is a primitive meaning – a metaphorical basis – that holds together these different senses of *break*. It is this cognitive structuring that enables us to perceive the conceptual unity embracing the various meanings.

We have contrasted two positions dealing with the relationship between the different meanings of a word. One fairly traditional view claims that although, historically, new meanings of a word may have had their origin in metaphor, any such connection is now 'dead' and what were once metaphorical meanings have evolved into independent, literal ones. Opposed to this position is the cognitive linguistic view. It too recognizes literal meanings but maintains that metaphor is still very much alive serving as the indispensable medium around which the different senses cluster conceptually. If we go back to the first quarter of the twentieth century, we can find similar contrasting views regarding the nature of corporate personality.

The philosopher, John Dewey, argued that 'person' is a purely legal notion and signifies whatever the law chooses for it to mean:

> In saying that 'person' might legally mean whatever the law makes it mean, I am trying to say that 'person' might be used simply as a synonym for a right-and-duty-bearing unit. Any such unit would be a person; such a statement . . . would convey no implications, except that the unit has those rights and duties which the courts find it to have. What 'person' signifies in popular speech, or in psychology, or in philosophy or morals, would be as irrelevant . . . as it would be to argue that because a wine is called 'dry,' it has the properties of dry solids . . . Obviously, 'dry' as applied to a particular wine has the kind of meaning, and only the kind of meaning, which it has when applied to the class of beverages in general. Why should not the same sort of thing hold of the use of 'person' in law?[65]

What matters for Dewey is that the law requires the notion of a right-and-duty-bearing unit, one that includes both human beings and corporations. If the law employs the word 'person' to describe that entity, this use does not imply any necessary connection, metaphorical or otherwise, between natural persons and institutions. One could just as well call this right-and-duty-bearing unit a robot, a table or anything else. The law had need of a concept for which no word previously existed, and so it chose an existing word to fill a gap in the lexicon. The legal meaning of 'person' covers a completely separate domain from that of its ordinary, everyday reference to humans. Moreover, Dewey's observation about the lack of a relationship between 'dry wine' and 'dry solids' is exactly analogous to the claim that the 'leg of a triangle' and the 'leg of a table' are no longer related to the anatomical 'leg', or that the various meanings of *break* have little or nothing in common.

Dewey's position that the law's use of the word 'person' does not imply any necessary connection – metaphorical or otherwise – between natural persons and institutions was refuted by a legal scholar, Arthur Machen, who observed:

> When a jurist first said, 'A corporation is a person', he was using a metaphor to express the truth that a corporation bears some analogy or resemblance to a person, and is to be treated in law in certain respects as if it were a person, or a rational being capable of feeling and volition.[66]

For Machen, the corporation is called a person, precisely because one treats it as a person. Furthermore, as a person, it can be conceived in ways not possible, had it been referred to in some other manner. Machen continues:

> If you can *imagine* that a corporate entity is a person, you can also imagine that this person has a mind. Consequently, corporations can be

guilty of fraud, of malice, or of crimes involving a particular mental state. [emphasis added].[67]

The choice of the word 'imagine' is particularly perceptive, for *imagining* is at the very foundation of metaphor. According to Machen, the law treats the corporation as though it were 'a rational being capable of feeling and volition'. To be rational is to have a mind or intelligence, to be capable of cognition. 'Feeling' and 'volition' are cognitive states, and in the linguistic treatment of institutional nouns it is precisely the cognitive verbs that can be attributed literally and liberally to these entities. We are also in a better position to appreciate Machen's further statement that, in the appropriate circumstances, we can imagine corporations to be guilty of fraud or of malice. Verbal expressions pertaining to fraud or malice would be included among activity verbs, and many of these, too, are compatible with institutional nouns, if we view the institutions as competent to perform the designated acts. Recall the discussion about corporations casting ballots. Although corporations are not permitted to vote in political elections, nonetheless one can conceive of that possibility. In an analogous way, we could create situations where it would be linguistically felicitous to impute fraud, malice or other criminal states of mind to a corporate body. In fact, the imputation of a criminal mind to the corporation itself is no longer so far-fetched, as the following excerpt illustrates.

Corporation ordered to pay $13 million criminal fine
On March 1, 2005, in San Diego, California, Titan Corporation, a San Diego-based military intelligence and communications company, *pleaded guilty to three felony counts*, including Foreign Corrupt Practices Act violations, *falsifying* corporate books and records, and *aiding* in the filing of a false corporate tax return . . . Titan *was sentenced* and ordered *to pay a criminal fine* of $13 million and *serve three years supervised probation*. [emphasis added][68]

An interesting question: what would happen should Titan violate its probation?

3 Speech Acts and Legal Hearsay

If the Rules of Evidence can be visualized as a castle,
the keystone in the main arch has to be the hearsay rule.
G. Michael Fenner[1]

A witness, taking the stand during a court trial, can testify about events directly perceived through any of the five senses: the witness can state that he or she saw the defendant leave the bank carrying a black bag; smelled gas on entering a room; ate oysters that had a peculiar taste; felt cold while sitting in a train compartment; or heard a loud explosion. However, if what a witness heard (or read) were the words spoken (or written) by someone else, then such utterances *may* constitute hearsay and, if so, will not be admissible as testimony. It is the 'rule against hearsay' that addresses this question: which statements related by a testifying witness count as inadmissible hearsay, and which ones do not and therefore may be admitted into evidence?

We shall begin with a brief overview of the rationale and the criteria for the hearsay rule. There are three broad types of statements – those falling within the definition of hearsay and consequently inadmissible as evidence; those not regarded as hearsay and therefore admissible; and those, although conforming to the definition of hearsay, nonetheless admissible as permitted exceptions to the rule. Our interest resides primarily with the first two types. So far as exceptions go, we shall only consider statements relating to state of mind.

We shall then introduce speech-act theory, a linguistic approach to meaning that investigates how speakers use language. Utterances perform specific functions within the communicative process. For example, speakers may report events or happenings, obligate themselves to some future course of action or bring about new states of affairs. We shall then show how this theory provides a novel means for determining which statements constitute hearsay and which ones do not. Of particular interest will be utterances reflecting state of mind. Although such statements are generally admissible, legal scholars have not always agreed on how to classify them. There are two conflicting views: state-of-mind assertions are non-hearsay to begin with; or they are hearsay but are permitted exceptions. Speech-act analysis will provide a unique solution to this question. Finally, we shall consider the contribution of speech-act theory to a better understanding of the nature of legal hearsay.

What is hearsay?

Hearsay is one of the topics covered by the rules of *evidence*. Within Anglo-American law, these rules are intended to uncover the truth by placing limitations on the kind of evidence permitted during a trial. When a jury is present, the judge and the jury have distinct responsibilities in evaluating the evidence. The judge determines whether the evidence is *admissible*, whether it may be presented to the jury. The jury then decides how much *weight* to give to the evidence, whether it is credible. In other words, the judge makes decisions about the law, and the jury applies the law to the facts of the case. A fundamental requirement is that the fact-finder – whether judge or jury – must decide the case entirely on the evidence presented within the courtroom.

Only *relevant* evidence may be admitted. ' "Relevant evidence" means evidence having any tendency to make the existence of any fact that is of consequence to the determination of the action more probable or less probable than it would be without the evidence.'[2] For example, an individual's extramarital affairs would be considered relevant evidence for the dissolution of a marriage in jurisdictions where infidelity constitutes grounds for divorce, but it is unlikely that such conduct would ever be admissible in a case involving a traffic mishap.

Evidence may be classified as *direct* or *circumstantial*, and as *real* or *testimonial*. Direct evidence is immediate. If believed, it automatically resolves the question before the court. Circumstantial evidence, even if believed, requires some additional reasoning before the issue can be resolved. Assume that at issue is whether Jones is the person who entered a bank, approached a teller, pointed a gun, demanded and received a wad of cash, stuffed it into a briefcase, and then swiftly walked out of the bank. At trial the teller identifies Jones as the person that robbed her. This is direct testimony. If the jurors believe the teller, the case is pretty much cut and dried: guilty!

Now let's change the scenario a bit. During the entire time he was in the bank, the robber had a stocking cap pulled tightly over his head. Hence, none of the employees or customers within the bank was able to identify the culprit. However, Jones became a suspect, was arrested, and is now on trial. The prosecution was able to find a witness who could testify at the trial. The witness states that as she was about to cross the street to enter the bank, she spotted Jones, a co-worker from a former job, hurriedly leaving the bank. He opened a briefcase and put inside what looked like a knitted cap. She called out to him, but he looked the other way and started running. Her recounting of this incident is circumstantial evidence, most importantly because she did not actually see the robbery take place. Still, the jury may find her story to be quite credible and to conclude that Jones is the robber. This conclusion, however, would require a crucial step in reasoning. Now, it is indisputable that the robber wore a stocking cap while in the bank and carried a briefcase. Anyone who was in the bank and saw the robbery can at least attest to these two facts. The critical step appeals to deductive reasoning: a woman claims to have seen a man rushing from the bank, carrying a briefcase and putting inside what looked like a cap. Moreover, this individual looked away, refusing to acknowledge someone who purportedly was a former acquaintance. Is it more likely than not that the robber is the person that fled from the bank, stuffed something into his briefcase, and then turned away and ran?

Real evidence concerns tangible things – documents, weapons – the proverbial 'smoking gun' in a homicide case. Testimonial evidence deals with witnesses' reports. In our two hypothetical situations about the bank robbery, the assertions from the bank teller or from the woman crossing the street are examples of testimonial evidence.

The purpose for the rules of evidence is to uncover the truth. The most effective tool for reaching this goal is without a doubt *cross-examination*. It is the ability to question rigorously an opposing side's witness that differentiates a trial in the English-speaking world from one taking place in Continental Europe or in Latin America. Let us see what could happen during cross-examination if a witness were to report what he or she heard from someone else. We need to keep in mind the difference between a *witness* and a *declarant*. The witness is the person speaking before the court, the one who has taken an oath 'to tell the truth, the whole truth, and nothing but the truth'. A declarant is the author of a statement that is offered as evidence for some issue at trial. Now, most of the time that person will be the witness. However, if the witness is reporting what someone else has said, then that other person is also a declarant. With this distinction in place, we are ready for a new, and different, scenario about the bank robbery, one containing testimony that could never be permitted in court.

Jones is on trial. For whatever reason, the woman who claims to have spotted him just before crossing the street is not available to appear in court. Instead, a friend has come to testify on her behalf. Jones's attorney wants to prove that the woman who was unable to be present was quite mistaken in identifying Jones as the alleged robber. The cross-examination of the 'proxy' witness is taking place:

Lawyer: You mentioned that when your friend was about to cross the street to go into the bank, she saw a man hurrying out.

Witness: Yes, that's right.

Lawyer: And she recognized him as someone she knew from her previous employment.

Witness: Yes, that's what she told me.
Lawyer: What time did your friend arrive at the bank?
Witness: I believe it was in the afternoon.
Lawyer: How far from the entrance was she when she saw the man coming
    out?
Witness: I don't know. She didn't mention anything to me about the distance.
Lawyer: What was the weather like that afternoon?
Witness: I really don't know.
Lawyer: Does your friend wear glasses?
Witness: Sometimes.
Lawyer: Was she wearing them then?
Witness: I don't know.

In answering any further questions, this witness is most likely to repeat:
'I don't know'. Because she can provide few details about what happened, it becomes almost impossible for the opposing lawyer to discredit
the friend's story or to cast doubt on the friend's perception of the events.
Had the friend been available to testify, she would have been able to
respond to the defendant's attorney and to provide a full account of the
events.

The rationale behind the 'rule against hearsay' is precisely to exclude
verbal evidence that is defective, that is unreliable and that consequently
does not assist the fact-finder (in general, the jury) in arriving at the truth.
The inability to cross-examine the person that made the statement makes
hearsay not trustworthy.[3] Moreover, because that person is not present in
the courtroom, he or she is not under oath to tell the truth, is not surrounded by the solemnity of the judicial proceedings, and cannot be
observed by judge or jury.

Not all out-of-court utterances count as inadmissible hearsay, but only
those offered to prove the truth of what is asserted. A statement offered for
any other purpose would not be hearsay. For example, consider the utterance, 'It's a beautiful day today'. If it is offered to prove that *the weather was
especially pleasant on a particular day*, the statement would be hearsay. If it is
offered instead to show that *the person making the statement was being cordial
and friendly*, it would *not* be hearsay.

Here is a more dramatic example. Andy, while walking down the street,
is horrified to find his friend Bill lying in a pool of blood. He bends over
Bill and asks: 'What happened?' Bill feebly replies: 'Charlie stabbed me',
and then expires. Charlie is on trial for the murder of Bill, and Andy has
been called as a witness. Andy relates to the jury the incident of his
strolling down the street and seeing Bill lying there covered in blood. The
principal issue, of course, is: who killed Bill? Andy would love to tell the
jury that Bill's last words were: 'Charlie stabbed me'. Bill is the declarant
of this statement, but he is not the witness nor will he ever be available to
testify, for he is dead. Hence, for the issue of who killed Bill, Bill's out-of-
court statement, no matter how useful it could be, is inadmissible hearsay

and Andy would not be permitted to offer it for the issue of the identity of the murderer. Why not? Because if you believe Bill's statement, then you believe that Charlie is the murderer – that is, Bill's out-of-court statement has been offered to prove as true what it asserts. Unfortunately though, the author of this incriminating statement, the dead Bill, cannot be cross-examined.

Now let us change the issue: was Bill ever conscious after being stabbed? Andy testifies that Bill was conscious for a short period. How does Andy know this? He responds: 'Because I leaned over Bill and heard him whisper, "Charlie stabbed me"'. Bill's statement is not being offered to identify the killer, but to show that Bill was able to speak. He could have said anything at all, in English or in any other language. All that matters is his having said something, anything, because the ability to speak is generally sufficient evidence of consciousness. The jury is not asked to believe the truth of Bill's statement but to believe only that he made a statement. Even if Bill were lying about who stabbed him, it would not change the fact that he said something and whatever he said – be it the truth or a lie – is evidence enough of consciousness. Moreover, the witness, Andy, can be properly cross-examined: is he sure Bill said something? Was there a lot of street noise at the time? How close was his ear to Bill's lips? We see, then, that the same statement may be hearsay in regard to one issue, but non-hearsay to some other one. This means that a statement cannot be analysed in isolation or out of context. *A statement must always be evaluated vis-à-vis a particular issue.* Consequently, the judge in this scenario will probably find it necessary to instruct the jury that they may entertain Bill's statement as evidence of his being conscious but not as evidence that Charlie did him in. I leave to the reader to mull over whether the hypothetical jury would be capable of ignoring what Bill's statement asserts.

Legal hearsay

The following definition of hearsay is found in the *Federal Rules of Evidence* (*FRE*), a document containing the rules used in the US federal courts and adopted by many of the states: '"Hearsay" is a statement, other than one made by the declarant while testifying at the trial or hearing, offered in evidence to prove the truth of the matter asserted'.[4] The terms 'statement' and 'declarant' are also defined: 'A "statement" is (1) an oral or written assertion or (2) nonverbal conduct of a person [such as nodding "yes"], if it is intended by him as an assertion'.[5] 'A "declarant" is a person who makes a statement.'[6] (Throughout this discussion, we shall use the terms, 'utterance', 'statement' and 'assertion' interchangeably.) The federal rules go on to state: 'Hearsay in not admissible except as provided by these rules or by other rules prescribed by the Supreme Court pursuant to statutory authority or by Act of Congress'.[7] The English characterization of 'hearsay' is similar: 'Evidence of a statement made to a witness . . . may or may not be hearsay. It is hearsay and inadmissible when the object of the evidence is to establish the truth of what is contained in the statement. It is not hearsay and is admissible when it is proposed to establish by the evidence, not the truth of the statement, but the fact that it was made'.[8]

It follows from these definitions that a statement will *not* be hearsay if presented other than to 'prove the truth of the matter asserted'. What are some of these other uses of out-of-court statements that traditionally are not considered hearsay? There are four general categories: (a) utterances that count as verbal acts or the verbal parts of accompanying physical acts, which have legal significance; (b) utterances offered to show their effects on a hearer or on a hearer's state of mind; (c) utterances that indirectly say something about the mental state of the speaker or about a speaker's knowledge or awareness; and (d) utterances whose interest resides in the fact that they were made *qua* statements, such as those viewed as defamation or perjury.

Let us begin by looking at some questions about hearsay that appeared (many years ago) on an evidence examination given during the summer term at Harvard Law School.[9] The exam had 75 questions, many of them dealing with exceptions to the hearsay rule. We have selected 13 questions, and the responses to 12 are either hearsay or non-hearsay. Only one is a possible exception to the rule against hearsay. Here are the questions, each of which pairs an *issue* with a *statement*. You may wish to test yourself. An analysis of each statement vis-à-vis the issue follows the exam.

The Harvard Hearsay Examination

Which of the following items is hearsay?

1. On the issue whether X and D were engaged to be married, D's statement to X, 'I promise to marry you on June 1'.
2. On the issue whether a transfer of a chattel from D to X was a sale or a gift, D's statement accompanying the transfer, 'I am giving you this chattel as a birthday present'.
3. On the issue in 2, D's statement the day following the transfer, 'I gave you the chattel as a birthday present'.
4. On the issue of D's adverse possession of Blackacre, D's assertion, 'I am the owner of this farm'.
5. On the issue of X's provocation for assaulting Y, D's statement to X, her husband, 'Y ravished me'.
6. On the issue of the reasonableness of X's conduct in the shooting of Y by X, D's statement to X, 'Y has threatened to kill you on sight'.
7. On the issue of X's knowledge of speedily impending death, D's statement to X, 'You have only a few minutes to live'.
8. On the issue in 7, X's statement, 'I realize that I am dying'.

9. On the issue of the sanity of D, a woman, D's public statement, 'I am the Pope'.
10. On the issue of D's ill feeling toward X, D's statement, 'X is a liar and a hypocrite'.
11. On the issue of D's consciousness after an attack, D's statement, 'X shot me, as he often threatened to do'.
12. On the issue of the identity of the shooter, D's statement in 11.
13. On the issue of whether X made threats to shoot D, D's statement in 11.

We discuss from a legal perspective the statements and issues from the Harvard exam.

Verbal act

'I promise to marry you on June 1.'
The issue concerns whether X and D were engaged to be married.

D's out-of-court statement is a promise. Moreover, we must assume that the witness who reported this statement personally heard the declarant, and we are interested only in the fact that a promise was made, not that the marriage – which is what the promise is about – will be carried out. As for relevance, a promise of marriage is certainly relevant for the issue of whether there is an engagement. Now, a promise is the type of statement that the law recognizes as a verbal act, one that may have legal consequences. (For example, within Anglo-American law, a promise is an indispensable ingredient in the formation of a lawful contract, which is the subject matter of Chapter 4.) Statements having legal effects do *not* constitute hearsay.

'I am giving you this chattel as a birthday present.'
D handed over a chattel to X. Was it gift or had he sold it to X?

We assume that a witness saw D hand over the chattel to X. Recall that a witness can report whatever he or she has personally observed. Yet, this action by itself does not necessarily substantiate whether the transfer was a gift or a sale. However, D's words accompanying the physical act will unambiguously clarify the purpose of the transaction. This type of statement too is considered a verbal act, one that explains the nature of a physical act. Accordingly, it is *not* hearsay.

'I gave you the chattel as a birthday present.'
Now we consider D's statement the day following the transfer.

Here D is telling X that the chattel given to X yesterday was a gift. This statement is not a verbal act caught as it was being produced but rather a description by D of an action taken on a previous occasion. It is being offered to 'prove the truth of the matter asserted'. Therefore, this statement *is* hearsay. Moreover, statements whose verbs are in the past tense almost invariably will turn out to be hearsay.

'I am the owner of this farm.'
The issue concerns D's adverse possession of Blackacre.

Adverse possession is the acquisition of title to someone else's land after occupying it for a prescribed period.[10] Squatting, for example, would be a type of adverse possession. One of the criteria for adverse possession is that the occupier must openly acknowledge the possession.[11] D's going around town announcing for all to hear that he is 'the owner of this farm' would be in accord with this requirement. Such a claim clearly has legal significance. D's words then constitute a verbal act and so his statement would *not* be hearsay.

Hearer's reaction and hearer's state of mind

'Y ravished me.'
The issue concerns X's provocation for his assault on Y.

The wife's out-of-court statement is not offered to prove whether she had indeed been 'ravished' (for all we know, she may have lied), but rather to show the effect it had on the husband. On hearing his wife tell about this incident, whether or not it was true, X became furious and turned his wrath against Y. It is *not* hearsay when a statement is offered to show its effect on a hearer.

'Y has threatened to kill you on sight.'
The issue concerns the reasonableness of X's conduct in shooting Y.

D told X that Y had threatened to kill X. After hearing D's statement, X felt compelled to defend himself. D's statement is *not* hearsay if it is offered to show its impact on the hearer X. Note, though, that there would be hearsay if the statement were offered for the purpose of proving that Y had threatened X.

'You have only a few minutes to live.'
The issue is whether X has knowledge of his speedily impending death.

When D tells X that he has only minutes to live, at that moment X acquires knowledge of what was related to him by D – irrespective of whether the information about the impending death is true. The statement is not presented for its truth, but again for its effect on the hearer. Accordingly, there is *not* hearsay. The law also considers this type of non-hearsay as indicative of the 'state of mind of the hearer'.

Speaker's indirect state of mind

'I am the Pope.'
The issue concerns the sanity of the woman who made this statement.

Obviously, one is not trying to prove that she is the Pope. Rather, the statement is presented as the ranting of a purported disillusioned individual. Her statement is offered for the purpose of inferring something about her mental condition. It is *not* hearsay to use an assertion as circumstantial evidence for a particular state of mind of the speaker.

'X is a liar and a hypocrite.'
We are concerned here with whether D has expressed ill-feeling towards X.

The statement is not offered to prove whether X is really 'a liar and a hypocrite', but to show that one who speaks thus about another harbours ill-will. We are interested in the fact that the statement was made and not whether it is true. Hence, there is *not* hearsay.

'I realize that I am dying.'
The issue is whether X had knowledge of his speedily impending death.

The issue here is the same as the one considered in a previous example. There, the out-of-court statement by D to X was: 'You have only a few minutes to live'. The statement was offered to show not its truth about how long X would live but rather its effect on X, and for that reason it did not constitute hearsay. Here, however, X himself asserts directly his awareness of his impending death. His statement appears to prove exactly what it asserts and, from that perspective, it should count as *hearsay*. Yet, X's statement concerns his 'state of mind'. Thus far, we have suggested that statements reflecting state of mind are *not* hearsay. So, is X's statement hearsay or not? For the moment, we leave aside the answer to this controversial question. We shall resolve it when we take up statements pertaining to state of mind.

Utterance qua *statement made*

'X shot me, as he often threatened to do.'
The issue concerns D's consciousness after an attack.

This statement is similar to one discussed previously: 'Charlie stabbed me'. The same analysis is valid here. The statement is offered purely to show that D could speak. His making some kind of utterance provides evidence of the likelihood of his being conscious. For this reason, there is *not* hearsay. However, D's statement does constitute *hearsay* regarding the other two issues raised in the Harvard exam – the identity of the shooter and X's threatening behaviour. Each clause of the statement is offered to prove what it asserts: 'X shot me' is intended to identify the shooter; and 'he often threatened to do [that]' reports threatening behaviour. However, although D's statement, 'X shot me', when offered to identify the shooter, is undeniably hearsay, it might nonetheless be admissible under an exception known as a 'dying declaration'. Why should there be this exception to the rule against hearsay, and why, in general, should there be any exceptions at all?

Exceptions to the hearsay rule

Suppose that at trial you needed to prove the place and date of your birth. What would be simpler than to produce a birth certificate? However, that document would be hearsay as it is an out-of-court *written statement* attesting to the facts to be proven. Instead, you would need to find a witness having personal knowledge of the 'where' and 'when' of your birth. Unfortunately, there might be no such individual still alive or available. Although the hearsay rule has as its *raison d'être* the exclusion of unreliable evidence, it would also exclude certain valuable pieces of evidence that seem quite credible, such as your birth certificate. For this reason, over the years, the courts have recognized various exclusions and exceptions to the rule against hearsay, evidence that nonetheless will be admissible. The exceptions are permitted either because of the need for the evidence or because of its reliability. The Advisory Committee for the Federal Rules of Evidence notes: '[W]hen the choice is between evidence which is less than best and no evidence at all, only clear folly would dictate an across-the-board policy of doing without'.[12]

There are some two dozen exceptions to the hearsay rule. We shall only mention a few of them: records of vital statistics, such as birth, marriage, or death certificates, and other family records; documents of regularly conducted business activities, such as bills of sale, credit-card receipts, letters or notices sent to clients; statements pertaining to medical diagnosis or treatment; public records or reports; learned treatises, such as the reference works used by expert witnesses; statements about reputation or about family history; statements concerning present sense impressions or excited utterances; statements about an existing mental, emotional or physical condition – the so-called 'state of mind' exceptions; and statements about belief of impending death.[13] Excluded as hearsay (not quite the same thing as an exception, but having the same purpose) are: prior statements by a witness and admissions by a party-opponent.[14]

Let us consider the exception for 'belief of impending death', also known as a 'dying declaration'. Potential candidates for this exception may be our hypothetical statement, 'Charlie stabbed me', as well as D's assertion from the Harvard exam, 'X shot me'. One can easily see the possible necessity for the admission of such a statement. There might be no other direct or circumstantial evidence pointing to the perpetrator of the crime, other than the dying victim's statement of the identity. However, before a dying declaration becomes admissible, three conditions must be met: (a) the trial where the out-of-court statement is presented must involve a prosecution for homicide; (b) the statement deals with the circumstances leading to the declarant's death; and (c) at the time of uttering the statement, the declarant had to believe that death was imminent.[15] We can assume that conditions (a) and (b) are satisfied for our hypothetical situations: Charlie and X are on trial for homicide, and the victims have identified them as the perpetrators of the crimes. The third requirement stipulates that the declarants must have *believed* that death was imminent. Several ways exist for demonstrating this belief. Someone attending to the victim might have told him: 'You're going to die', or (as in the Harvard exam) 'You have only a few minutes to live'. Alternatively, the victim himself could have said (as in the

Harvard exam): 'I realize that I am dying', or even something as indirect, such as, 'I want to see a priest'. The victims' statements, 'Charlie stabbed me' and 'X shot me', although hearsay, would be admissible as 'dying declarations' provided all three criteria are met.

Now we face a new dilemma. The statements, 'I want to see a priest' and 'I realize that I am dying', are quite different in regard to their admissibility for the issue of belief. The former utterance is not problematic. Previously, we noted that statements that allow inferences about a speaker's mindset – such as, 'I am the Pope' and 'X is a liar and a hypocrite' – are not hearsay. The statement, 'I want to see a priest', is analogous. Thus, someone who asks to see a priest, probably for the administration of last rites, most likely believes that he or she is going to die shortly. It is *not* hearsay when an assertion is used as circumstantial evidence for a particular state of mind. On the other hand, as noted in the discussion of the Harvard exam, the utterance, 'I realize that I am dying', is not a circumstantial statement, for it speaks directly to the issue. Therefore, it ought to be hearsay and ought to be inadmissible as evidence. However, this utterance will be admissible, but for an entirely different reason. It will qualify as a *state-of-mind* exception.

State-of-mind exceptions

One of the most important exceptions to the rule against hearsay concerns a declarant's statement about his or her own 'state of mind' – such as, 'I am crazy' or 'I hate my husband', as well as (from the Harvard exam), 'I realize that I am dying'.[16] Each of these statements is offered to prove the truth of what it asserts: the questionable sanity of D; D's ill feeling toward her spouse; and X's knowledge of impending death. Although the reliability of such statements at times may be questionable, the need for the evidence may be overwhelming for often there may be no other way to prove a declarant's mental state.

Let us look in more detail at the utterance from the Harvard exam: 'I realize that I am dying'. The introductory words, '*I realize*', directly assert awareness. Therefore, concerning the issue of knowledge of impending death, this utterance precisely satisfies the definition of hearsay – an out-of-court statement offered to prove what it asserts. Suppose instead that X had said, 'I am about to die', a statement with no explicit introductory reference to a state of mind. Without the opening words, 'I realize', the utterance, 'I am about to die', becomes an indirect statement about mindset and hence would not count as hearsay. It is analogous to the statement: 'I am the Pope'. Both utterances provide circumstantial evidence of the declarants' states of mind.

It is bizarre that slight differences in the wording of an assertion – the presence or absence of a prefatory 'I realize' or 'I believe' – determine whether there is hearsay. This inconsistency may be of little practical importance, for, no matter how the statement is worded, it will be admissible, simply because 'state of mind' has always been one of the well-recognized exceptions to the hearsay rule. Nonetheless, this dilemma concerning the vagaries in the phrasing of a statement is of theoretical interest if we wish to arrive at a coherent view of hearsay. We shall see that speech-act theory provides an interesting solution to this problem.

What are speech-acts?

Speech-act theory is an approach to meaning that deals with the way 'words relate to the world'.[17] We tend to think of sentences as descriptive statements about events, as assertions that are verifiable: 'Henry beats his wife'; 'It will rain tomorrow'; 'George wanted to buy my car'; 'The cat looks sick'. However, the philosopher, John Austin, observed that in uttering a sentence, a speaker does not necessarily make a true or false statement, but instead may be engaging in the very act designated by the words – acts, such as making a promise, declaring a new state of affairs or expressing an emotion about some event.[18] A speaker who says, 'I promise you that I will pay back the money I owe', in uttering these words, performs an act of creating the special type of obligation known as promising. A justice of the peace, duly authorized to perform marriage ceremonies, creates the marital status by means of the words, 'I now pronounce you husband and wife'. In saying, 'I congratulate you on your promotion', the speaker is not asserting the truth or falsity of a proposition – in fact, it is presumed to be true that the promotion has taken place, but rather the speaker is performing an act of congratulating. Austin referred to these kinds of utterances as *performative*, because the speaker *performs* the action denoted by the verb, in contrast to those he called *constative*, where the speaker does describe an event or a state.[19]

Austin pointed out several interesting grammatical properties of English performative utterances. The subject of the sentence must be first person ('I' or 'we'), there is often an expressed or implied second person ('you'), and the *performative verb* must occur in the simple present tense – e.g. 'I congratulate you on your promotion'. Compare this utterance to a non-first-person form, 'she congratulates you on your promotion', or to the past-tense form, 'I congratulated you on your promotion', where the speaker is no longer congratulating, but is either transmitting the congratulations of another or is reporting the occurrence of a previous act of congratulating. (Note, though, that the utterance, 'she congratulates you on your promotion', would be acceptable as a performative in a situation where the speaker acts as her agent. However, we are concerned only with the constative interpretation, where the speaker is reporting someone else's congratulations.) It is the simple present-tense verb 'congratulate', embedded in the appropriate linguistic frame ('I ____ you') that brings off the performative act of congratulating. Austin proposed the 'hereby' test as a further means of identifying some performative utterances. Verbs that convey performative acts often allow the inclusion of the word 'hereby' in their sentences, but the same verbs when they occur in constative utterances do not. Thus, one can say, 'I hereby swear to tell the truth', but not, 'I hereby swore to tell the truth'.

John Searle, also a philosopher, has expanded on Austin's notion of 'performative'. Searle's theory of speech act provides a comprehensive account of the use of language by speakers and hearers. His term 'speech act' is particularly a propos as it emphasizes that the performance of an act can come about through speech. It is significant that a speech act may be as valid as a physical act. It may stand alone or occur along with non-verbal acts. Thus, one may propose to bet on the outcome of a sporting event by uttering the words, 'I bet you that Barcelona will beat Madrid', or by offering a handshake, or even by performing both acts – the verbal and the physical – simultaneously. Consider, as another example, the legal act of the swearing-in of a witness at trial, where the witness may raise his hand while uttering the words, 'I swear to tell the truth'.

According to Seale's theory, which we adopt for our analysis of hearsay, every speech act has four essential components: illocutionary, perlocutionary, locutionary and state of mind. (The terms 'perlocution' and 'locution' are originally due to Austin. The terms 'illocution' and 'state of mind' come from Searle. His term 'utterance act', which we shall not use, is similar to Austin's 'locution'.) The principal attribute, around which the others cluster, is the *illocution*. It corresponds more or less to Austin's performative – that is, a speaker *does something in saying something*. Now a speaker's illocution may affect a hearer in various ways. It is the *perlocution* that refers to the resulting effects. Moreover, because an illocution is expressed through language it must have linguistic properties. It is the *locution* that characterizes these language aspects. In a lighter manner of speaking, the trio of locution, illocution and perlocution may be summed up as: 'what I say, what I mean, [and] what you think I mean'.[20] Searle notes further that in uttering an illocution, the speaker, at the same time, tacitly expresses a particular *state of mind*. The illocution becomes an outward expression of the speaker's belief, intent, desire or feeling about the content being expressed through the illocution. These four elements – illocutions, perlocutions, locutions and states of mind – will constitute the building blocks for our analysis of hearsay. Let us consider each of them.

Illocutions

In what kinds of illocutionary acts may a speaker engage? Searle recognizes five types: *assertive, commissive, directive, declarative* and *expressive*.[21]

ASSERTIVES

In producing an assertive illocution, the speaker states a proposition that represents some state of affairs that in principle could be true or false – for example, 'I *claim* that speech-act theory provides an elegant account of hearsay'. Some English illocutionary verbs that function as assertives are:

assert, claim, report, maintain, predict, inform, admit, accuse, remind, testify, confess, state, swear. These verbs differ from one another by their *illocutionary force* or the strength of their asserting. For instance, claiming is a stronger mode of asserting than merely informing, and swearing is stronger yet, but all these verbs still constitute different ways of making assertions. The event or state of affairs described by an assertive may occur in the past, present or future tenses: 'I testify that Jones *left* the bank in a hurry'; 'I maintain that Jones *is* not innocent'; 'I predict that the jury *will find* Jones guilty'. Each of these assertive sentences contains two parts: an *illocutionary clause* containing a first-person pronoun with a following performative verb – e.g. 'I claim', 'I testify', 'I predict' – and a *propositional clause* describing some event, condition or state of affairs – e.g. 'that speech-act theory provides an elegant account of hearsay'; 'that the jury will find Jones guilty'; etc. We shall refer to these types of two-clause sentences as *explicit* illocutions. However, many assertive illocutions do not exemplify this two-part structure. They fail to begin with an explicit assertive verb. What we find instead looks like a propositional clause without the introductory 'that' – for example, 'Jones left the bank in a hurry'. We shall refer to these kinds of one-clause sentences as *implicit* illocutions. Although they do not contain an assertive illocutionary verb, nonetheless we still understand them as making assertions. They are equivalent to the utterances that Austin called 'constative'. We will have more to say about the properties of explicit and implicit illocutions after our discussion of the different types.

Most illocutions have an associated state of mind. For assertives, it is *belief*. Thus, one who makes an assertion, with no intention of deceiving or lying, believes the proposition asserted, even though it may be factually false. Ethical and religious statements are frequently of this type. Thus, if I sincerely say, 'I maintain that the earth is 6,000 years old', then I believe that the earth is 6,000 years old, even though scientific evidence belies this assertion. It is important to keep in mind that a false assertion is not necessarily a lie. For an assertion to be a lie – and for there to be perjury in a legal situation – the speaker must *not believe* what he or she asserts and must *intend* to deceive.[22]

COMMISSIVES

In producing a commissive illocution, the speaker commits himself or herself to perform or not to perform some future course of action – e.g. 'I promise you that I will pay back the money I owe'; 'I vow that I will not take revenge'. Some verbs that function as commissives are: *promise, vow, offer, pledge, guarantee, swear*. (The verb 'swear' functions as a commissive in the utterance, 'I swear that I will tell the truth', but it functions as an assertive in the utterance, 'I swear that I was in New York last Tuesday'; hence, a verb may have more than one illocutionary value.) Whereas the verb of the propositional clause for an assertive could occur in any of the three tenses, the verb of the propositional clause for a commissive can only be in the future tense. In other words, one cannot commit oneself to the performance of a past or present act. This restriction on tense makes sense. A speaker who says, 'I promise you that I will pay back the money I owe', by uttering the verb 'promise' in the present tense, is performing right now the speech act of promising. However, the repayment of the money can take place only subsequent to the making of the promise.

The state of mind that accompanies a commissive is *intent*. Thus, if I promise to pay back the money, then I intend to do so. Unlike assertive illocutions, commissives are neither true nor false. Thus, should I fail to pay back the money, you would normally say that I 'broke' my promise as opposed to saying that the promise was false. This distinction requires some clarification. To be sure, the expression 'false promise' on occasion does refer to a promise that was not kept. Although a promise, as an illocutionary act, has no truth value – that is, it is neither true nor false, there is a sense in which its propositional clause has a truth value. Let us compare the propositional clause of a commissive with that of an assertive. Consider first the truth value of a prediction, a type of assertive – for example, 'I predict that there will be an earthquake next week'. If no earthquake occurs the following week, then the propositional content will turn out to be false, as it describes an event that will not have taken place. In an analogous fashion, if I promise that next week I will pay back the money I owe, but I fail to do so, then the propositional clause of that promise also will fail to match an event that was *supposed* to occur. It is in this sense that the propositional content of a promise may be true or false, whereas the promise itself does not have this property. This distinction between an illocution and its propositional content will be crucial for our analysis of hearsay: we shall see that hearsay will occur whenever the propositional content is extracted from its illocution and is offered as evidence for the occurrence of an external event.

DIRECTIVES

In producing a *directive* illocution, the speaker directs the hearer to perform or not to perform some future course of action – e.g. 'I order you to be present in court promptly at 8:00 tomorrow'; 'I advise you not to drive after drinking'. Some verbs that function as directives are: *ask, order, command, request, recommend, advise, suggest*. The individual who is to carry out a directive cannot engage in a present or past activity. This restriction follows from the same logical reasoning that was noted for a commissive speech act. A speaker who says to a hearer, 'I order you to be present in court promptly at 8:00 tomorrow,' by uttering the verb 'order' in the present tense, is performing right now a speech act of ordering. But the hearer's action or inaction can occur only subsequent to the issuing of the order.

The state of mind that accompanies a directive is *want* or *desire*. Thus, if I order you to be in court at 8:00, it is because I want you to be there at that time. Directives, like commisives (but unlike assertives), are neither true nor false. Thus, I can say that you 'disobeyed' my order if you failed to show up at 8:00, but I would not say that my order was false. It should be evident that commissive and directive illocutions have much in common. The principal difference resides in which participant is to perform or refrain from performing a future act: for a commissive, it is the speaker, the one who utters the illocution; for a directive, it is the hearer, the one to whom the illocution is directed.

DECLARATIONS

In producing a declarative illocution (also called a declaration), the speaker brings about, as the very words are being spoken, the state of affairs described in the proposition – e.g. 'I now pronounce you husband and wife' (declared by a minister or a justice of the peace at a wedding); 'I name this ship the *Queen Mary II*' (declared by Queen Elizabeth at the ship's christening); 'The defendant is guilty' (declared at trial by a judge or a jury). And let us not forget the most spectacular declaration of all time, the one reported in *Genesis* 1.3: 'God said: Let there be light! And there was light'. As these examples vividly illustrate, not just anyone may engage in a particular declaration. Often only certain persons under specific conditions have the authority to do so. Some verbs that function as declarations are: *declare, name, bless, christen, pronounce*. Because a state of affairs that did not exist previously is created at the very moment of the declaration, the verb describing that state of affairs can occur only in the present tense.

Declarations have no accompanying state of mind, other than the speaker's purpose to bring into fruition the situation being declared. Furthermore, declarations are neither true nor false. They do not describe a worldview or some existing state of affairs, but rather if they are performed successfully – by the right person under the right circumstances – they create a new state of affairs simultaneously with their being uttered.

It is important not to confuse a 'declarative' illocution with a grammatical declarative sentence. With the exception of imperatives and questions (which function as implicit directive illocutions), most illocutions are expressed grammatically as declarative sentences. To obviate any misunderstanding, we shall refer to declarative illocutions as declarations. Note also that some legal treatises use the term 'declaration' to mean 'statement' (or 'utterance', in our terminology). Again, this usage should not be confused with the speech-act term.

EXPRESSIVES

In producing an expressive illocution, the speaker expresses an emotion or feeling about a proposition that is generally presumed to be true – e.g. 'I congratulate you on your promotion'; 'I apologize for being angry with you'. In the former utterance there is a presupposition that you have

Kinds of speech acts

Table 3.1   Illocutions, states of mind and permitted tenses

Type of illocution	Accompanying state of mind	Permitted tenses of propositional clause
Assertive	Belief	past, present, future
Commissive	Intent	future
Directive	Want	future
Declaration	[none]	present
Expressive	Feeling	past, present, future

received, or even will receive, a promotion and in the latter that I have been angry with you. Some verbs that function as expressives are: *congratulate, thank, compliment, apologize,* and verbal expressions such as *be happy, be surprised, be angry* – e.g. 'I am surprised that the jury reached a decision so quickly'. The verb of the propositional clause of an expressive can occur in any tense. For example, I can thank you for something you did in the past, for something you are doing now or for something you will do in the future. In this regard, expressives resemble assertives, the other illocutionary type permitting all three tenses. But that resemblance is as far as it goes. The truth conditions of the two types are radically different. The propositional clause of an assertive is either true or false, whereas the propositional clause of an expressive is presumed to be true.

The state of mind that accompanies an expressive corresponds to the speaker's internal subjective *feeling* or *emotion* that has elicited the illocution. Thus, one who apologizes sincerely feels an appropriate degree of remorse or regret, and one who congratulates has a positive, good feeling about some event.

Table 3.1 summarizes the five kinds of illocutions, their accompanying states of mind, and the tenses that may occur in their respective propositional clauses.

Perlocutions

When an illocutionary act is performed successfully it will always produce one or more effects on hearers. The perlocutions are these effects. One consequence of a perlocution is that the hearer is put on notice concerning the propositional content of the illocution. If I inform you that it is raining outside, you then know that it is raining. If I promise to drive you to the airport, then you are made aware of my commitment. Persuading, threatening and frightening someone are also kinds of perlocutionary effects. A perlocution may be manifested either as a physical response or as its own illocutionary act. If someone in a crowded theatre shouts 'Fire!', a possible perlocutionary effect could be trampling by those trying to escape. In contract law, an offer, which is a type of commisive illocution, can elicit an acceptance, a rejection or a counter-offer, all of which are perlocutions to the offer; yet, at the same time, they are illocutions because the hearer or offeree, in responding, has taken on the role of a speaker. There can be any number of back-and-forth counter-offers emanating from an original offer. Each subsequent counter-offer will function simultaneously as a perlocutionary effect to the immediately preceding offer and as an illocution for a new offer. We shall see that statements that function as perlocutions do not constitute hearsay.

Locutions

Because illocutionary acts are expressed through language, they have linguistic properties, such as sounds or letters, words, grammatical features and meanings. The way speakers use language and their knowledge about usage also count as locutionary characteristics. Consider, for example, the accusation: 'Smith cheats on his income tax'. Some of the trivial locutions of this assertive illocution are: it is a sentence of English; it is composed of six words; it contains the verb 'cheats'; and the first word begins with an s-sound. The following locutions are perhaps somewhat more interesting: the topic of this sentence concerns Smith; it comments on his behaviour; and this kind of utterance can be defamatory. We shall see that statements offered for their locutionary properties do not constitute hearsay.

Explicit and implicit illocutions

We touched briefly on this topic in the discussion about assertives. Recall that an explicit illocution is composed of two grammatical clauses: an *illocutionary clause* that contains a first-person subject, a performative verb and an optional second-person pronoun, followed by a *propositional clause* that expresses the content of the illocutionary act: '[I promise (you)] [(that) I will pay back the money I owe]'. (In English the propositional clause may begin optionally with the word 'that'.) Other grammatical means exist for expressing explicit illocutions. Some propositional clauses begin with an infinitive construction ('to' + verb) instead of a *that*-clause. This type of grammatical structure is frequent with directives: '[I order you] [to be in court at 8:00 tomorrow]'. Commissives also may be expressed in this way: '[I promise] [to pay back the money I owe]'. Although these two infinitive structures look superficially similar, they differ regarding the person who is *understood* to carry out the act: the understood subject of an infinitive clause is always 'you' for a directive illocution, and it is 'I' for a commissive one. Declarations and expressives allow still other types of grammatical structures after their performative verbs: '[I name] [this ship the *Queen Mary II*]'; '[I congratulate you] [on your promotion]'. In spite of the varying grammatical forms, all of these are examples of explicit illocutions, because they begin with a first-person subject and a verb indicating the precise type of illocution.

However, illocutionary acts are not generally rendered in such an exact manner. Often the propositional content alone, or an equivalent wording of it, will suffice for enabling the hearer to deduce the type of illocution intended by the speaker – for example, 'It was raining that day' (an assertive); 'I will pay back the money I owe' (a commissive); 'Be here tomorrow at 8:00' (a directive); 'You're guilty!' (a declaration). Questions of all types are considered to be directives. If I inquire, 'What time is it?', my question is equivalent to the explicit directive illocution: 'I ask you to tell me the time'. In fact, imperative and interrogative sentences are the most common ways of implicitly expressing directive illocutions. Occasionally, even one word may suffice for indicating the type of illocution: 'Guilty!' (a declaration by a judge); 'Out!' (a declaration by an umpire). Only expressive illocutions have no corresponding implicit variants. Because the speaker of an *expressive* illocution must state an emotion or feeling about a proposition, the hearer normally has no way of deducing the exact nature of that emotion or feeling unless the speaker explicitly states what it is.

How does a hearer figure out the appropriate type of implicit illocution? Most utterances do not occur as isolated sentences but as part of a social interaction with other utterances in a conversational setting. In a face-to-face encounter, it is evident which participant is the speaker and which one is the hearer. The person engaging in an implicit illocutionary act must be the understood 'I' of that speech act, and the recipient of those words must be the 'you'. The social situation, the linguistic context and the grammatical structure of the speaker's utterance all contribute to enabling the hearer to deduce the intended illocutionary act, even though an explicit verb is lacking. Nonetheless, a sentence in isolation may be potentially ambiguous. For example, the utterance, 'I will take you to Paris next year', could be a promise, a statement of intent or even a prediction. To resolve an ambiguity, a speaker may even state, as an afterthought, the speech act intended – for instance, 'I will take you to Paris next year. That's a promise'. Or else the hearer may ask for disambiguation: speaker: 'I will take you to Paris next year'; hearer: 'Is that a promise?'.

Figure 3.1 provides, for each illocutionary type, examples of: (a) an explicit illocution with its performative verb underlined; (b) a corresponding implicit illocution; and (c) a statement of the accompanying state of mind with its verb italicized. Note that all three versions of an illocutionary type contain the same propositional content.

An implicit illocution not only replaces an explicit one but it also expresses the corresponding state of mind. One who says, 'The grey car went through the red light', at the same time asserts and believes that the grey car went through the red light. Thus, from an implicit illocution, one can derive the corresponding explicit illocution and statement of state of

Explicit and implicit illocutions and states of mind

Assertive
I <u>affirm</u> that the grey car went through the red light. The grey car went through the red light. I *believe* that the grey car went through the red light.

Commissive
I <u>swear</u> that I will tell the truth. I will tell the truth. I *intend* to tell the truth.

Directive
I <u>request</u> that you deliver the documents to the court. Deliver the documents to the court. I *want* you to deliver the documents to the court.

Declaration
We <u>declare</u> that the defendant is guilty. The defendant is guilty. [no associated state of mind]

Expressive
I <u>regret</u> that the lawsuit has not been settled. [no implicit form] I *feel regret* that the lawsuit has not been settled.

Figure 3.1   Types of illocutionary acts

mind – i.e. 'I assert that the grey car went through the red light', and 'I believe that the grey car went through the red light'. In our analyses we shall often find it insightful to convert an implicit illocution into one of its correlates. In an analogous fashion, from an explicit illocution one can always construct an implicit one and a statement of state of mind; and from state of mind one can arrive at both types of illocutions. Because an explicit illocution requires the presence of a performative verb, in order to derive an explicit illocution from an implicit one or from a statement about state of mind, it is necessary to supply some kind of performative verb. In such a situation one can appeal to a 'generic' verb – for instance, 'assert' for assertives, 'commit (oneself)' for commissives, 'direct' for directives and 'declare' for declarations. Because of the interconvertibility among the three kinds of utterances, we will find it convenient to view the different versions as equivalent expressions. The equivalence will play an important role in our speech-act analysis of hearsay.

A speech-act analysis of hearsay

Here is how the analysis will work: if a witness offers an out-of-court statement for its illocutionary value, its perlocutionary effects, its locutionary properties or its associated state of mind, it will *not* be hearsay. If offered solely for its propositional content, then the statement *will be* hearsay.

Assertive illocutions as hearsay

The *FRE* characterize 'hearsay' as a *statement*. It further defines a 'statement' as 'an oral or written *assertion*'.[23] Note, though, that the *FRE* term 'assertion' is not identical to the speech-act term 'assertive'. All five illocutionary types can qualify as *FRE* assertions, although without doubt, most assertions will be speech-act *assertives*, if only because the majority of utterances tend to be of this type.

The primary feature differentiating an assertive illocution from the other types is its relation to the propositional content: it presents the content as being true or false. In our analysis, hearsay will occur whenever the propositional content of an assertive is 'offered in evidence to prove the truth of the matter asserted'.[24] Now, it should make no difference whether the statement occurs as a fully-fledged explicit assertive, as a truncated implicit assertive or even as a statement about state of mind. Regardless of version, the propositional content remains the same, and so long as it is offered for its truth value we have hearsay.

Consider the case of *State* v. *Hargrave*.[25] A young lad was looking for a horse stolen from his father. Upon seeing the animal in someone else's possession, the son was overheard to exclaim: 'That's father's mare'. A lower court admitted the statement as evidence for the identification of the horse. On appeal, the appellant claimed that the statement was inadmissible hearsay, and the lower court's decision was overturned. Let us see exactly why the boy's statement is hearsay from a speech-act perspective. His statement functions as an implicit assertive. However, he could just as well have uttered an explicit assertive, 'I claim that's father's mare', or he could even have chosen to report his state of mind, 'I believe that's father's mare'. It makes no difference! All three utterances contain the same propositional content – i.e. 'that's father's mare', which is being offered to prove that the horse identified by the son belonged to his father. Hence, the son's statement, whether expressed explicitly, implicitly or as a state of mind, is a paramount example of hearsay and, consequently, would be excluded as evidence for the identity of the mare.

Not all assertive illocutions are automatically hearsay but only those whose *propositional content is presented for its truth value*. There will not be hearsay whenever an assertive is offered for its perlocutionary effects, its locutionary properties, its associated state of mind or solely for its illocutionary value. We shall consider shortly these various functions of assertives, but first let us look at the other illocutions.

Verbal acts: commissives, directives and declarations

The law recognizes that statements giving rise to legal consequences – called 'verbal acts' – do not constitute hearsay. The term 'verbal act' is not equivalent to 'speech act'. The latter covers much more territory, for it includes all types of illocutions along with their locutions, perlocutions and states of mind. Legal verbal acts, though, will generally correspond to one of the following illocutions: commissive, directive or declaration. Accordingly, speech acts containing these illocutions will not be hearsay, provided they are offered for their illocutionary value and not for the propositional content alone. Austin remarked on this special property of the illocution.

> It is worthy to note that . . . in the American law of evidence, a report of what someone else said is admitted as evidence if what he said is an utterance of our performative kind [i.e. an illocution]: because this is regarded as a report not so much of something he *said*, as which it would be hear-say and not admissible as evidence, but rather as something he *did*, an action of his. [emphases in the original][26]

Assume that in *State* v. *Hargrave* one of the issues was whether the father had offered to sell the horse to the man who later purportedly stole it and the son had heard his father say to the man, 'I offer to sell you my mare for $1,000'. So long as that out-of-court statement would have been presented purely for its illocutionary value – that is, to show that the father was performing a speech act of making an offer, there would be no hearsay.

In a case involving an insurance claim, an employee had taken out an insurance policy on his life.[27] After several months of paying the premiums, he decided to drop the coverage. He told the manager of his company: 'I want to discontinue my group life insurance policy'. The manager notified the insurance company and the policy was rescinded. Shortly thereafter, the employee was killed in an automobile accident and his beneficiary sought payment under the policy. The insurance company refused to pay and the beneficiary went to court. The insurance company introduced the employee's statement to his manager: 'I want to discontinue my group life insurance policy'. This is a statement of state of mind, and it corresponds to an explicit illocution, such as: 'I request that you discontinue my group life insurance policy'. The insurance company was able to introduce the employee's statement for its illocutionary value as a directive. Not being hearsay, it was admissible as evidence.

In the case, *Safeway Stores, Inc.* v. *Combs*, a customer while shopping for groceries slipped on ketchup that had spilled on the floor from a broken bottle.[28] She sued the store for injuries. Safeway contended that there was contributory negligence because the customer had failed to heed a warning from the store manager. The manager's wife, who just happened to be shopping in the store when the accident occurred, claimed to hear her husband call out to the customer: 'Lady, please, don't step in the ketchup'.

The manager's utterance has the grammatical form of an imperative construction – i.e. 'don't step' – which functions as an implicit directive. Hence, it was not hearsay for the store to offer the utterance for the issue of whether the manager had warned the customer. The act of warning is a directive illocution.

In the case of *Hanson* v. *Johnson*, Hanson owned and leased farmland to a tenant. In return the tenant was to give two-fifths of his corn crop to Hanson.[29] The tenant had taken out a mortgage for the crops that he owned. He defaulted on his loan and the bank holding the mortgage subsequently sold at auction all of the crops stored on the property. The plaintiff, Hanson, in order to prove that some of the crops had belonged to him, testified, over the bank's objection of hearsay, that when his tenant had finished husking the corn, he pointed to some of the stacks of corn and said: 'Mr Hanson, here is your corn for the year, this double crib here and this single crib here is your share for this year's corn; this belongs to you, Mr Hanson'. The court acknowledged that the tenant's statement was not hearsay. From the perspective of speech-act theory, his utterance functions as a declaration. By pointing to specific cribs of corn while announcing 'here is your corn', those particular cribs become the property of the plaintiff. In other words, ownership was created simultaneously with the uttering of these words. Here is an example where a verbal act – a declaration – is accompanied by an associated physical act – pointing to specific piles of corn. Within the law the words that clarify a physical act are frequently referred to as the 'verbal part of an act'.

Note that the utterances in *Hanson* v. *Johnson* and in *State* v. *Hargrave* have a very similar grammatical structure: 'here is your corn' and 'that's father's mare', respectively. Although both are implicit illocutions, the former is a declaration, and the latter an assertive. The tenant, in making his statement while pointing to some cribs of corn, creates the legal ownership of those cribs for Mr Hanson. The son, in making his statement while pointing to the mare, is not creating ownership of the mare for his father, but instead is claiming that the horse belongs to his father. For the respective issues of who owns the corn and who owns the mare, the former utterance is not hearsay, but the latter one is.

It is important to keep in mind that in order for an illocutionary verb to indicate a particular kind of illocution it must occur in the present tense. A past-tense verb can function only as an assertive about a past illocution. Thus, the present-tense utterance, 'I promise to pay back the money I owe', is a bona fide commitment. On the other hand, the past-tense statement, 'I promised to pay back the money I owe', does not constitute a present act of commitment, but instead it is an implicit assertive reporting a commitment that was made in the past. Its corresponding explicit form would be: 'I assert that I promised to pay back the money I owe'.

We can readily see how this distinction in tense applies to some of the cases cited in this section. If the manager in the Safeway episode had been heard to utter, 'Lady, I told you not to step in the ketchup', that utterance would be hearsay concerning the issue of whether the manager had warned the customer. This hypothetical out-of-court utterance is no longer a directive illocution – a warning as it is being delivered – but an assertive about a past act of warning. Or consider the case involving the distribution of the cribs of corn. If the tenant had said, 'Mr Hanson, I pointed out to you yesterday the cribs of corn that are yours', the utterance would indeed be hearsay concerning the issue of what belonged to Hanson.

Expressive illocutions

For an *expressive* illocution the speaker states his or her emotion or feeling about a proposition presumed to be true – e.g. 'I am happy that Harry got a promotion'; 'I am sorry that I caused this horrible accident'. This kind of illocution expresses a particular state of mind of the speaker. Recall that there are also states of mind associated with the other illocutions – i.e. 'belief' with assertives, 'intent' with commissives and 'want' with directives. I shall postpone a discussion of the hearsay implications of expressive illocutions and will treat them when discussing other states of mind.

Assertive illocutions as non-hearsay

We noted that hearsay occurs whenever the propositional content of an assertive is presented for its *truth value*. However, there will not be hearsay where an assertive is offered for its *illocutionary value* – that is, as a statement *qua* statement without regard to whether it is true or not. However, most often, this kind of illocution will be offered for one of its associated functions: as perlocution, locution or state of mind.

Perlocutions

A statement may affect a hearer or hearers in various ways. These effects are the perlocutions that arise from a speaker's illocution. For example, what the speaker has said may cause the hearer to become anxious, to be frightened, to feel threatened or to be provoked. Reactions of anxiety, fear, feeling threatened or being provoked relate to the hearer's state of mind, and from a legal perspective statements eliciting such reactions do not constitute hearsay. The speech-act analysis agrees: a statement offered for its perlocutionary effects is never hearsay. Consider the emotion experienced by a woman who slipped in the lobby of a hotel, severely injuring herself and suffering from a collapsed lung.[30] In a lawsuit for pain and suffering, she testified that the doctor had 'told me that I would have to live with myself and to be careful never to strain myself'. This out-of-court assertive statement by the doctor was not hearsay because it was offered to show its perlocutionary effect on the patient – that is, on hearing the doctor's assertion the woman became anxious and afraid.

In the Harvard exam, the following statement was not hearsay: 'On the issue of X's provocation for assaulting Y, D's statement to X, her husband: "Y ravished me"'. D's statement caused Y's antisocial physical response, the perlocution. Or consider the situation where people rush out of a theatre trampling one another as they leave. The issue concerns the event that caused the panic. Various people state that they heard someone in the theatre shout, 'There's a fire on stage'. This implicit assertive illocution is not being offered for its propositional content – to prove that indeed there was fire on the stage – but for its perlocutionary effect of causing a panic. Defamatory statements tend to be assertive illocutions – for example, 'Jones is a disreputable businessman who will cheat you'. This kind of statement is not offered for the truth value of the propositional content, which in fact can be a defence for a charge of defamation. Rather, such a statement is typically offered as a perlocution, as evidence that some of the hearers believed what they heard and subsequently behaved in a manner detrimental to the plaintiff's reputation, welfare, or business interests.[31]

When a speaker asserts something to a hearer, the hearer then *knows* the information conveyed. This means of acquiring knowledge can be an important perlocutionary effect of an assertive, and accordingly, whenever a statement is offered for that purpose, it too is not hearsay. A question of this type arose in the Harvard exam: on the issue of X's knowledge of speedily impending death, D's statement to X: 'You have only a few minutes to live'. Assuming that X was conscious and understood D's statement, D's utterance would not be hearsay for the issue of X's knowledge. Or consider a driver who is having his car checked over and is told by the mechanic: 'The brakes are bad'. The driver decides to wait a week before having the brakes repaired. That afternoon he gets into a severe accident. To show his negligence of continuing to drive after learning about the condition of the brakes, the insurance company introduces the mechanic's out-of-court statement to the driver: 'The brakes are bad'. This statement, although an assertive illocution, will not constitute hearsay provided it is not offered for the truth of its propositional content – that the brakes are bad – but rather for its perlocutionary effect – for showing that the driver had knowledge of what was told to him. If the brakes are indeed bad, this fact will have to be determined in some other way.

Locutions

Illocutionary acts are performed through language. Consequently, every illocution has linguistic or grammatical properties. It is not hearsay for a statement to be offered for its locutionary aspects. Consider impeachment. The issue is whether the President had been lying. During an interrogation by the Senate Ethics Committee he admits, 'I had sex with M.L.'. To prove impeachment the prosecution brings in a prior out-of-court statement: 'I never had sexual relations with that woman, M. L.'. The credibility of the witness is now at stake.[32] The earlier out-of-court statement has been resurrected for the purpose of impeachment – to show that the witness has made contradictory assertions. A comparison of the two statements reveals

that although they have a similar propositional content, one of the utterances asserts that the propositional content matches an outside event of
having sex with M.L., whereas the other utterance denies such a match. The
locutionary interest of these two utterances lies precisely in their grammatical and logical inconsistencies.

Defamatory statements may be offered not only for their perlocutionary
effects on hearers but also for their locutionary values as tokens of language. Consider again the assertive illocution: 'Jones is a disreputable businessman who will cheat you'. The highly charged words 'disreputable' and
'cheat' are the kinds of words that the law recognizes as possibly defamatory. Such language is indicative of an assertive illocution functioning as a
defamatory statement. In fact, in the common law there was a presumption
that certain kinds of statements were slanderous per se – such as accusing
a woman of not being chaste, stating that one has a loathsome disease,
asserting that one has committed a crime. Note the particular kinds of
vocabulary items found in these assertive illocutions.[33] The Harvard exam
provided two examples of assertives offered for their locutions: (1) On the
issue of the sanity of D, D's public statement: 'I am the Pope'. The claim
that one is the Pope, Napoleon, Jesus Christ, or any other famous or historical personage exemplifies the type of linguistic utterance typically
ascribed to delusional individuals. (2) On the issue of D's consciousness
after being attacked, D's statement: 'X shot me . . .'. D's statement has the
property of an utterance produced in the English language. This locutionary property is offered for establishing D's consciousness. Anything that D
might have uttered – whether in English or in another language – would
serve just as well for this locutionary purpose.

Summary: illocution, perlocution and locution versus propositional content

Let us summarize our analysis of hearsay up to this point. If a statement is
offered for its illocutionary value – the speaker asserts something, commits
himself or herself to do something, directs the hearer to do something, or
declares the existence of something, that statement, whether offered as an
explicit illocution, an implicit illocution or a statement of state of mind, is
not hearsay. It is hearsay, though, if offered solely for its propositional
content – that is, to prove that the 'something' part of the illocution by itself
is true. The following hypothetical scenario exemplifies these points.

A street vendor is prosecuted for selling handbags that are purportedly
knocked-off Gucci bags but were being sold as the authentic brand. Various
passers-by testify in court that as they walked past the vendor's cart he
pointed to several handbags, saying, 'These are Gucci handbags'. (This
implicit assertive illocution is of course equivalent to an explicit one, such
as 'I assert that these are Gucci handbags'.) The statements by the passers-
by, repeating the vendor's words, are not hearsay provided the statements

are being offered not to prove that the bags are Gucci, but solely to show that the vendor was making such a claim to the public. This example is particularly interesting, as the utterance, 'These are Gucci handbags', is presented purely for its illocutionary value as an assertive illocution, and not for its perlocutionary effects or its locutionary properties.

Now suppose that some of the passers-by actually did buy bags, *believing* that they were authentic Gucci. The same statement by the vendor would still not be hearsay, for now it is presented for its perlocutionary effect on the hearers – to show that they believed what the vendor was asserting. Suppose further that in his defence the vendor states that he belongs to a religious sect where it would be a mortal sin for him to tell a lie. Since he claims only to tell the truth he tenders his out-of-court assertive illocution, 'These are Gucci handbags', as proof that the bags are authentic. This time the statement is presented solely for its propositional content – to make the claim that the words reflect reality. Hearsay!

This view about the propositional content of an assertive as the basis for hearsay should hold as well for other kinds of illocutions. Consider, for example, a directive illocution uttered by a woman to her stockbroker: 'I request that you sell all my shares of ImClone stock', or the equivalent implicit directive, 'Sell all my shares of ImClone stock'. For the issues of whether the woman gave a directive, whether she instructed her broker to unload her shares, or even whether she wanted [state of mind] to divest herself of the shares, the illocution would not constitute hearsay. Previously, we noted that a directive illocution is neither true nor false. For that reason there can be no question of hearsay. But what if the issue instead concerned whether the broker in fact had sold the shares? Then I contend that the statement, 'I request that you sell all my shares of ImClone stock', *would* count as hearsay because the issue now concerns exclusively the propositional content of the illocution, totally ignoring its directive function or its associated state of mind. In other words, the propositional content is being presented solely for its truth value, as though it were the propositional content of an assertive.

A commissive illocution presents an analogous situation. Consider the explicit commissive, 'I promise to pay back the money I owe', or its implicit variant, 'I will pay back the money I owe'. For the issues of whether a commitment has been made, whether the speaker has promised to repay the money, or whether the speaker intends [state of mind] to repay the money, the illocution would not constitute hearsay. But for the issue of whether the speaker had actually repaid the money – which looks only at the propositional content as though it were an assertive – there would be hearsay, although (as we shall note shortly) an exception has been carved out for a particular type of intent statement.

Commissive and directive illocutions, then, rarely raise questions of hearsay, because these particular speech acts are neither true nor false. Only if the propositional content were to be extracted from one of these illocutions would a hearsay problem arise. However, this claim about the relation between propositional content and hearsay does not apply to declarations. Consider, for example, a declaration made by an umpire who has called a player 'out'. An explicit version of this declaration would be, 'I declare that you are out'. It is the very nature of a declaration to bring into existence the state of affairs declared in the propositional content. That is, the act of declaring and the fulfilment of the propositional content are simultaneous. Hence, the propositional content of a declaration is always an inextricable part of its illocution and cannot be logically separated from it. For this reason, the propositional content of a declaration will never be hearsay when offered 'to prove the truth of the matter [declared]'. Recall the *Hanson* case, where the issue was whether the cribs of corn belonged to the plaintiff. His tenant had declared: 'Mr Hanson, here are your cribs of corn'. Note how the content of this declaration, although clearly not hearsay, nonetheless speaks directly to the issue of who is the owner of the corn.

State of mind

Within speech-act theory, *'state of mind' refers exclusively to the speaker*. It is the mental state associated with an illocution. A hearer's mental state, on the other hand, is always the result of a perlocution. We can state unequivocally that whenever a statement addresses an issue relating to the hearer's state of mind, that statement will *not* be hearsay precisely because it is offered for its perlocutionary effect. However, one cannot make a similarly incontrovertible assertion about the speaker's mental state. Some instances of speaker's state of mind are definitely *not* hearsay, whereas other cases remain controversial. Legal scholars are divided on this issue. Some treat the controversial utterances as hearsay, but which may be admitted into evidence as permitted exceptions; other scholars are of the opinion that such statements are never hearsay. Speech-act theory has its own solution to this debate.

Speaker state of mind can be expressed either indirectly or directly. An indirect expression asserts one thing while at the same time suggesting something about the mental condition of the speaker – for example, 'I am the Pope'. Direct expression comes in two variants: (a) the speaker relates his or her state of mind in regard to some *external* event – such as 'I believe that these are Gucci handbags' or; (b) the speaker asserts precisely the nature of a current state of mind, emotion, or *inner* feeling – such as 'I am depressed'. We begin with indirect expressions, a topic touched on previously.

Indirect state of mind

An assertive illocution has 'belief' as its accompanying state of mind. Apart from deliberate lying, one who asserts something, believes it. This belief may then be indicative of other mental conditions, such as fear, anxiety or delusion. The Harvard exam provided an example of indirect state of mind:

'On the issue of the sanity of D, D's public statement: "I am the Pope"'. Here D asserts that she is the Pope; hence, she believes that she is the Pope. Because her belief is at odds with that of the dominant culture, her statement may well be viewed by others as a reflection of a disoriented condition. It is not hearsay when an assertive is offered as circumstantial evidence for indirectly establishing a particular state of mind for the speaker. Previously, we noted the locutionary aspect of the utterance, 'I am the Pope', a statement representative of the kind of language often associated with a delusional state. Hence, there may be more than one way of analysing an utterance. Yet the result is the same. In either case one infers from that statement something about the speaker's mental condition.

There is a famous case that provides a stunning example of this kind of indirect state of mind.[34] A divorced woman, who had two children, was living with a man named Caporale. He was suspected of killing her son. Her other child, a daughter, was in foster care. In the meantime a custody battle was going on between the mother and the natural father. The foster caretaker told the child that she had read in the newspaper that the natural mother had married Caporale. On hearing this news the child exclaimed: 'He killed my brother and he'll kill my mommy too'. From this assertive it follows that the young girl believed that Caporale had killed her brother and that he would do the same thing to her mother. This belief was admitted as circumstantial evidence for the state of mind relevant to this case – namely, that the child was *afraid* of Caporale, and hence it would be unwise for her to be placed in the custody of her mother.

Now we turn to what is perhaps the most interesting aspect of the application of speech-act theory to hearsay: utterances where the speaker directly states a state of mind. Are such statements non-hearsay to begin with, or are they technically hearsay but nonetheless admissible as permitted exceptions to the rule against hearsay? This distinction may not be of real practical importance since in any case there is always the state-of-mind exclusion, but the distinction is of theoretical interest for an explanatory account of the rule against hearsay. To answer this question we shall consider two types of statements: one where the speaker states his or her state of mind in relation to some external event; and the other where the speaker directly asserts a state of mind in and of itself.

State of mind about an outside event

Recall the three ways of expressing the propositional content that refers to an event: as an explicit illocution, as an implicit illocution or as a statement about state of mind. For example:

Explicit illocution: 'I maintain that these are Gucci handbags.'
Implicit illocution: 'These are Gucci handbags.'
Statement about state of mind: 'I believe that these are Gucci handbags.'

I have claimed that *regardless of which version is offered* the question of hearsay or non-hearsay should be consistently decided for any particular issue. Recall our previous discussion of this point in the case of *State* v. *Hargrave*, where the issue concerned a son's identification of a mare belonging to his father. The son's statement was hearsay, irrespective of whether it would have been expressed as an explicit illocution, as an implicit one or as a state of mind – i.e. 'I claim that's father's mare'; 'That's father's mare' or 'I believe that's father's mare'.

The same reasoning ought to apply where the issue itself concerns a state of mind. To illustrate this claim, let us return to our hypothetical scenario of the Gucci handbags.[35] The vendor of the alleged knocked-off handbags is on trial. The prosecution decides to conduct a survey. Six fashionable women are shown for the first time some of the vendor's handbags and they are asked to identify the brand. After carefully examining the handbags, three of the women state, 'These are Gucci handbags'; two say, 'I believe that these are Gucci handbags'; and one boldly asserts, 'I maintain that these are Gucci handbags'. The prosecution wants to show that these well-dressed women were duped and that all six believed – erroneously – that the handbags were authentic.

Now under the traditional view of hearsay, as encompassed in the FRE definition, the statement, 'I believe that these are Gucci handbags', creates an interesting paradox for the issue of belief about the authenticity of the bags. On the one hand, it appears that this statement is being offered precisely 'to prove the truth of the matter asserted' – that is, that the speaker *believes* that the handbags are Gucci, and therefore, according to the FRE definition, the statement should count as hearsay. Yet the corresponding explicit and implicit illocutions, 'I maintain that these are Gucci handbags', or simply, 'These are Gucci handbags', would not be considered hearsay where the statements are offered only to show belief on the part of the speaker (and not to prove the authenticity of the handbags, for which any of the three versions would be hearsay). Such differences in interpretation should not at all depend on the vagaries of speakers' choices in stating their beliefs – that is, whether the propositional content of a statement is or is not preceded by the words, 'I believe'.

This dilemma of inconsistent interpretation does not arise in a speech-act analysis where a statement can be expressed by means of one of three variants, all of which function equivalently in regard to a particular issue. There is no question that for each of the women who reported her state of mind, regardless of which version of the statement she happened to utter, it was her intention to express her belief that the handbags were authentic. Nor has the law been entirely immune to this view of state of mind. Rothstein *et al.* consider the problem of type of utterance vis-à-vis the FRE definition, and these authors also reach the conclusion that the form of a variant should not affect the interpretation.[36] Mueller and Kirkpatrick arrive at a similar conclusion. They compare two hypothetical statements made by a woman: 'He tripped' and 'I think he tripped'. They then go on to say: 'Obviously the two statements are substantially identical and should be treated the same if the purpose is to prove what she thought or what happened'.[37]

The preceding examples have dealt with a speaker's 'belief'. Let us consider now other kinds of mental conditions. Among these are expressive illocutions, whose role in regard to hearsay we have not yet considered – e.g. 'I am happy that Harry got a promotion'; 'I am so sorry that I caused this horrible accident'. An expressive illocution has three unique properties: (a) it does not have an implicit variant; (b) in its explicit formulation it reflects a speaker's attitude, emotional behaviour or feeling about some state of affairs put forth as the propositional content; (c) its propositional content is presumed to be true. That is, for the cited utterances there is a presupposition that Harry was promoted and that the speaker caused the accident. It is easy to see that the propositional content reported in the past tense refers to an event that is presumed to have already happened. However, what about a propositional content reported in the future tense – for example, 'I am happy that Harry will get a promotion next month'? The fact that the promotion has not yet taken place is irrelevant to the nature of expressives. There remains nonetheless the presupposition regarding Harry's eventual promotion, and it is the speaker's emotion vis-à-vis this presupposed future event that is important. Because the propositional content of an expressive illocution is presumed to be true, it is unlikely that the event described by it would ever be at issue. Rather, the issue would concern the speaker's attitude towards the event. Let us make this situation more concrete. Suppose that a defendant has been found guilty of speeding, causing an accident that resulted in the death of a child. During the sentencing phase for this crime, the issue arises whether the defendant has shown remorse. A witness reports having heard the defendant say shortly after the accident, 'I am sorry that I caused this horrible accident'. This statement is being offered exclusively for its *illocutionary value* as an expression of remorse, and as such would *not* constitute hearsay.

It is the presupposition about the truth of the propositional content that distinguishes expressive illocutions from those states of mind associated with assertive illocutions. Compare, for example, the two superficially similar utterances: 'I am happy that Harry got a promotion', and 'I believe that Harry got a promotion'. Only the former statement, an *expressive illocution*, carries a presupposition about Harry's promotion; the latter, a *statement about the state of mind* that goes with an assertive illocution, does not.

There is yet another kind of statement that looks grammatically similar to an expressive illocution, but whose content is not presumed to be true. As an example, consider the utterance, 'I am afraid that my husband will kill me'.[38] The clause stating the cause of the fear – 'that my husband will kill me' – is not presupposed to be true. Moreover, the relation between the enunciated state of mind and the following event is different from that of an expressive. For the expressive, 'I am happy that Harry will get a promotion', the speaker expresses his or her feeling *about* the propositional content. For the utterance, 'I am afraid that my husband will kill me', the speaker states the *cause* or reason for her fear – i.e. that her husband intends to kill her. In fact, there are several other linguistic differences between the two utterances. For the sentence, 'I am happy that Harry will get a promotion', 'will' denotes exclusively an event presumed to take place in the future. On the other hand, for the sentence, 'I am afraid that my husband will kill me', 'will' indicates intent of a future act. The utterance would be equivalent to: 'I am afraid that my husband intends to kill me'. In addition, negating the first clause of a sentence with a presupposition does not negate the presupposition. For the sentence, 'I am *not* happy that Harry will get a promotion', there is still a presupposition that Harry will be promoted. However, for the sentence, 'I am *not* afraid that my husband will kill me', the speaker no longer necessarily holds the belief that her husband intends to kill her. These differences, although subtle, are significant.

From a legal perspective, the significance concerns those aspects of an utterance that will be admissible for state of mind under *FRE* 803(3). Fenner notes that, according to a traditional analysis of hearsay, the first part of the statement (i.e. 'I am afraid') would be admissible, but the second part (i.e. 'that my husband will kill me') would not. He mentions two reasons for the exclusion of the part of the statement that explains the nature of the fear. First, it is in violation of a requirement known as the 'no-elaboration rule', which permits 'an out-of court statement of a state of mind . . . but not an accompanying statement of the underlying reasons for that state of mind . . .'.[39] Second, it 'is a statement of someone else's intention to do something in the future' and a statement of another's intention is not admissible as an exception to the hearsay rule. [40] We can agree partially with Fenner's observation. The speech-act explanation relies on how the propositional content will be put to use. If it is being offered for its truth value – i.e. that the husband does intend to kill his wife, then that part of the statement would be inadmissible hearsay. On the other hand, if the issue is about her fear, then one could argue that the complete utterance, 'I am afraid that my husband will kill me', is an admissible statement about state of mind. Fenner, in fact, concedes this latter point: 'It may well be that the "elaboration" part of [the statement] will be admissible. Depending on the facts, there may be an argument that the elaboration is not hearsay in the first place or that it fits under some other exception . . .'.[41]

State of mind for itself

What happens where the issue concerns solely the declarant's mental state or condition per se and the declarant's out-of-court statement is a direct assertion of that mindset? Assume, for example, that the issue is whether X is depressed and X's out-of-court statement straightforwardly is: 'I am depressed'. Because this statement precisely asserts what is at issue, again it ought to be hearsay according to the traditional definition. Even though it would be admissible as a permitted exception under *FRE* 803(3), our interest here is to determine whether such a statement constitutes hearsay under a speech-act analysis.

From the perspective of speech-act theory, direct statements about a current state of mind, feeling or emotion – such as 'I am depressed', 'I feel ill' or 'I hate my husband' – function as assertive illocutions. As assertives they have 'belief' as the corresponding state of mind, which can be rendered, respectively, as: 'I believe that [I am depressed, I feel ill, I hate my husband]'. Here we have a statement of belief about some other state of mind, feeling or emotion.

Belief statements dealing with state of mind per se differ in an important respect from the indirect type and from state of mind about an external event: the difference resides in the nature of the propositional content. Let us look again at the three types.

1. Indirect state of mind: 'I believe that [I am the Pope]'
2. State of mind about an external event: 'I believe that [these are Gucci handbags]'
3. State of mind for itself: 'I believe that [I am depressed]'

Recall that statements 1 and 2 do not constitute hearsay for the issue of the declarant's sanity and for the issue of the declarant's belief that the handbags are authentic Gucci. The utterances are offered as statements of belief, and *not* for the truth of their propositional contents. For statement 3, however, the propositional content *does* speak directly to the issue, and we have maintained that it is this correspondence that entails hearsay within a speech-act analysis. Yet the propositional content of 3 is embedded within the larger statement about 'belief'. Because statements of belief such as 1 and 2 do not constitute hearsay, could this view about 'belief' be extended to a statement like 3, so that it too would not constitute hearsay?

In pursuit of this endeavour, we present three possible analyses: the first draws an analogy between statements such as 3 and those like 1, treating the former as similar to an indirect state of mind. The second analysis claims that the nature of the propositional content of a statement such as 3 is diametrically different from that of a statement like 2, and for that reason the former would be formally excluded from the definition of hearsay. The third proposal argues that a statement such as 3 and its 'belief' counterpart are more or less equivalent, and therefore it should not constitute hearsay at all.

State of mind as an indirect type

One considers state of mind per se as analogous to indirect state of mind. The statement, 'I am the Pope', was presented as circumstantial evidence for the issue of the declarant's sanity. In an analogous fashion, the statement 'I am depressed' is to be offered as circumstantial evidence for the issue concerning the declarant's state of depression. Just as the fact of believing oneself to be the Pope is relevant to the issue of sanity, the idea of believing oneself to be depressed is relevant to the issue of depression. Under this analysis we are not concerned with the truth of what is asserted – that is, whether the declarant is truly depressed according to current medical or psychological opinions. Rather, we are interested solely in the declarant's belief about his or her asserted state of mind.

Lily suggests the possibility of analysing state of mind per se as circumstantial evidence:

> These [kinds of] declarations appear to fall clearly within the hearsay rule . . . It could be argued, however, that these statements, even if untrue, have some circumstantial probative force . . . a probative value quite aside from the literal truth of the statement[s]. The use of the words gives rise to an inference of an underlying state of mind consistent with the statement, even though the statement may not be literally true.[42]

Because of the subtleties of this kind of analysis, Lily does not wholeheartedly commit himself to this view but instead defers to classifying such statements as hearsay and admitting them into evidence as Rule 4803(3) exceptions.

State of mind as an internal event

There is good reason to treat the propositional content about state of mind per se as completely different ontologically from the propositional content about an external event. The former – e.g. 'I am depressed' – refers to the 'subjective' inner world of an individual's thoughts, beliefs, emotions or feelings, whereas the latter – e.g. 'those are Gucci handbags' – refers to the 'objective' outer world of people, things and happenings. Such a distinction has the potential of dramatically affecting the interpretation of the meaning of the term 'matter' within the *FRE* definition of hearsay as a statement 'offered in evidence to prove the truth of the *matter* asserted'. A revised definition would have the term 'matter' referring uniquely to entities and events of the external world.

Rothstein *et al.* note that '[c]ourts vary on the definition of "matter" under the FRE', and the authors suggest that '[t]here is some reason to define "matter" as "external matter" or "external fact", because then the covered situation is most like a witness giving testimony in court . . .'.[43] This restricted sense then would exclude any statements about internal states of mind and, consequently, these kinds of statements would no longer fall within the purview of hearsay. Such an analysis is actually not so far-fetched from the traditional view concerning state-of-mind statements. The law has long recognized that individuals have a special privity with their own internal mental workings, and generally statements about current states of mind are deemed to have a sufficient degree of trustworthiness. Perhaps it is for this reason that, within the traditional view of hearsay, state-of-mind statements have always constituted well-accepted exceptions to the 'rule against hearsay'.

Equivalence of internal state of mind and belief

A direct assertion about a state of mind *is equivalent to* a statement of belief about that state of mind. Consider again a speaker who asserts, 'I am depressed'. We assume that he or she has uttered this assertion due to some kind of inner mental turmoil associated with a feeling of depression. The implicit assertive statement, 'I am depressed', has as its corresponding statement of state of mind, 'I believe that I am depressed'. However, one who believes oneself depressed must perforce feel depressed. That is, it would be a contradiction to believe that one is depressed but not experience any of the angst of depression. Hence, either a statement of belief about depression or a direct assertion about depression serves to describe the same inner state of mind – namely, depression. Yet, in spite of this equivalence, the assertion, 'I am depressed', still creates an interesting paradox within a speech-act analysis. Because the propositional content speaks directly to the issue, there ought to be hearsay. However, if an assertion about some underlying state of mind is deemed equivalent to a statement about the belief of that mindset, then there should not be hearsay. It is this latter interpretation of the paradox that must ultimately prevail in order for a direct assertion of state of mind to be directly admissible as non-hearsay.

Utterances of state of mind per se do not comprise the only kinds of possible paradoxical statements. Consider, for example, the issue of whether X knows some English. X's statement, 'I know some English', would be hearsay if offered for the truth of its propositional content; however, it would not be hearsay as a locution, as an utterance whose words come from the English language. It would be up to its proponent to argue for its locutionary function if the statement were to be admitted into evidence.

State of mind merely relevant: intent

A commissive illocution has 'intent' as its associated state of mind. Thus, the commissive illocution from the Harvard exam, 'I *promise* to marry you on 1 June', has as its corresponding statement of state of mind: 'I *intend* to marry you on 1 June'. However, not every statement of 'intent' entails a corresponding 'commissive' illocution. For example, the utterance, 'I intend to go to Rome next week', does not imply a commitment to the hearer, unlike the statement, 'I intend to marry *you* on 1 June', which does.

A case well known to law students provides a fascinating account of the legal consequences of 'independent state-of-mind' intent.[44] The story begins in Kansas in 1879 and involves three men: Hillmon, Walters and Brown. Two of them head west on horseback. One of the men is Brown, but no one is sure who the other one is. After several days of travel they reach the town of Crooked Creek in Colorado. The man who is not Brown dies from a gunshot incident and is buried by Brown. The interesting twist to this tale is that both Hillmon and Walters have disappeared. Subsequently,

Hillmon's wife comes forward claiming that the fellow who died at Crooked Creek is her husband and that she is the beneficiary of his insurance policies. The insurance companies deny payment contending that the dead man is not Hillmon, the husband, but rather the other missing person, Walters. At trial, to prove their claim that the body buried by Brown was that of Walters, the insurers introduce a letter written by Walters to his fiancée. In the letter he says in effect, 'I intend to go to Crooked Creek with Hillmon'. The insurance companies' argument proceeds as follows: Walters told his fiancée of his intention to go to Crooked Creek. If he told her this, then he really did intend to go there. If he truly intended to go there, then he probably did go there. And if he was there, then he was the one shot and buried by Brown. Hence, the dead man is Walters, and not Hillmon.

Walters' written statement to his fiancée shows his state of mind – i.e. his intent to go to Crooked Creek, and it would be admissible as evidence, either as a permitted exception to the hearsay rule (according to *FRE* 803(3)) or as non-hearsay (according to our speech-act analysis). Although it is relevant, Walters' state of mind is not the issue in contention between the two parties. The real issue concerns his actual presence at Crooked Creek. From a statement of intention can one conclusively deduce the occurrence of the event that is intended? For example, from a prior statement, 'I intend to marry you on 1 June', are we to conclude that a marriage actually took place on that date? I believe we must say no. No matter how sincere one's intention may be, its fruition may be thwarted by an unexpected event occurring between the stated intention and its projected fulfilment.

From the perspective of speech-act theory, a statement of an intention as evidence for the occurrence of the intended event should unequivocally be inadmissible hearsay. Walters' statement has two components: a clause directly indicating state of mind and an infinitive clause expressing the object of intention: '[I intend] [to go to Crooked Creek with Hillmon]'. Now, for the issue of Walters' intention to go to Crooked Creek there would not be hearsay, as statements about state of mind do not count as hearsay. However, for the issue of Walters' actually having gone to Crooked Creek there indeed would be hearsay, as the propositional content of the intent statement is being offered for its truth value. Such a statement could become admissible only if regarded as some kind of exception, which is precisely what the Supreme Court did in the *Hillmon* case. The court decided that this kind of statement, even though admittedly hearsay, was admissible evidence. By allowing it, the court in essence carved out a new exception to the hearsay rule: *state of mind merely relevant*.[45]

Courts are divided as to whether the declarant's statement of intent to engage in some activity with another party can serve as evidence that the other party also engaged in that activity. Under the 'state of mind merely relevant' exception, can Walters' statement, 'I intend to go to Crooked Creek with Hillmon', be offered as circumstantial evidence that Hillmon also went to Crooked Creek? Generally courts will require independent corroborative evidence that the other individual participated in the event.

The 'state of mind merely relevant' exception is embodied within *FRE* 803(3). It states that the following is *not excluded* by the hearsay rule: 'A statement of the declarant's then existing state of mind, emotion, sensation, or physical condition (such as intent, plan, motive, design, mental feeling, pain, and bodily health), but not including a statement of memory or belief to prove the fact remembered or believed . . .'. In other words, the exception permits a statement of a 'forwards-looking' state of mind to prove the fact intended, but not a 'backwards-looking' state of mind to prove the fact believed.

The pivotal case for this distinction involved a doctor charged with poisoning his wife.[46] At the murder trial, the wife's nurse testified that Mrs Shepard, after drinking some whisky, stated that 'it tasted strange', and then said: 'Dr Shepard has poisoned me'. The latter statement unequivocally was hearsay. The Supreme Court in its comments drew a distinction between permissible statements pointing to the future, as in the *Hillmon* case, and impermissible ones looking to the past, as in the *Shepard* case. Justice Cardozo wrote: 'There would be an end, or nearly that, to the rule against hearsay if the distinction were ignored'.[47]

The relevance of speech acts to hearsay

The 'hearsay problem' bears on the correspondence between an out-of-court utterance and the event to which it refers: it questions the veracity of such a statement when made by a declarant not subject to in-court contemporaneous cross-examination. Of course, not every statement poses a hearsay issue, but only those utterances that present as true what they purportedly assert. Consequently, for the legal practitioner – whether trial lawyer or judge – it is imperative for him or her, during the rapid-fire interrogation of a witness, to have the uncanny ability for differentiating practically instantaneously the types of statements permitted into evidence from the kinds to be excluded. In addition, one runs up against the myriad exceptions to the rule against hearsay, statements that technically satisfy its definition but nonetheless will be deemed admissible. The multitude of cases involving decisions about hearsay that have ended up in appeals courts amply testify to the difficulty often experienced by legal practitioners. To facilitate the task of evaluating a witness's utterances, various scholars have presented novel ways for approaching the hearsay issue.

Lawrence Tribe, a law professor at Harvard, proposed to unravel the hearsay problem by viewing it as a 'chain of inferences' that begins with a declarant's out-of-court statement.[49] The first link proceeds from the statement to an underlying belief, and the second link from the speaker's belief to the conclusion that there is an actual external event that triggered the belief. Tribe depicts this chain as a triangular configuration, as shown in Figure 3.2.

Tribe's testimonial triangle

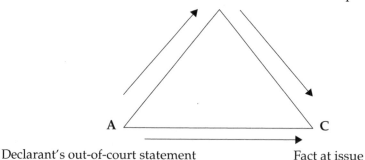

B Declarant's belief responsible for A

A

C

Declarant's out-of-court statement   Fact at issue

Figure 3.2   Hearsay triangle

Each path along a leg of the triangle is indicative of the kind of inference that a fact-finder must make in determining whether there is a hearsay problem. One begins the triangular odyssey at the lower-left vertex of the triangle (A), which represents the declarant's out-of-court statement. The path proceeds to the upper vertex (B), which corresponds to the declarant's belief underlying the statement. The path continues to the lower right vertex (C), which represents an external reality that purportedly is responsible for the declarant's belief. A traditional hearsay problem arises whenever A is used to prove C along the path through B. A hearsay issue does *not* exist with either of the following two routes: a path from A to B (without a continuation to C), or a direct path from A to C (without a detour through B).

As illustrations of these various routes, consider the utterance from the Harvard exam, 'I am the Pope'. One begins the trip around the testimonial triangle with the utterance situated at point A. At point B one enters the head of the speaker of this utterance, the woman who said, 'I am the Pope'. She made this statement because apparently she *believes* herself to be the Pope. That belief is supposed to emanate from a true outside event (located at point C), and if that state of affairs were the issue (i.e. is she the Pope?), one would have a real hearsay problem. That is not the issue, of course, in the Harvard exam. The issue there is whether the woman is delusional (i.e. does she think she is the Pope?). In this situation one need only proceed as far as point B. The journey to point C is unnecessary, as one is not trying to establish a connection between her belief and the outside event of being the Pope. Now assume, instead, that the issue is whether this same woman was ever conscious after having been struck on the head. Here one can advance from point A – her having said something (albeit bizarre) – directly to point C (the issue of her being conscious) as her erroneous belief at point B has nothing to do with her state of consciousness.

The path from A to B, without continuing to C, appropriately characterizes as non-hearsay instances of indirect state of mind, such as the Pope assertion.

Hearsay as a speech-act

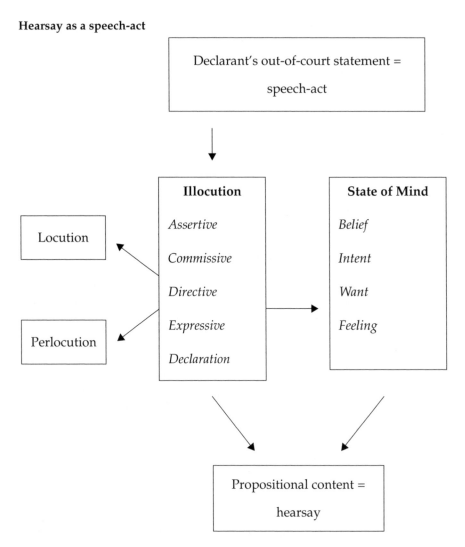

Figure 3.3   Hearsay quadrilateral

The other non-hearsay path – from A to C without passing through B – has to cover all of the remaining types of non-hearsay: verbal acts, hearer's state of mind, hearer's reactions and utterances *qua* statements, such as those that are defamatory or are offered for the purpose of impeachment. What do these disparate categories have in common? At most, the words by themselves, regardless of the veracity of the statements, are deemed relevant to the issues.

Within a speech-act analysis of hearsay, the various categories of non-hearsay are much more sharply delineated. Figure 3.3 depicts the speech-act treatment of hearsay.

This diagram contains three levels. The box on the top level represents a declarant's out-of-court statement. Because it is a speech act, it comprises one of five possible illocutions (shown on the middle level). Every illocution has locutionary and perlocutionary aspects (the arrows to the middle-level boxes on the left) and, for four of them, an associated state of mind (the arrow to the middle-level box on the right). There will not be a hearsay problem whenever an out-of-court statement is offered for one of the purposes within any middle-level box. However, if a statement, whether rendered as an explicit illocution, an implicit illocution or a statement of state of mind, is offered solely for its propositional content, then there will be hearsay (as noted by the arrows pointing to the bottom-level box).

Comparing the speech-act diagram to the triangular one, we see that the middle level of the former is much more detailed regarding the types of utterances that count as non-hearsay. Categories that are distinguished in the speech-act diagram have been lumped together in the triangular one. In particular, the commissive, directive and declarative illocutions, the locutions and the perlocutions have as their correlate the single A-to-C path of the triangle. Although both diagrams explicitly acknowledge the state of mind of the speaker, the range of utterances covered by that classification differs considerably in the two systems. The traditional view, as suggested by Tribe's triangle, sanctions 'indirect state of mind' – that is, statements such as 'I am the Pope,' statements offered as circumstantial evidence for the mindset of the speaker. More controversial are those utterances overtly expressing state of mind – such as 'I believe that those are Gucci handbags' or 'I am depressed', as these statements directly assert the matter to be proven. In the speech-act analysis, *all* statements pertaining to state of mind, whether indirect, about an external event, or concerned with state of mind for itself, *do not constitute hearsay*. This approach also eliminates the undesirability of different statements, although having an identical purpose, nonetheless not being treated uniformly. For example, in regard to the issue of one's belief whether certain handbags are authentic Gucci, the statement, 'Those are Gucci handbags', would typically be treated as non-hearsay within a traditional analysis; yet the corresponding direct statement, 'I believe that those are Gucci handbags', would technically count as hearsay. It may be deemed admissible, but only because 'state of mind' is one of the recognized exceptions to the rule against hearsay.

We have presented hearsay from two different perspectives: a traditional legal treatment and a speech-act approach. Table 3.2 summarizes the comparison. It pairs up the four kinds of statements that the law has traditionally recognized as non-hearsay with their various correlates within a speech-act analysis.

Are the legal treatment of hearsay and the speech-act approach simply alternative analyses of the facts? Is the speech-act analysis more than just an interesting intellectual exercise? There are two ways to handle data. One can examine utterances, inductively note their similarities and differences,

Non-hearsay statements as speech acts

Table 3.2 Non-hearsay statements and their speech-act correlates

Types of non-hearsay statements	*Corresponding speech-acts*
1. Verbal act (statement with legal effects)	Commissive illocution Directive illocution Declaration
2. Effect on hearer (including state of mind)	Perlocution
3. State of mind of speaker (circumstantial)	Indirect state of mind
	Locution
4. Utterance *qua* statement	Assertive illocution Locution

and then set up arbitrary classifications for the observed properties. The grouping of hearsay statements into the four basic categories traditionally recognized by the law exemplifies this course. The other way to account for data is by means of an independent theory whose original purpose was the treatment of particular phenomena, but that subsequently handles new facts from another domain. A speech-act treatment of hearsay exemplifies that approach. Hearsay data played no role in the theory's formulation. Yet, speech-act theory has shown itself to be a valuable resource for investigating hearsay issues. As we shall see in the next chapter, it also accommodates other areas of the law.

4   Promise and Contract Formation

> A contract is a promise or a set of promises for the
> breach of which the law gives a remedy, or the
> performance of which the law in some way recognizes
> as a duty.
>
> Restatement of the Law Second, Contracts 2d[1]

The notion of 'promise' has intrigued both jurists and philosophers. The lawyers' interest arises from a classical view of contract law, one that puts promise at the foundation of contract formation and enforceability. The language philosophers' interest has been primarily from the perspective of speech-act theory, which is concerned with how speakers put language to use. Although the two groups generally have widely different worldly concerns, it happens that they share remarkably similar views about the nature of promise, because the concept of promise in contract law raises many of the same issues about meaning that have emerged in the study of language.

Why, in contract law, does promise hold the pivotal position that it does? It has figured in a long-standing debate between those who continue to adhere to a version of 'contract as promise' and those who profess 'the death of contract' – that is, the inadequacy of classical contract theory.[2] We shall begin with a summary of these opposing views. Then we shall look at the three fundamental features of a contract: offer, acceptance and consideration. The latter doctrine requires that a promisor, in exchange for his or her promise, receive something of value from a promisee. This requirement, alien to many ordinary, everyday promises, will become a major theme of the present chapter. In our analyses of the various elements of a contract, we shall turn once again to speech-act theory, concentrating exclusively on 'commissive' speech acts – those where a speaker makes a commitment to carry out a future course of action. We shall then take up the problem of 'infelicitous' communication. What happens when a speech act misfires – that is, when the wrong person produces it or it is defective is some way? We shall discuss the conditions that must be met in order for a commissive speech act to be valid or 'felicitous'. We shall see that those constraints are appropriate as well for determining adequate consideration within the law.

Legal promises and the formation of contracts

We fill our lives with obligations, goals and aspirations. Yet we find that we cannot always carry out all our desired projects entirely through our own sweat and effort. We may be unable physically to perform the required work or, more likely, we have never acquired the necessary expertise. Assume that I need the roof of my house repaired but I have no idea how to go about doing it, although I am an excellent house painter. You need your house painted, but that is one boring job you seem to find no time for. It just so happens, though, that you are good at repairing roofs. Therefore, it makes sense that we might get together. I will paint your house, if you will repair my roof. (Of course, you might instead repair my roof in exchange for an agreed-upon sum of money.) We could shake hands, making it a 'gentlemen's agreement', or we could draw up a written contract. By whichever means we have reached accord, essentially we have each made a promise: I promise to house-paint and you promise to roof-repair. Because we have exchanged promises, each of us trusts the other to carry out his or her end of the bargain.

'Contract as promise' or 'death of contract'?

Arthur Corbin states at the outset of his monumental work on contract law: 'That portion of the field of law that is classified and described as the law of contracts attempts the realization of the reasonable expectations that have been induced by the making of a promise'.[3] Why should promise reside at the very heart of contract law? Charles Fried, an advocate of the thesis of 'contract as promise', maintains that morality and ethics ultimately explain the privileged place of promise.[4] An individual, in soliciting others to help him accomplish his goals or in assisting others in their projects, may freely choose to be bound to a future course of action. This duty to carry through with a commitment does not come from an outside source; rather, it is a self-imposed obligation.

The idea of a voluntarily elected commitment is essential to a promise. Yet a promise is more than just an obligation to a future course of conduct, for it represents at the same time an inducement to another person for complete trust in that commitment. It is the principle of promise – of a self-imposed and communicated obligation, where none had existed previously – that requires the promisor to render performance as promised. Contractual duty follows directly from the moral precept that we should honour our agreements. In other words, 'our word is our bond', and one who violates this trust has a legal obligation to make restitution for having thwarted the other's expectations.[5]

Fried contends that the breaking of a promise is as reprehensible an act as the telling of a lie, perhaps even more so.[6] The liar and the promise-breaker both abuse the bonds of trust. A lie is the product of a present act of speaking; but a broken promise extends all the way into the future, beyond the moment that the promise was made. In order *not* to tell a lie, one must, at the moment of speaking, believe what one asserts, while harbouring no intention of deceiving the other person. In order *not* to break a promise, one must, at the moment of making the promise, intend to carry through with it at some future time, while retaining no right to change one's mind later.

The pivotal role of promise in contract law has not gone unchallenged.[7] Most of the general principles upholding the classical view of contracts evolved throughout the eighteenth and nineteenth centuries. The opponents of 'contract as promise' attribute its demise to sweeping changes in economic conditions and in social policies throughout the twentieth century. Three factors underlie the shift away from the classical view.[8] The first is the widespread use of standard forms, whereby the consumer has substantially no input into the wording of an agreement. Insurance policies, regulations governing commercial travel, the right to use computer software – these come easily to mind as obvious examples of such contracts. The second factor, somewhat related to the first, is the declining importance of free choice and intention as bases for legal obligation. One-sided contracts undermine the classical principle that a contract comes about though the mutual agreement of the parties. The third factor, perhaps a consequence of the other two, is the emergence of consumer protection, which becomes a way of redressing some of the inequalities between large institutions and ordinary citizens. An example of this redress would be the rule of law that settles an ambiguity in an insurance contract in favour of the insured. Other types of consumer protection include legislation governing product liability, fair advertising practices and landlord–tenant relations, where requirements imposed by the law supersede any counter-provisions that the dominant party might want to include in a contract.

Advocates of the 'death of contract' perceive contract enforcement as obligation imposed, not so much from within the individual, but more often from outside – in the form of legislative or judicial justice or else in the interests of public policy. Viewed from this perspective, economic considerations then dictate that one who has suffered a detriment through undue reliance on another's promise merits relief; or conversely, one who has received a benefit where no gift was intended ought to be required to compensate his benefactor. The doctrine of 'promissory estoppel' has been increasingly used by courts to enforce promises not supported by consideration, particularly in situations where the promisee has relied to his or her detriment on the promise. These views do not necessarily entail that the making of promises no longer enters into the formation of contracts.

Rather, the presence of promises or the lack of them is not by itself a sufficient reason for enforcing or not enforcing agreements.

This brief overview of the controversy between those subscribing to a more traditional view of 'contract as promise' and those professing 'the death of contract' indicates that in contemporary legal discussions the role and value of promise are very much in the limelight. Still, classical contract law continues to play an important part in the education and training of lawyers and – in theory, if not always in practice – promise still stands solidly as a cornerstone of the institution of contract. One place where the relevance of promise is quite evident is in some of the definitions and discussions found in the *Restatement of the Law Second, Contracts 2d*.[9] This US compendium of principles that have evolved from the Anglo-American common law pertaining to contract formation and enforcement represents much of classical contract theory. The *Restatement* definition of a contract, cited at the head of this chapter, embodies the notion of 'a promise or a set of promises' worthy of legal recognition, and the idea of promise figures conspicuously in some of its other definitions as well.[10] We adopt this classical view of contracts for our analysis.

Offer and acceptance

A contract is an agreement that the law will enforce in some way. It is presumed that the parties will have entered into it willingly – without coercion, fraud, or unlawful purposes – and that they are competent to understand the terms of their agreement and to realize the consequences of a breach; hence, the law will excuse minors or the mentally incapacitated from the bargaining table. The law further assumes that there has been 'mutual assent' to the agreement. Most often, this assent will come about through an 'offer' and an 'acceptance'.

A 'valid' offer must contain at least one *promise*. Suppose I, the offeror, say to you: 'I promise to paint your house next week, if you repair my roof today'. It is this expressed commitment to carry out a future performance that constitutes one of the essential elements of a bona fide offer. However, my promise represents only half of the requirement. I must also stipulate what I expect you, the offeree, to give me in return. In this particular example, I have offered my promise in exchange for your performance. The law refers to an offer with only one promise as a 'unilateral' agreement. Of course, nothing prevents my proposing that both of us make promises, what is known as a 'bilateral' agreement: 'I promise to paint your house sometime next week, if you will promise to repair the roof also sometime next week'. It makes no difference whether the two jobs are done on the same day or on different days; and if on different days, it matters not which job is done first. Such is the power, flexibility and utility of an exchange of promises. In fact, most contractual agreements tend to be bilateral. We shall have more to say about unilateral versus bilateral contracts towards the end of this chapter.

An offer always demands some kind of response from the offeree. Let us say that we are face to face and I make the following offer: 'I will sell you my car for $2,500'. There are four possible ways that you might respond: (a) you could *accept* the offer by saying, 'I accept' or 'Okay', or even by reaching into your pocket and handing me the full amount right there on the spot; (b) you could *reject* the offer by saying, 'No, thanks' or 'I'm not interested'; (c) you could make a *counter-offer*, by saying, for example, 'I'll give you $2,350 for the car'; or (d) you could remain *neutral*, saying, 'I'm not sure' or 'I'll think about it', or even saying nothing at all.

If you accept my offer, we then have a valid agreement: I must hand over to you the title to the car and you must give me $2,500. If you reject the offer, the deal is off. Nor am I obligated to sell the car to you for $2,500 if you should come back later expressing interest in buying it. If you make a counter-offer, the tables have suddenly turned. Your counter-offer is effectively a rejection of my original offer, but at the same time, it blossoms into a new and different offer, this time one made by you instead of by me. We could continue to go back and forth – you, $2,350; me, $2,450; you, $2,400 – with each counter-offer rejecting the previous offer and, in turn, serving as a new offer. Eventually, one of the other three responses has to happen: one of us will accept the last counter-offer, outright reject it or want to mull it over. Finally, what happens in the neutral situation? The offeror can do one of two things: he or she could leave the offer open, feeling there is a good chance that the other party will come back later to accept the original offer. Alternatively, the offeror is free to withdraw the offer at any time. After all, there is no guarantee that the other party will in fact return, and there just might be another willing buyer waiting in the wings.

It is important to note that the offeror, having made a promise, becomes a promisor. It is for that reason that he or she is obligated to carry out the promise once the offer is accepted. There are, of course, many details and fine points about offer and acceptance, topics for a contracts class at a lawschool. We shall not delve further into these intricacies. Our purpose here is to relate these legal concepts to the notion of promise.

Consideration

In addition to an offer and an acceptance, a valid agreement requires a third element: *consideration*. In its simplest form, consideration is something of value that the promisee must give in exchange for the promise – for instance, your repairing my roof for my promising to paint your house; or your giving me $2,500 in exchange for my promise to turn over the title of my car to you. The *Restatement* asserts: 'To constitute consideration, a performance or return promise must be bargained for [by the promisor]'.[11] What this means is that a promise will be part of a 'bargain' when the promisor explicitly offers it to the promisee in exchange for the latter's giving back something of value. In other words, consideration is a kind of *quid pro quo*.

Why is consideration necessary? The presence of consideration suppos-edly indicates that the parties really did intend to have a legal agreement, and further it serves to differentiate promises that will be enforceable from those that will not. The law does not choose to enforce every kind of promise. For example, the promise of a gift is generally considered 'gratu-itous' – that is, without legal import. There is a classic US case on this issue.[12] The plaintiff is a widow with several children and the defendant is her brother-in-law. He wrote to her saying: 'If you will come down and see me, I will let you have a place to raise your family . . .'. She accepted the offer and made the trip. Two years later, he told her to leave. The court found that she had given no consideration in exchange for his promise. The bargain element was lacking. The brother-in-law did not invite his sister-in-law because he *wanted to see her*. Rather, from his perspective, he was just being a congenial guy trying to help out the bereaved widow of his brother. It would be somewhat similar to your saying to an acquaintance, 'If you visit me, you can stay in my flat'. In our day-to-day dealings with family, neighbours and friends, we make these kinds of promises, and hopefully, we do feel morally and ethically bound to keep them if we wish to stay on good terms with our relatives and acquaintances, but in the eye of the law such promises nonetheless are gratuitous, and hence, they are unenforce-able. Unfortunately, the sister-in-law had incurred some expenses in making the move. Ordinarily, the law would view these outlays as condi-tions that she had to meet in order to accept her brother-in-law's 'gift' of a place to live. Now, if the facts of the case had been somewhat different – for example, if the brother-in-law had offered his sister-in-law a place to live in exchange for her doing some housekeeping, then the court would very likely have interpreted his promise as part of a legitimate bargain.

Is there any recourse for an unfortunate promisee who has suffered a substantial detriment by reasonably relying on a gratuitous promise? The typical textbook situation deals with a gratuitous promise of real estate/property or of the renewal of a lease. The promisee, in reliance, goes ahead and makes significant improvements on the property. Another well-defined area involves charitable subscriptions. There is a promise to make a donation for educational, religious or other charitable purposes. The charitable organization then proceeds with a project on the assumption that the funds will be forthcoming. Courts have frequently enforced such prom-ises, particularly when the promisor should have foreseen the subsequent action taken by the promisee. There is no question that a promisee in this situation has suffered a detriment, and some commentators have found this disadvantage to constitute a sufficient reason for maintaining that there is consideration.[13] Others have questioned this inclusion of 'reliance on a promise' under the guise of consideration. Since the performance by the promisee was never bargained for, the courts, by enforcing such a promise, in reality are operating under a doctrine other than consideration, such as 'unjust enrichment'. In fact, the court awarded $200 to the woman that visited her brother-in-law, but it was careful to point out that this compensation was not due to any breach of contract, as there was no contract from the outset.

Generally, we think of consideration as constituting something of value: money, property, tangible assets or providing a service. Nevertheless, one's giving up something or not acting in a certain manner can also comprise valuable consideration, as illustrated by the famous case of *Hamer* v. *Sidway*.[14] An uncle promised his nephew that if the latter 'would refrain from drinking, using tobacco, swearing and playing cards or billiards for money until he became twenty-one years of age he would pay him a sum of $5,000'. The nephew assented and, to the best of our knowledge, abstained from engaging in any of those activities. On his 21st birthday he wrote his uncle a letter stating that he 'in all things fully performed his part of said agreement'. The uncle answered back, informing his nephew that the money was definitely his, but the uncle went on to say that he was willing to keep the money invested for him until the time came when the nephew was ready to do something worthwhile with it. The young man was agreeable to this new proposal. Two years later, the uncle died. The deceased's estate refused to honour the agreement, contending that it was without consideration and therefore invalid. The estate argued that the nephew, by refraining from drinking, gambling and carousing, had not suffered any detriment, a requirement of consideration, but rather he had even benefited physically and morally from his forbearance. The court did not buy this argument. It was inconsequential whether the nephew may have benefited by changing his lifestyle. The court went on to say: '[T]he promisee [had] used tobacco, occasionally drank liquor, and he had a legal right to do so. That right he abandoned for a period of years upon the strength of the promise of the testator that for such forbearance he would give him $5,000 . . . It is sufficient that he restricted his lawful freedom of action within certain prescribed limits upon the faith of his uncle's agreement . . .'. The court was responding to one of the traditional precepts of consideration: the consideration passing from the promisee to the promisor should be a detriment for the former and a benefit to the latter. Because the nephew had given up activities that were not unlawful, his forbearance was sufficient to qualify as a legal detriment. In return, the uncle benefited, for he received great pleasure in seeing his nephew refrain from activities that the older gentleman had perceived as unwholesome.

Absence of consideration

Now let us look at some situations where it may seem that there should be consideration but where the law does not recognize any. A service performed or something of value already given before the making of a promise does not constitute valid consideration. A case with a surprising outcome illustrates this point.[15] A young man, 25 years old, became gravely ill while travelling. He was cared for by a stranger 'acting the part of the good Samaritan, giving him shelter and comfort until he died'. When the young man's father learned about the stranger's generosity, the father wrote to him promising to pay for all the expenses that had been incurred. Subsequently, the father broke his promise, refusing to pay anything at all. The stranger sued; but the father prevailed. Because the stranger had performed his good deeds before the father made his promise, they were not given in exchange for the promise. Hence, there was no consideration. The court noted that, notwithstanding the father's morally reprehensible behaviour, there was little redress it could make: 'The rule that a mere verbal promise, without any consideration, cannot be enforced by action, is universal in its application, and cannot be departed from in individual cases in which a refusal to perform such a promise may be disgraceful'. The law frequently refers to an act performed by a promisee before the promise has been made as 'past consideration', but the law also recognizes the dictum that 'past consideration is no consideration'.

Another type of non-consideration is when one promises to do something that one is already legally obligated to do; such an act does not constitute the kind of detriment necessary for consideration. Law students frequently find out about this restriction, known as a 'pre-existing duty', from the well-known English case of *Stilk* v. *Myrick*. A ship leaves London to go to the Baltic and back. In the course of the voyage, some of the seamen desert ship and the captain is unable to find replacements. He promises the remaining crew to divide among them the wages he would have paid to the deserters. When the ship returns to London the captain reneges on his promise. The court favours the captain, finding his promise to be void for want of consideration:

> There was no consideration for the ulterior pay promised to the mariners who remained with the ship. Before they sailed from London they had undertaken to do all they could under all the emergencies of the voyage . . . But the desertion of a part of the crew is to be considered an emergency of the voyage as much as their death, and those who remain are bound by the terms of their original contract to exert themselves to the utmost to bring the ship in safety to her destined port.[16]

On the other hand, had the captain promised the extra wages on condition that the crew perform some extra duty beyond what they were already committed to do, such as paint the vessel, then this 'fresh' consideration, when added to the pre-existing duty, would suffice for a claim for an increase in wages. Nonetheless, one might question whether the additional labour required of the remaining crew in performing the work that would have been done by the deserted seamen was not sufficient consideration for the promised payment.[17]

There are a few additional types of promises resulting in insufficient consideration. One of them is 'sham' or nominal consideration. A promisor makes a promise in exchange for a paltry sum of money or some worthless object. Here is an example from the *Restatement*:[18]

> A desires to make a binding promise to give $1000 to his son B. Being advised that a gratuitous promise is not binding, A offers to buy from B for $1000 a book worth less than $1. B accepts the offer knowing the purchase of the book is a mere pretense. There is no consideration for A's promise to pay $1000.

Note that it is evident to both parties that the purported consideration is a sham.

Another kind of invalid consideration involves a promisee who does nothing in exchange for the promise although at first blush it may appear otherwise. Consider the following hypothetical example.

> A has applied for admission to several lawschools, including Harvard and Yale. Her fate now rests entirely on the decisions of the admissions committees. During this state of limbo, B, her uncle, an alumnus of Harvard, says: 'If you get admitted to Harvard Law School, I'll give you $1,000'. A's subsequent acceptance by Harvard is not consideration for B's promise.

A had applied to Harvard *before* her uncle made his promise; hence, the act of making application (i.e. past consideration) cannot be a valid consideration for the promise. After the uncle made his promise, A engaged in no further act that contributed to her admission to Harvard. The decision rested entirely with the committee. Essentially, her admission was a fortuitous event, something that just happened to her. There can be no consideration where the outcome is fortuitous. Now contrast this hypothetical situation with the following one.

> A is contemplating lawschool. B, her uncle, says: 'If you apply and get admitted to Harvard, I'll give you $1,000'. A decides to apply, spends a week writing an incredible essay on why she should be admitted to Harvard, and sends it to the admissions committee along with her application. The committee is duly impressed and admits her. A's acceptance by Harvard is consideration for B's promise.

This time A applied to Harvard *after* the uncle made his promise. The acts of writing the essay and submitting it to the committee were not only instrumental to her admission but were also undertaken in response to the uncle's promise.

Finally, there will not be consideration if the promisee is asked to do something that the promisor truly did not bargain for. We have already seen an example of this requirement in the case where the brother-in-law had said more or less: 'If you come see me, I will let you stay here'. His motivation for making a promise was not a deep desire for a visit from his sister-in-law. Her undertaking the trip was a condition on her accepting his largesse – what the law calls a 'condition precedent'.

The following are five hypothetical proposals. Test yourself. Do the following offers constitute promises backed by consideration?

1. An employee has reached retirement. Her employer says: 'In view of your 30 years of faithful service to our company, I will give you a retirement bonus of $8,000'.
2. A father, who is unhappy with his daughter's choice of a mate, says: 'I'll send you on a holiday to Europe, if you break off your engagement to Philip'.
3. Mary is expecting a baby and tests have determined that it is a boy. John promises Mary $5,000 if she will name her baby 'John'.
4. Bertha thought she would stay in bed the morning of the final exam in her physics class. Her father says to her: 'If you go and take your physics exam, I'll buy you a convertible sports car'.
5. Eleanor says to her neighbour, Theodore: 'I will wash your dishes tomorrow morning, if you're not feeling well'.

Here are the answers to the hypothetical situations.

For 1, there is *no* consideration. The employee had already completed all work prior to the employer's promise. This is an example of 'past consideration', which is no consideration.

For 2, there *is* consideration. The daughter has the choice of staying engaged to Philip or of breaking off the engagement. The latter choice constitutes a valid detriment, similar to that of the nephew who gave up smoking, drinking and gambling.

For 3, there *is* consideration. Mary is free to name her child whatever she chooses. By agreeing to call him 'John', she gives up this freedom, an acceptable detriment in exchange for a promise of $5,000.

For 4, there is *no* consideration. One of the requirements of enrolling in the physics course is to take the exams. Hence, the daughter has a 'pre-existing duty' to show up for her final exam.

For 5, there is *no* consideration. Eleanor is not bargaining for Theodore to be ill. The possible illness functions simply as a 'condition precedent' on a gratuitous promise.

We are ready now to consider the various linguistic features of a promise and how those features relate to particular legal elements of contracts.

The linguistic speech act of making a promise

It will be helpful first to clarify some terminology. Throughout the discussion we shall refer to 'speakers' and 'hearers' and to 'promisors' and 'promisees'. In the philosophy of language, 'speaker' and 'hearer' are the traditional terms for the participants in speech acts. Although these words may carry the connotation of applying to the spoken language, their use is by no means limited to oral promises but covers written ones as well. In legal discussions, the 'promisor' takes the place of the speaker and the 'promisee' of the hearer. We shall employ both sets of terms interchangeably.

In speech-act theory a speaker who makes a commitment to the hearer engages in the kind of illocutionary act known as a *commissive*. This class includes promises, offers, vows, pledges and guarantees. Promise probably has the strongest illocutionary force among these various commissives – that is, a promise is one of the most powerful types of commitment that a speaker can undertake. Although in this chapter we shall be concentrating exclusively on the nature of 'promise', this illocution still conforms to all of the properties presented in Chapter 3 that govern speech acts. Here is a summary of the principal characteristics. (See also Figure 3.1 of Chapter 3, on p. 116)

1. Every statement contains an **illocution**: *assertive, commissive, directive, expressive* or *declaration*.
2. An **explicit illocution** contains two parts: (a) an *illocutionary force* (the type of illocution) – such as 'promise', 'offer', 'vow', 'pledge', 'guarantee' for the commissive, and (b) a *propositional content* (the subject matter of the illocution) – for example, *I offer* [illocutionary force] *to drive you to the airport tomorrow* [propositional content].
3. An explicit illocution has the following linguistic structure – first-person actor (speaker) + simple present-tense verb + second-person addressee (explicit or understood) – for example, *I promise (you)* that I will be home by midnight. (Note: If there is a non-first-person subject or a past-tense verb, then one is dealing with an *assertive* about an illocution made in the past.)
4. Most illocutions can be stated implicitly (usually by means of the propositional content alone) – for example, 'The defendant was in the bank at the time of the robbery' (assertive); 'I will drive you to the airport tomorrow' (commissive); 'Be here promptly at noon' (directive); Guilty! (declaration).
5. Every illocution (except a declaration) has an associated state of mind – *belief* for assertive, *intent* for commissive, *want* for directive, *emotion* for expressive.
6. For every illocutionary statement (whether explicit or implicit), one can derive a statement describing the corresponding state of mind – for examples, 'I *believe* that the defendant was in the bank at the time of the robbery' (assertive); 'I *intend* to drive you to the airport tomorrow' (commissive); I *want* you to be here promptly at noon' (directive); I *feel sad* that my neighbours are getting a divorce' (expressive).

Searle's felicity conditions

Every promise involves two acts: a present illocutionary act of promising; and a proposed future act of performing or forbearing. If a promise is to be felicitous, then both its present and future acts have to satisfy certain constraints. Searle has proposed four necessary and sufficient conditions for non-defective promises.[19] He refers to them as the *propositional content* rule, the *preparatory* rule, the *sincerity* rule and the *essential* rule. They serve to evaluate all types of illocutionary acts, but our main concern will be with their application to promise. Let us look at each of these rules.

The propositional content rule

This condition focuses on the particular act promised. Consider the following utterance.

I promise you that *I will drive you to the airport tomorrow.*

Two qualifications are in order here. First, the speaker must be the one to perform (or to refrain from) that act. In other words, I cannot promise someone else's act. Notice the bizarre quality of the following utterance. (A question mark preceding a sentence denotes that it is deviant in some way.)

? I promise you that George will drive you to the airport tomorrow.

This sentence becomes acceptable, however, if it is interpreted as: 'I promise you that *I will see to it* that George will drive you to the airport tomorrow' – that is, what I promise to do is to exert my influence on George. This interpretation is then in accord with the propositional content rule. The *Restatement* also remarks on this type of promise: 'Words are often used which in terms promise action or inaction by a third person, or which promise a result obtainable only by such action. Such words are commonly understood as a promise of conduct by the promisor which will be sufficient to bring about the action or inaction or result . . .'.[20]

In addition to the requirement that the speaker be the one performing or forbearing, the other half of the propositional content rule requires that the performance or forbearance take place in the future. We shall refer to this aspect of the propositional content rule as the *futurity condition*. This requirement means that I cannot promise to do a past act. Consider the strangeness of the following utterance.

? I promise you that I drove you to the airport yesterday.

The verb 'promise' can be used to express other kinds of speech acts that are not commissive. The preceding quoted sentence could be interpretable as a strong affirmation, as an assertive illocution, equivalent to: '*I swear* to you that I drove you to the airport yesterday'. Here I vouch for the performance of a past act. This use of the word 'promise' works best where the hearer has no apparent knowledge of the act, as illustrated by the following utterance.

I promise you that I have deposited sufficient funds into the account.

In spite of the word 'promise', this clearly is not an example of the commissive speech act of promising. Notice that the propositional content rule is just another way of stating what constitutes a commissive speech act: the speaker is to undertake the performance of a future act.

The preparatory rule

This condition covers presuppositions pertaining to the fulfilment of the proposed act. There are two aspects of this rule. First, the hearer must be favourably disposed to having the act done. We shall refer to this aspect of the preparatory rule as the *benefit* condition. Hence, whatever I promise to do (or not to do) must benefit you in some way and not be counter to your interests. For this reason, the following utterance, as a promise, is defective.

? I promise you that I will beat you.

This sentence would normally be interpreted as a threat, another subsidiary use of the verb 'promise'. If, however, the hearer were a masochist and found enjoyment in being beaten, then that utterance indeed could be a bona fide promise. As Searle notes, one promises to do something *for* someone (i.e. a benefit), but one threatens to do something *to* someone (i.e. a detriment).[21]

The second aspect of the preparatory rule stipulates that the speaker normally would not perform the act in the ordinary course of events. We shall refer to this aspect as the *non-expectancy* condition. Thus, there is something decidedly bizarre about my promising to do something that I have already promised to do, or that I habitually do, or that I would do under normal circumstances. As Searle aptly observes, a happily married man who promises his wife that he will not leave her the following week is likely to provoke more concern than comfort.[22]

The sincerity rule

This condition has two requirements. One of them is that the speaker must have the necessary physical or mental competency to perform the act. If I promise to help you prepare for your calculus examination, I have to know how to do calculus. Should I lack the appropriate skills, it is unlikely that I could effectively carry out my promise. We shall refer to this aspect of the sincerity rule as the *ability condition*. A second requirement is that the speaker must *intend* to perform the act. It is evident that if I do not intend to keep a promise or if I have made one in jest, then I am insincere in making that promise. We shall refer to this aspect of the sincerity rule as the *state-of-mind* condition. Recall from the previous chapter that 'intent' is the state of mind that is associated with a commissive illocution.

The essential rule

This condition establishes the purpose of the speech act. What is the point of my saying, 'I promise you . . .'? In uttering these words, not only do I commit myself to the performance of a future act, but also, at the same time, I convey to you my intention of carrying out that obligation. It is a strange kind of promise where the promisee is not aware of the promise. For this reason, the commitment is always between speaker and hearer (and never a third person). Thus, the following utterance is defective because it is not addressed to the hearer.

? I promise your sister that I will drive her to the airport tomorrow.

This sentence could have an acceptable interpretation in a situation where you are acting as agent for your sister but, even then, the promise is being made to you. You become the conduit carrying the promise back to your sister. Although promises are made to hearers, third persons often are the real beneficiaries, as shown by the following utterance.

I promise you that I will drive your sister to the airport tomorrow.

Where there is a third-party beneficiary, it is not the case that that person necessarily wants the act performed. For example, if I promise that I will take your child to the doctor's, there is a good chance that the child does not want me to undertake this endeavour. Nonetheless, there is still the requirement that the hearer wants the act done.

To summarize: the propositional content and preparatory rules relate to the future act of performance: the former concentrates on the promisor's performance of a future activity, while the latter stipulates certain presuppositions for its successful fulfilment, such as the promisee wanting the performance and the promisor not already obligated to do it. The sincerity and essential rules pertain to the present act of promising: the former establishes the promisor's ability and good intention; whereas the latter provides an explicit communication of a commitment to the promisee.

Among the four rules, the essential rule and the propositional content rule are primary, in the sense that they define their respective acts: the former stipulates that the present speech act is to count as a promise, whereas the latter specifies the precise content of the future act. Furthermore, it is elements of these two rules that are directly expressed in sentences having the grammatical structure of an explicit illocution – e.g. 'I promise you that I will drive you to the airport tomorrow', where the verb 'promise' of the main clause states the illocutionary force of the utterance, while the propositional clause, 'that I will drive you to the airport tomorrow', denotes the nature of the future act. On the other hand, features of the sincerity and preparatory rules are not explicitly coded and so these rules play secondary roles. This distinction between primary and secondary rules has important repercussions whenever the rules are violated. Violations of the primary category vitiate the act of promising, whereas violations of the secondary type preserve the promises but will leave them defective in some way. For example, should one ignore the essential rule by not undertaking an appropriate commitment to the hearer, or should one disregard the propositional content rule by not proposing the performance of a future act, then one has simply failed to make a promise. On the other hand, should one abuse the sincerity rule by not intending to go through with the commitment or should one misjudge an aspect of the preparatory rule, such as thinking that the hearer wants the act done when in reality he or she does not, then one has succeeded in making a promise but either has made one insincerely or else has been mistaken about the hearer's desire to receive the benefit being promised.

Felicity conditions and their legal correlates

Because a valid legal agreement requires at least one promise, it would be interesting to see whether contract law has principles similar to the speech-act conditions for felicitous promises. In fact, it has. The futurity condition of the propositional content rule stipulates that the promisor is to undertake a future act. This condition corresponds to the legal requirement that a contract must be 'executory' – that is, one or both of the parties must agree to perform or to refrain from an act whose performance or forbearance is to take place in the future. Suppose that I were to hand over to you the title to my car while simultaneously receiving $2,500 from you. Such a transaction contains no promise by either of us for a future performance. The deal would be fully 'executed' and, consequently, there would be no contract. On the other hand, had I promised to transfer title to you, and either you had paid the $2,500 or else had promised to pay it, there would be a contract, since at least one of the performances was to take place in the future.

The preparatory rule contains two requirements: the *benefit* condition stipulates that the promisee must be favourably disposed to having the promisor do the act; and the *non-expectancy* condition requires that the promisor not be likely to perform the act in the ordinary course of events. These two conditions have their analogues in the law. When we take up again the notion of consideration, we shall see that one of its requirements is that the recipient of a promise should reap some benefit from it. The non-expectancy condition is similar to the legal proviso of 'pre-existing duty' – that is, one cannot contract to do what one is already legally obligated to do. For example, I may not enter into a private agreement with my students for them to pay me for instruction that I am required to give them under my university contract.

The sincerity rule requires that the promisor intend to do what has been promised and has the ability to do it. One of the necessary conditions for a legal agreement is that the parties intend to have a contract. Now, intent has always been problematic for the law. Not being mind-readers, judges cannot establish directly someone else's 'subjective' state of mind. Hence, courts try to rely on some 'objective' standard, such as the notion of a 'reasonable person', for determining intention. One asks how a reasonable person in the shoes of the other party would interpret his adversary's manifestations of intention. In other words, one must infer intent from language, behaviour and actions. The law also expects participants to deal with one another in 'good faith'. If at the time of entering into a contract, I know that I am not capable of performing in the future as required, then clearly I have failed to operate with the requisite standard of good faith.

The essential rule establishes the presence of a commitment. The legal equivalent of this rule requires that the promisee be aware of the promisor's intention to contract. Once again, the parties need not reach agreement subjectively – that is, in their minds. The promisee need only reasonably believe that the promisor's actions denote an intention to enter into a contract. However, where the promisee is unaware of a commitment, there can be no legal promise. For instance, if John promises a reward for the return of a lost article, and if Mary, having no knowledge of the reward, returns the article to him, he need not follow through with the payment. Mary's unawareness of the existence of a reward means that she has not been properly apprised of John's commitment to a promise. However, some jurisdictions do allow an unknowing performer to collect the reward, particularly in those situations where there is a 'standing offer' by a governmental body.

Table 4.1 summarizes the felicity conditions and their legal correlates.

Types of felicity conditions

Table 4.1   The felicity conditions and their legal correlates

Felicity conditions	*Legal correlates*
1 Propositional content rule **Futurity condition:** The *promisor* must perform (or refrain from) a *future act*.	A contract requires at least one *promise* of a *future* performance (or forbearance).
2 Preparatory rule **Benefit condition:** The promisee *desires the act*.	The promisee must receive some *benefit* from the promisor.
Non-expectancy condition: It is *not obvious* that the promisor will do the act in the normal course of events.	The promisor cannot contract to do what he or she is already *legally obligated* to do.
3 Sincerity rule **Ability condition:** The promisor is *able* to do the act.	The promisor acts in *good faith* that he or she will be able to undertake the promised performance.
State-of-mind condition: The promisor *intends* to do the act.	The promisor *intends* to carry out his or her end of the bargain.
4 Essential rule The promisee is *aware* that the promisor has made a commitment.	The promisee must *know* of the promisor's promise in order for there to be a contract.

A linguistic analysis of consideration

The philosophers and linguists who have investigated promises as speech acts have largely restricted themselves to unconditional promises. Such promises place no restrictions on the performance, nor do they require anything in return from the promisee. Searle's felicity rules for well-formed promises, in their original formulation, treated only unconditional promises. However, legal promises are more complex and so the challenge before us will be to adapt the felicity rules to promises with various types of conditions. To accomplish this goal, we start with an analysis of unconditional promises, move on to simple conditional ones, and then turn to promises that propose exchanges, the latter being the kinds of promises backed by consideration.

Unconditional promises

The following utterance, with which we are very familiar by now, is an example of an unconditional promise, one with no strings attached:

'I promise you that I will drive you to the airport tomorrow.'

This kind of utterance – an explicit illocution – is not the only way, or necessarily even the most common form, of making a promise. The following two sentences represent possible alternative versions: the first expresses the propositional content by means of an infinitive construction; and the second resembles a propositional clause standing alone.

'I promise to drive you to the airport tomorrow.'
'I will drive you to the airport tomorrow.'

Essential elements that are present in the explicit illocution are missing in these alternative utterances. The first version lacks in its illocutionary clause the object pronoun 'you' and in its propositional clause the pronoun 'I' and the auxiliary 'will'. However, because this utterance still contains the illocutionary verb 'promise', the type of speech act remains evident and, consequently, the missing terms can be readily inferred. The second sentence is an *implicit illocution*. In form, it closely resembles a propositional clause occurring all by itself. It is the auxiliary 'will' that helps to establish that the speaker is still making a promise. The three sentences, of course, are equivalent in meaning, differing from one another in the degree of explicitness in expressing various components of an illocution. Due to their semantic equivalence, they are reducible to a single logical form, which we shall represent as follows:

I hereby promise you [I will do X]

This formula is intended to show unequivocally that the speaker/promisor ('I') is engaging in a present speech act ('hereby') of a particular type of commitment ('promise') addressed to the hearer/promisee ('you'). The nature of the obligation is shown by the text in square brackets: the speaker/promisor ('I') at some future time ('will') is to perform an act ('do'), whose content is represented by the variable X.

Conditional promises

Unconditional promises place no restrictions on performance, nor do they require anything in return from the promisee. But many everyday promises do not encompass such generosity. Promises often are conditional: some other event must (or must not) transpire before the promisor need perform: 'I will take you shopping this afternoon, if it stops raining . . . if I decide not to go to work; . . . if you meet me on Oxford Street . . . if you tidy up my office'. Linguistically, a conditional promise typically contains a conditional clause headed by 'if' or an equivalent conjunction, such as, 'provided', 'providing', 'on condition', 'in case', 'unless', 'lest'. Where there is an exchange of money or goods, the preposition 'for' frequently serves this function: 'I will sell you my car for $2,500'. This type of sentence can always be paraphrased by means of an if-clause: 'I will sell you my car, if you pay me $2,500'.

To see how conditionals restrict the act of promising, compare the following two sentences. The first has a subordinate clause that is *not* conditional; the second a clause that is.

'I will take you shopping, *when* it stops raining.'
'I will take you shopping, *if* it stops raining.'

In the first sentence there is a presupposition that it will stop raining later. The purpose of the when-clause is to specify a projected time of future performance. There is no question that the speaker intends not only to make a commitment to the hearer but also to perform unequivocally the future act. Hence, the utterance, although grammatically a complex sentence, still counts as an unconditional promise. In the second sentence, there is no presupposition that it will stop raining. The purpose of the if-clause is to constrain the future performance to the occurrence of this outside event. Furthermore, the specified condition is not necessarily linked to any envisaged time of performance. For instance, if the speaker had uttered the sentence in the morning, and a few minutes later it had stopped raining, he or she would be obligated to take the hearer shopping any time subsequent. The speaker would be released from the obligation to go shopping only if it were not to stop raining.

Conditions may be fortuitous outside events (what the *Restatement* calls 'aleatory') – for example, '. . . if it stops raining', or they may be under various degrees of personal control – such as '. . . if I decide not to go to work; . . . if you meet me on Oxford Street; . . . if you tidy up my office'. However, a conditional promise will be 'illusory', and hence infelicitous, whenever its condition is ill-formed. There are three kinds of illusory conditions.

1. A condition that renders performance entirely optional is ill-formed, such as '. . . if I feel like it'. This type of condition allows a promise to be undone at any time at the whim of the promisor; hence, such a conditional promise is equivalent to no promise at all.
2. An impossible condition yields an illusory promise, such as '. . . if I live to be 200 years old'. Short of a miracle, such a promise has no chance of ever being actualized.
3. A condition whose outcome is already known is unacceptable. Note the following example from the *Restatement*:

> A promises B to pay him $5000 if B's ship now at sea has already been lost, knowing that the ship has not been lost. A's promise is illusory.[23]

Although a well-formed condition must be at least possible, it need not be very probable – for example, 'I will give you $3,000 if I win the lottery'. This condition, despite its statistical improbability, nonetheless is well formed. The following example of a reasonable condition is also taken from the *Restatement*.

> A says to B, 'I will employ you for a year at a salary of $5000 if I go into business.' This is a promise, even though it is wholly optional with A to go into business or not.[24]

A's decision to go into business may well depend on various outside events or economic conditions over which he has little or no control.

Note that even unconditional promises are by no means immune from fortuitous outside events. Humans are not immortal or omniscient beings. Consequently, their lives are subject to unforeseen circumstances that may thwart the realization of any promise: somebody dies, becomes ill or insolvent; there is a family crisis; a war breaks out; an earthquake occurs. When a catastrophic event or an emergency situation happens between the making of a promise and its projected fulfilment, a promisor will often be relieved of having to carry out the obligation. The law, too, recognizes 'impossibility of performance' and 'frustration of purpose' due to unforeseen circumstances, and in such situations a party may be discharged from having to perform the contract.

Conditional promises differ from unconditional ones in the relationship between the commitment and the performance. Promise as a speech act, as it has been traditionally construed, requires a present commitment to a future course of action that in principle will transpire. Only an unconditional promise satisfies this requirement. A conditional promise, on the other hand, constitutes a present commitment to a future course of action that is contingent on some other event, and the promise 'ripens' only on the occurrence of that event. We posited the following logical form for an unconditional promise:

> I hereby promise you [I will do X]

The structure for a conditional promise must stipulate that the future act is contingent on the occurrence of some previous event.

I hereby promise you [Y will occur > I will do X]

Recall that the material enclosed in square brackets indicates the nature of the obligation. For an unconditional promise, the obligation was a future performance. For a conditional promise, the obligation becomes the entire implication holding between a future event and a future performance (indicated in the formula as the two propositions connected by the logical operator >). Moreover, the order of the three propositions reflects their temporal sequencing: the speech act of promising precedes the obligation, and within the latter the conditional event precedes the performance. An appropriate paraphrase of the formula would be: 'I promise you that where there will be an occurrence of Y it will be followed by my doing X'.

The logical formulae satisfy the 'truth conditions' of formal logic. A promise will be broken when the object of the promising has a 'false' truth value. For an unconditional promise, the promise is broken whenever the proposition [I will do X] is false. For a conditional promise, the entire implication [Y will occur > I will do X] must be false. In formal logic, an implication is false only when the conditional (the Y proposition) is true and the consequent (the X proposition) is false; however, the implication will always be true whenever the conditional is false (regardless of the value of the consequent). What all of this means is that I have broken my promise only if Y has occurred and I do not do X; however, if Y has not occurred, then I am free to do or not to do X.

Conditional promises that propose the exchange of an act

Just because somebody has made a promise, it does not mean that the promisee has recourse to a legal remedy in the event of breach. The distinction between unconditional and conditional promises is particularly significant for the law, because in general it does not acknowledge the former class of promises. Although in mundane affairs with family, neighbours and friends, we may feel morally and ethically bound to unconditional promises, in the eye of the law they are 'gratuitous'. This does not mean, however, that all promises with conditional clauses will be legally valid. There is an important additional qualification – *consideration*: the promisor is willing to make a commitment, provided he or she gets something in return, either from the promisee or from someone else. Here are three conditional promises. The first one is gratuitous; the other two are not.

'I will take you shopping, if its stops raining.'
'I will take you shopping, if you tidy up my office.'
'I will take you shopping, if your sister tidies up my office.'

The latter two examples constitute 'unilateral' agreements: the promisor proposes to exchange his promise for someone else's performance. In those cases where the consideration comes from a third party, it would seem that there must be some kind of communication between the promisee and the other party, for in accepting the promisor's offer the promisee implicitly agrees to see to it that the performance will be rendered by the other person. Generally, though, it will be the promisee who provides the consideration.

A promise may contain more than one condition:

'I will take you shopping, if it stops raining and if you tidy up my office.'

Of course, I am obligated to perform only if *both* conditions are satisfied. What happens, though, if you should tidy up the office while it is raining, but then the rain doesn't stop? Unfortunately for you, I don't have to take you shopping, and fortunately for me, I end up with a tidied office. This result may seem unfair but, in actuality, there is nothing wrong with taking a chance on a contract and losing. Isn't that precisely what occurs with the purchase of a lottery ticket? The State promises a large sum of money if you first give it a considerably lesser amount and – here is the clincher – provided your number happens to get drawn. A similar situation obtains with a life insurance policy. In exchange for paying a yearly premium, the insurance company will give your beneficiary a considerable sum of money, but on condition that first you die.

A promise that proposes an exchange is a special kind of conditional promise. We posited the following logical form for a conditional promise:

I hereby promise you [Y will occur $>$ I will do X]

To insure a request for someone else's future performance, we must stipulate that the condition, 'Y will occur', take the form: 'Someone (S) other than the promisor (i.e. either you or a third party) will do Y'. Here is the complete logical structure for a promise proposing the exchange of an act:

I hereby promise you [S will do Y $>$ I will do X]

Conditional promises that propose an exchange of promises
A proposed performance is not the only way of satisfying the requirement of consideration. The promisor instead may choose to bargain for a promise in return for his or her own promise, what is known as a 'bilateral' agreement.

'I will take you shopping, if you promise that you will tidy up my office.'
'I will take you shopping, if you promise that your sister will tidy up my office.'

There is no question about the utility of a promisor wanting a return promise. Consider the situation where I propose to take you shopping in exchange for your tidying up the office. It might be impractical for me to wait around to see whether you start performing. Alternatively, I may have no particular reason for preferring that the office-tidying episode precede the shopping expedition, just so long as my office is straightened up. Therefore, I have good reason to desire a commitment from you in exchange for my commitment. The flexibility, the convenience and the utility afforded by a return promise expand considerably the power of contracting, and in no way should it be surprising that most legal contracts will be of this type.

A conditional promise that requests a performance had the following logical form:

I hereby promise you [S will do Y] > I will do X]

If there is to be an exchange of promises, then the conditional, 'S will do Y', must be part of (i.e. embedded in) a promise made by the promisee. Here is the logical structure for an exchange of promises:

I hereby promise you [you will promise me (S will do Y) > I will do X]

There are several ordering dependencies here: the speaker's speech act precedes in time the conditional obligation [which is everything enclosed in square brackets]; within the obligation, the hearer's future promise to do Y or to have someone else do Y, which is everything from the left square bracket to the symbol >, must precede the speaker's future performance of X; and the hearer's act of promising must precede the requested performance (which is the material in parentheses). The logical form, however, imposes no dependency on the two future performances by the speaker/promisor and the hearer/promisee.

Felicity conditions and consideration

Searle's original felicity conditions handled unconditional promises. We shall need to adapt his rules to conditional promises with consideration. We repeat the various conditions, stating them now in terms of a promisor and a promisee.

1. **Propostional content rule**

   Futurity condition: The *promisor* must perform (or refrain from performing) a future act.

2. **Preparatory rule:**

   Benefit condition: The *promisee* wants the act done.
   Non-expectancy condition: It is not obvious that the *promisor* would do the act in the normal course of events.

3. **Sincerity rule:**

   Ability condition: The *promisor* must be able to do the act.
   State-of-mind condition: The *promisor* intends to do the act.

4. **Essential rule:**

   Essential condition: A commitment is established between the *promisor* and the *promisee*.

For unilateral agreements, those conditional promises that look to another person's performance, the four rules will still apply to the promisor and his or her performance, but they have nothing to say about the conditional part of the promise – that is, the appropriateness of the other person's performance. Some additional criteria are necessary in order for there to be a valid exchange. Consideration for a unilateral promise will be 'sufficient' whenever the *requested performance* – what the promisee is to do – satisfies the following four conditions.

The criteria for a valid exchange

1. **Futurity:** *Someone (other than the promisor)* must perform (or refrain from) a future act.
2. **Benefit:** The *promisor* wants the act done.
3. **Non-expectancy:** It is not obvious that the *other party* would do the act in the normal course of events.
4. **Ability:** The *other party* must be able to do the act.

These criteria, governing the act done by the promisee or by some other person, are similar to four of the six conditions on the promisor's performance. Note that there are no corresponding constraints to the essential condition or the state-of-mind condition. For a unilateral contract, the promisor is the only one making a promise, and so these two additional conditions must apply to that speech act. They are not relevant, however, for the other person's conduct, for he or she has not made a promise and will be engaged uniquely in a performance (or a forbearance).

The criteria for a valid exchange will also accommodate bilateral agreements, where there is an exchange of promises. The notion of consideration requires that someone other than the promisor perform (or refrain from) a future act. One of the central ideas of speech-act theory is that a speech act, although verbal, nonetheless is as much an act as any other kind of action. Thus, a promisor, in requesting an act in exchange for his or her promise, can have that request met through the promisee's giving of a speech act: 'I will take you out to dinner, if you *nominate* me for the presidency of our club; . . . if you *invite* me to the debutantes' ball; . . . if you *ask* Charlie to lend me $10; . . . if you *tell* my boss that I'm not feeling well today'. It goes without saying that if a promisor can request the performance of an illocutionary act, he or she can bargain just as well for a promise:

'I will take you shopping, if you will *promise* to tidy up my office.'

Notice that a requested promise satisfies the four criteria for a valid exchange: (a) someone other than the promisor (i.e. the promisee) will perform the future act of promising; (b) the promisor wants the promise made; (c) it is not obvious that the promisee would make such a promise in the normal course of events; (d) the promisee is able to make the promise.

However, not just any promise whatsoever will constitute consideration. A promisor who requests a return promise desires more than just the mouthing of words. His or her ultimate interest is in the other party's performance of a specific act, and it is the nature of that act that should decide whether the promise qualifies as valid consideration. Here is what the *Restatement* has to say about this kind of promise: '[A] promise which is bargained for is consideration if, but only if, the promised performance would be consideration'.[25] This quotation emphasizes that where a promisor seeks, not a future performance, but instead a return promise of a future performance, the promised performance must still constitute a valid exchange.

For a bilateral agreement, the promisor requests a promise from the promisee. But by specifically performing the illocutionary act of making a promise, the promisee perforce has become also a promisor. Consequently, the entire set of felicity conditions ought to be fully effective. The illocutionary part of the return promise will have to conform to the state-of-mind clause of the sincerity rule and to the essential rule, while the proposed act must continue to satisfy the remaining rules. Because we are dealing here with a return promise, the rules, of course, now apply to someone other than the original promisor.

To summarize the speech-act requirements for consideration: for a unilateral agreement, the promisor's promise must satisfy all of the felicity conditions, and the promisee's act must satisfy the criteria for a valid exchange (which, in actuality, are nearly identical to four of the six felicity conditions). For a bilateral agreement, both parties' promises must satisfy all of the felicity rules. This brings us to our next topic: how these two sets of linguistic requirements relate to the legal doctrine of consideration.

The nature of consideration

For several centuries, it has been customary to maintain that an informal promise without consideration is not enforceable. It is not only within the Anglo-American common law that promissory words alone are insufficient for enforcing promises. In Roman jurisprudence, for example, a *nudum pactum*, a bare promise, was not enforceable. In order to turn it into a *pactum vestitum*, an agreement invested with the proper form for enforceability, there had to be present some other *causae*, or factors.[26]

Although, within contract law, there is no simple definition of consideration, over the years certain principles have emerged for evaluating the sufficiency of the consideration.[27] They include: (a) an agreed exchange or a bargain; (b) a benefit accrued by the promisor; (c) a detriment incurred by the promisee; and (d) a *quid pro quo* or an equivalence in performances. These different requirements are interrelated. (a) The promisor offers his promise in exchange for the promisee's performance or promise of performance. (b) In order for that exchange to be valid, the promisor is supposed to reap some benefit from the other person's performance. (c) Conversely, the promisee, in expending effort or funds in carrying out the requested act, suffers a detriment. (d) Benefit and detriment, however, turn out to be reciprocal relations. The promisee, being the recipient of a promise, will also derive some benefit from the act that has been promised, whereas the promisor, by making the promise, will bear a detriment. Hence, there is a certain *quid pro quo*, an equivalent give and take. For example, if I offer to you sell you my car for $2,500 and you accept my offer, I will benefit by having an additional $2,500 in my bank account but I will suffer a detriment by no longer owning a vehicle. Conversely, you will accrue a benefit in acquiring the car, but you will bear a detriment in being $2,500 poorer.

Foremost among the various requirements for consideration is the notion of an 'exchange' or a 'bargain'. The *Restatement*, in fact, adopts the view that 'a performance or a return promise must be bargained for' and, according to the *Restatement*, this requirement is the only one really relevant for consideration.[28] Its 100-page chapter devoted to consideration is an elaboration and emendation of this position. The promisor desires a certain action or forbearance and, as an inducement for that performance, he or she promises to do something that the promisee would want. The idea of a bargain is central too to the framework proposed here. We have characterized a promise backed by consideration as a conditional promise that proposes an exchange. Indeed the element of exchange finds direct expression in the linguistic form of this type of promise: the main clause of a conditional promise stipulates the performance promised by the promisor – for example, 'I will take you shopping', while the if-clause specifies the other party's act that is to be given in *exchange* – namely, 'if you tidy up my office'.

The requirements for consideration

The four criteria for a valid exchange interestingly enough correspond to certain of the legal principles for consideration that were mentioned in the preceding section. For convenience, we shall repeat the criteria and then show how they relate to the legal principles.

Criteria for a valid exchange

1. Someone (other than the promisor) must perform (or refrain from) a future act.
2. The promisor wants the act done.
3. It is not obvious that the other party would do the act in the normal course of events.
4. The other party must be able to do the act.

Criterion 1 eliminates any acts that the other party has already performed at the time of the promise. (We shall take up the notion of 'past consideration' in a moment.) Criterion 2 plays two roles: it encompasses elements of 'benefit' and of 'bargain'. The promisor wants something from another person. The satisfaction of that desire – the promisor's obtaining the requested performance – will provide a benefit to him or her. This criterion is relevant too for the 'bargain' aspect. It is the desire for that performance that ultimately motivates the promisor to make a promise as part of a bargain. Criterion 3 deals with 'detriment'. The other person is to perform an act that he or she need not do otherwise. One bears a legal detriment by either engaging in an act that one is not legally obligated to do or else by refraining from an act that one is legally privileged to do. Criterion 4 requires that the other person be able to carry out the agreement by doing something in furtherance of the promisor's request, which means that the individual must have some volitional control over the requested performance.

Recall that similar constraints apply to the promisor's act, as encompassed in the felicity conditions for a well-formed promise. The promisor will act in the future; the promisee will derive some benefit from the promise; the promisor is to do something not otherwise required; and the promisor must be capable of performing. Together, the *rules for felicitous promises* and the *criteria for a valid exchange* accommodate the concept of *quid pro quo*. This notion encompasses substantially more than just the idea of something given in exchange for something else. Rather, there is an equivalence of sufficiency of the two performances. Even though the content of the respective acts will be different and, in some cases, there may be substantial inequality in their monetary worth, nonetheless the requirements governing the legitimacy of the content are identical. There is complete reciprocity: each party is to perform in the future; each desires something from the other; the other person is not expected to perform the act in the ordinary course of affairs; and each has reason to believe that the other is capable of doing the required performance.

The notions of 'benefit' and 'detriment' can be somewhat problematic if the benefit must come uniquely to the promisor and the detriment proceeds solely from the promisee. Problems crop up whenever third persons enter the picture. Consider the following two examples:

> 'I promise to take you shopping this afternoon, if you wash my brother's car.'
> 'I promise to take you shopping this afternoon, if your sister washes my car.'

For the first example, how will I benefit from your performance? According to criterion 2, the promisor wants the other person's performance, but there is no requirement that the performance must benefit the promisor directly. Of course, getting what one wants can be construed as a benefit, as we saw in the case of *Hamer* v. *Sidway*, where the uncle wanted to see a change in his nephew's behaviour. For the second example, what kind of detriment will *you* undergo? According to criterion 4, someone is to undertake an unexpected act, but that person need not be the promisee. In other words, the detriment can lie elsewhere. In those cases where the consideration does come from a third party, there must be some communication between the promisee and the other party, for in accepting the promisor's offer the promisee implicitly agrees to see to it that the performance will be rendered by the other person. This guarantee by the promisee is not unlike that of a promisor who promises action by a third party. Consequently, the concepts of 'benefit' and 'detriment' must take the following forms: a benefit will accrue to the promisor whenever he or she obtains the performance of the other party, but not necessarily a personal advantage resulting from that performance; and a detriment will be incurred by the other person, who may or may not be the promisee, whenever the performance is not otherwise required. This is how benefit and detriment are to be understood in contract law, a view that is consistent with the *Restatement*'s position: 'The performance or return promise may be given to the promisor or to some other person. It may be given by the promisee or by some other person'.[29]

The sufficiency of the consideration

A favourite style of examination for first-year students of contract law is the presentation of hypothetical illustrations of proposed bargains. The examinee must decide whether there is sufficient consideration. The speech-act criteria for valid exchanges can be useful for analysing the different situations. We shall examine the various types of examples traditionally recognized within the law of contracts – past consideration, pre-existing duty, sham consideration, condition on a gift and fortuitous occurrence.[30]

Past consideration

A promisor makes a promise in exchange for an act already performed. Consider the following examples from the *Restatement*:

(A) A receives a gift from B of a book worth $10. Subsequently A promises to pay B the value of the book. There is no consideration for A's promise. This is so even though B at the time he makes the gift secretly hopes that A will pay him for it.[31]

(B) A gives emergency care to B's adult son while the son is sick and without funds far from home. B subsequently promises to reimburse A for his expenses. The promise is not binding.[32]

Let's see how the *criteria for a valid exchange* (see p. 162) apply to these situations. Criterion 1 states that the other person's act must take place in the future – that is, subsequent to the promisor's speech act of promising. Examples (A) and (B) disregard this criterion. In a common sale of goods, A promises to pay for goods if B transfers ownership to him. In example (A), there is a reversal of this state of affairs. B's transfer of ownership has preceded A's promise to pay. Hence, the transfer counts as a gift and so there can be no promise to buy. Example (B) is based on the famous case involving a sick son cared for by strangers. B promises to pay A for an act that A has already performed. Of course, had A communicated with B at the time the son fell ill, and had B at that time promised payment, A's subsequent caring for the son would have constituted valid consideration for B's promise.

A promise of 'past consideration' is easy to identify linguistically. Its subordinate clause will always have a past-tense verb and will generally not be conditional: 'I will pay you $500 because you took care of my sick son', or 'I will pay you $500 for having taken care of my sick son'. The purpose of the subordinate clause here is to state the speaker's reason for promising a gift of $500. A subordinate clause with a past conditional is also ineffective: 'I will take you shopping this afternoon, if you have tidied up my office'. This sentence can only be a gratuitous promise with a condition precedent, provided the condition is not illusory – that is, at the time of making the promise the speaker must not yet know whether the condition has occurred. In order for there to be consideration, the linguistic structure of a conditional clause requires a non-past verb: 'I will pay you $500, if you (will) take care of my sick son'.

Pre-existing duty
A promisor makes a promise for an act that the other party is already committed to do. Here are two examples:

(C) A offers a reward to whoever produces evidence leading to the arrest and conviction of the murderer of B. C produces such evidence in the performance of his duty as a police officer. C's performance is not consideration for A's promise.[33]

(D) A, an architect, agrees with B to superintend a construction project for a fixed fee. During the course of the project, without excuse, A takes away his plans and refuses to continue, and B promises him an extra fee if A will resume work. A's resumption of work is not consideration for B's promise of an extra fee.[34]

Criterion 4 for a valid exchange requires that the other party not be expected to perform the requested act. Whenever the other person has a legal obligation to do so, there is a violation of this criterion. In example (C), C has an obligation to apprehend criminals as part of his contractual duties as a police officer. In example (D), A had a previous agreement with B to do certain work. Hence, A cannot enter into a valid new contract with B if, in the new contract, he must do exactly what is already expected of him. However, the consideration will become valid whenever the other person can perform the act outside of his current contractual duties or whenever he does more than he is currently obligated to do. Note the next two examples:

(E) In illustration [C], C's duties as a police officer are limited to crimes committed in a particular state, and while on vacation he gathers evidence as to a crime committed elsewhere. C's performance is consideration for the promise.[35]

(F) A owes B $5. B promises to give A a book if A will pay the $5 and $1 in addition. A pays the $6. B's promise is binding, although A's payment of the $5 which he owed would not of itself have been consideration.[36]

Let us turn to the linguistic features of pre-existing duty. This type of invalid consideration represents a violation of the presuppositions of the if-clause. An if-clause, by its very nature, carries the presupposition that the event in question is not habitually expected. For example, let us assume that you wash my car every Saturday morning. In this situation it would be inappropriate for me to say: 'I will take you out to lunch, if you wash my car on Saturday morning'. The conditional clause is infelicitous here, because it presupposes that you would not ordinarily wash my car on Saturday, a situation not supported by the facts. Similarly, had you previously promised to wash my car, it would be just as strange for me to say: 'I will take you out to lunch, if you promise to wash my car'. However, if you had expressed only an intention to wash it, then it would not necessarily be inappropriate for me to utter the preceding sentence. These are the effects of criterion 4 in non-legal dealings. The consequences are precisely the same in legal contexts. To see this more clearly, let us recast examples (C) and (D) as promises.

(C') 'We will pay you a reward if you [policeman] provide information leading to the arrest and conviction of the murderer of B.'
(D') 'I will pay you X dollars more, if you [architect] promise to do the work you previously promised to do.'

The if-clause of (C') presupposes that the police officer need not provide information about felons, a presupposition that undoubtedly is not in accord with the terms of his employment. In (D'), the infelicity of the conditional becomes blatantly transparent: one cannot promise felicitously to do what one has already promised to do.

Sham consideration

A promisor makes a promise in exchange for a trifle or a ridiculously small sum of money. Consider the next example:

(G) In consideration of one cent received, A promises to pay $600 in three yearly instalments of $200 each. The one cent is merely nominal and is not consideration for A's promise.[37]

In general, the law does not look into the economic value of the consideration, and there are clearly contracts where the parties exchange things that do not have equivalent monetary worth. For example, one may offer to sell an item at a price considerably beneath its market value. If value is not at issue, then why should a peppercorn or a cent not qualify as appropriate consideration? Criterion 2 for a valid exchange stipulates that the promisor wants the act done. Should the promisee's performance not be really desired by the promisor, there will be a violation of this criterion. In example (G), it is highly unlikely that A is eager to pay B $600 because A really wants B to give him one cent. Of course, if A has a gap in his coin collection, he indeed may want B to give him a certain penny in exchange for a promise to pay $600. There is no question then of the adequacy of B's consideration. That is not the case here. We can say, then, that what is characteristic about sham consideration is the insincerity of the promisor's wanting the other person's performance. The expression 'not wanting' does not mean 'lacking in enthusiasm'. For example, A may not really want to sell his house to B, but a divorce compels him to do so. Nonetheless, he still 'wants' B to give him his price. It is the latter sense of 'want' that enters into criterion 2. Even where circumstances force A to sell his house substantially under its market value, there is nonetheless a presumption that he wants his price, a presumption that is absent in the cases of sham consideration.

Condition on a gift

The sincerity requirement by itself in not a sufficient characterization of criterion 2 for a valid exchange. The bargain element must also be present. The promisor may indeed be sincere in wanting the promisee to do something, but if that act is viewed only as a necessary condition on the promisee's acceptance of the promisor's gift, and not as something given in exchange for the promise, there can be no consideration. Consider the following example:

'I will buy you a coat this afternoon, if you meet me on Oxford Street.'

Under normal circumstances, this utterance would be a gratuitous promise. In order to go shopping, we have to go to a part of town where there are shops. My request for you to meet me on Oxford Street is not an unusual one. I assume that you are physically able to find your way there and the distance for you to travel is reasonable. I am *not* asking you to meet me there in exchange for my promise, but rather as a condition for you to enjoy the fruits of my generosity.

Now let us construct a different scenario. Suppose that you happen to be a recluse suffering from agoraphobia, and my real motive for having you meet me on Oxford Street is to get you out of the house and into the open. In this case, your meeting me on Oxford Street could conceivably be construed as valid consideration for my promise.

How do the criteria for valid exchanges handle these two situations? In both instances, the three criteria pertaining to the other person are satisfied: you will meet me on Oxford Street, you are able to do it and you are not otherwise expected to be there. The difference in the two scenarios hinges entirely on criterion 2 – the motivation for my 'wanting' you to meet me on Oxford Street. If that desire is what induces my promise, there should be consideration; otherwise, there should not be. In the 'recluse' scenario, my wanting you to meet me on Oxford Street becomes primary from my perspective. I have an interest in getting you there, an interest that is separate from the promise to buy you a coat. In the other situation, it is the promise that becomes primary. It is motivated entirely out of my amicable desire to buy you something. I have no interest in your meeting me other than for this purpose.

Fortuitous occurrence

The *Restatement* has no well-defined category corresponding to violations of criterion 3, which requires that the other party be able to perform the requested act. It is easy enough to concoct absurd examples – for instance, 'I will take you out to dinner, if you swim to France'. An impossible condition of any sort yields an illusory promise. There is, however, a more interesting side of criterion 3. The other person must expend some effort in performing the act requested or alternatively be able to exercise some control over the outcome. Where it is entirely fortuitous, there can be no consideration. The promisor too must have control over the act that he or she promises to do. Notice the oddness of the following utterance: 'I promise to win next Saturday's lottery'. If this is to be a felicitous promise, it implies that the promisor has some way of either predicting or influencing the draw of the numbers. Contrast the two following hypothetical examples, which are not from the *Restatement*.

(I) A has applied for admission to the Yale Law School complying with all their application requirements. B, his aunt, an alumna of Yale, says to him: 'If you get admitted to Yale, I'll give you $5,000.' Subsequently, A gains admission. A's acceptance by Yale is not consideration for B's promise.

(J) A has applied for admission to several lawschools. Both Harvard and Yale have accepted him. Now he needs to decide which lawschool to choose. B, his aunt, says: 'If you go to Yale, I'll give you $5,000.' A's subsequent choosing of Yale over Harvard is consideration for B's promise.

In example (I), A had applied to Yale before his aunt made her promise. Afterwards, he engaged in no act to further his admission to Yale. The decision for admission was completely out of his control. Essentially, it was a fortuitous event. In example (J), A had applied to Yale before his aunt made her promise, but he had also applied to Harvard. Once the aunt found out that her nephew had been admitted to both institutions, she offered him $5,000 in exchange for his choosing Yale over Harvard. Because A had control over which lawschool he would eventually attend, his choice of Yale would constitute consideration for B's promise.

Summary

The speech-act felicity conditions serve to differentiate between promises that are felicitous or well formed from those that are defective in some way.

We established analogous constraints governing the requirements of a promisee's performance for the class of promises that propose exchanges. These joint requirements for both promisors and promisees have direct application for determining the adequacy of consideration in contract law. Failure to respect the futurity condition or a preparatory rule will result in one of the forms of inadequate consideration – past consideration, sham consideration or pre-existing duty. On the other hand, violations of the sincerity rules or the essential rule will lead to contracts that are voidable, fraudulent or even non-existent. Table 4.2 summarizes the relationship between speech-act felicity conditions and legal outcomes.

A condition that proposes an exchange plays three simultaneous roles: it operates as a condition precedent, it specifies the consideration required for

Speech-act analysis of consideration

Table 4.2 Felicity conditions and consideration

Felicity conditions	*Legal correlates*
Failure to respect this felicity condition	*Results in the following legal consequence*
1. Futurity rule Each party must perform (or refrain from performing) a **future act.**	**Past consideration** A party has already performed the requested act.
2. Preparatory rule **Benefit condition:** Each party **desires an act** to be performed by the other party.	**Sham consideration:** A party is not 'truly' bargaining for the act.
Non-expectancy condition: It is **not obvious** that a party would do the act in the ordinary course of events.	**Pre-existing duty:** A party is already under a legal obligation to perform the act.
3. Sincerity rule **Ability condition:** A promisor **is able** (physically and/ or mentally) to perform the act promised.	**Voidable contract:** A party is deemed unable or unfit to perform the required act.
State-of-mind condition: A promisor **intends** to do the act promised.	**Fraud:** A party has acted in bad faith and with intent to deceive.
4. Essential rule A **commitment** exists between the promisor and the promisee (i.e. the promisee is aware of the promisor's commitment).	**No contract** An individual was unaware of the promisor's promise.

the promisor's promise and it turns the promise into an offer. Consider again the situation where I promise to take you shopping if you tidy up my office. There is a condition precedent because my future performance of taking you shopping is contingent upon your prior performance of tidying up the office or, alternatively, of promising to do so. Furthermore, because the condition stipulates what you must do in order to consummate the bargain, it functions as the consideration for my promise. Finally, because the condition is not fortuitous, but under your control, you are free to accept or reject its terms and, as I shall argue, this kind of promise is equivalent to an offer.

Offer or promise?

In traditional contract law, an offer turns into a binding agreement only after it has been accepted. If not accepted immediately, or within a period stipulated by the offeror, then the latter is free to withdraw the proposal. Now, a withdrawal generally poses no particular problem in the case of a bilateral agreement, where the offeror has requested a return promise. If one is not forthcoming and the offer is withdrawn, the offeree will have suffered no real detriment. However, the consequences for a unilateral agreement, where the offeror has requested a return performance, may not be so benign. Consider the following hypothetical example humorously employed by some contracts professors to drive home this point.[38]

> The professor offers to pay a student a sum of money if the student rides a bicycle across the Brooklyn Bridge. The student takes up the challenge and begins cycling across the bridge. The professor is secretly waiting on the other side and just as the student is about to finish traversing the bridge, the professor jumps out and shouts, 'I revoke'.

The professor's offer constitutes a unilateral agreement: in exchange for his promise to pay a sum of money, the student must perform an act of cycling across the bridge. What exactly constitutes an assent to this kind of offer? According to the classical view of contracts, an offeree can accept such a proposal only by a completed performance of the requested act. This means that in order to accept the professor's offer, the eager student must cycle across the entire length of the Brooklyn Bridge. However, at any time before full completion, the devious professor is free to revoke the offer and therefore will be under no obligation to pay up.

Alternatives to the traditional view

Laypersons doubtless consider a revocation at the last moment as quite unjust and many legal scholars certainly would agree with them. Consequently, there have been various proposals for ameliorating the harsh effects of the traditional approach.[39] One suggestion resorts to the legal notion of 'estoppel'.[40] An offeree who begins performance is clearly relying on the offeror to keep his or her end of the bargain. Because of this reliance, the offeror will be 'estopped' or prevented from revoking the offer once the offeree begins to act. The *Restatement* also adopts the view that an offeror is bound to a unilateral agreement as soon as the offeree tenders partial performance.[41] The *Restatement* accomplishes this goal in a novel manner: the commencement of performance creates an 'option' contract, whose effect is to keep the original offer open until completion of the act. Notice, though, that both proposals continue to uphold the doctrine that acceptance of a unilateral contract takes place only when the offeree completes performance. The estoppel and the option element of these proposals function as stopgap measures for preventing an unscrupulous offeror from taking advantage of a naive offeree once the latter has begun performance.

Other commentators have suggested that acceptance of a unilateral contract should take place, not on completion, but on commencement. According to this proposal, the hypothetical unilateral agreement between the professor and the student would have gone into effect as soon as the student began pedalling across the bridge.[42] Hence, the professor would no longer have the opportunity to jump out and revoke the agreement at the last moment. The notion that the ability to revoke ceases with the offeree's commencement of performance has pretty much replaced the traditional rule allowing revocation until full performance. No matter which solution one adopts for resolving the issue of an unjust revocation, it is still the case that the offeror's duty to carry out his or her end of the bargain is contingent on the offeree's total performance of the requested act. Although all the various alternative proposals succeed in protecting a promisee's interests once performance has commenced, they fail to accommodate any expenditures of time, effort or money in preparation for the act.

Unilateral contracts as promises

Peter Tiersma has undertaken an in-depth study of the various issues surrounding unilateral contracts.[43] He maintains that the problem of unjust revocation arises from the mistaken view that such contracts come about through the traditional mode of offer and acceptance. According to Tiersma, this model is appropriate only for bilateral agreements. By saying 'I accept', or uttering other comparable words indicating a promise, the offeree has agreed to the terms of the proposal and both parties are then bound to carry out their respective sides of the bargain. The claim here is that acceptance is essentially a matter of language and not of action. An offeree accepts by uttering the appropriate words (or alternatively by an act equivalent to words, such as a handshake). It is precisely this linguistic feature of acceptance – that is, the rendering of a commissive speech act – that is sought by an offeror in quest of a bilateral contract. Because a unilateral agreement, by asking for a performance, does not look to a verbal response, it fits awkwardly into the offer-and-acceptance mould. How, then, is one to characterize a unilateral contract if it does not contain an offer?

Tiersma maintains that an individual who proposes a unilateral agreement is not making an offer, but rather is making a *promise* – to be more exact, a promise with a condition precedent. To see how this proposal works, let us compare the following two utterances.

'I will take you shopping, if it doesn't rain.'
'I will take you shopping, if you tidy up my office.'

The first sentence is a gratuitous promise; the second could qualify as a unilateral agreement. Yet each contains a condition precedent and so for either situation the promisor is committed to uphold his or her end of the bargain if the condition occurs first. This proviso still permits the promisor of a unilateral agreement to undertake his or her performance only after completion by the promisee. The important point, though, is that when viewed as a promise, a unilateral proposal will not necessitate any kind of acceptance. In making a promise, a promisor is immediately committed to honouring his or her proposal. Hence, the controversy concerning the moment at which a unilateral agreement can no longer be revoked, whether on commencement of the requested act or on its completion, does not arise at all with a promise. Tiersma's suggestion has the additional merit that any expenses incurred by a promisee in preparation for his or her performance will not be in vain. This result follows from the very nature of promise as a commitment. A promise goes into effect immediately when made and from that moment a promisee may rely on a promisor to keep his or her part of the bargain.

If the condition precedent of a promise has failed to occur, then of course the promisor is under no further obligation to perform. The promise has terminated or lapsed; it has not been revoked. This distinction is important. Revocation is a wilful speech act by the promisor. By uttering the words, 'I revoke', he or she declares no intention of carrying out the promise. Termination, on the other hand, is not due to a speech act but rather to the non-fulfilment of the condition precedent over which the promisor typically has little or no control, such as 'if it rains'. However, in the case of a unilateral proposal, the condition is no longer a fortuitous outside event but rather one whose control is vested in the promisee, for the latter is free to perform or not to perform the condition. If the choice is for non-performance, or the promisee simply fails to take any action, then the promise must ultimately terminate. However, exactly when it will lapse is not always so evident. Consider the following conditional promises:

'I will pay you $25, if you wash my car this afternoon.'
'I will pay you $25, if you wash my car.'

For the first example, it is clear enough that as evening approaches and you have failed to wash my car, then I cease to have an obligation to pay you anything. However, what about the second example where the promisor has specified no time limit? How long must he or she wait for a possible response from the promisee? A day, a week, a month? We certainly cannot expect the condition to remain in effect for ever. If the promisor has not stipulated a period of time and if there is to be no breach of contract, then we might suppose that a court or the legislature or even an agreed-upon arbitrary period could designate a reasonable longevity for the condition precedent. The point is that after some period the promise must terminate.

Promise versus offer

We have seen that a conditional promise that proposes an exchange is relevant for consideration. This kind of promise is interesting for another reason: it is formally equivalent to an offer. In order to show why this equivalence holds, we need to examine possible responses to the various kinds of promises.

Let us go back to the unconditional promise. Suppose I say, 'I will take you out to dinner tonight'. You could respond in one of three ways. First, you might react positively by exclaiming, 'Wonderful!', or by doing something non-verbal like jumping up and down with glee. Second, you could react negatively by retorting, 'I don't want to do that', or by screwing up your face in disgust. Third, you might remain neutral, saying or doing nothing. In the first case, where you were enthusiastic, there can be no question whatsoever that my promise is binding. The second situation is quite different. Your negative reply effectively releases me from any further obligation to carry out my prospective programme. Recall the benefit condition of the preparatory rule. Not only must I think that you would like me to take you out to dinner, but also that you indeed want me to do so. A mistaken belief on my part about your desire would violate this important presupposition. In such a situation, my original promise turns out to be infelicitous. Later, if you change your mind and decide it might not be so bad after all to have dinner with me, you cannot accuse me of breaking my promise should I no longer wish to dine with you. In the third case, where you do nothing, I am nonetheless committed to the promise. If I am mistaken about your wishes, I cannot know that fact, unless your views are communicated to me in some fashion. Hence, silence must be construed as a tacit confirmation of your desire for the promised act. This result follows from the nature of the unconditional promise as a speech act. Unless something interferes to render the promise infelicitous, it takes effect with the speaker's utterance of it.

Notice that in the first case, your positive response was *not* an acceptance. As we noted in the discussion of Tiersma's proposal, one cannot accept a promise. A positive response from you is nothing more than an overt confirmation of my assessment of your desire for me to take you to dinner. Charles Fried, taking an opposite stance, observes correctly that one cannot 'thrust' one's promise onto an unwilling promisee but he concludes from that observation that in order for a promise to be valid the promisee must 'accept' it.[44] From the speech-act perspective, the attempted foisting of a promise on an unenthusiastic promisee represents a violation of the benefit condition that the hearer wants the act performed. We conclude that such a promise is deviant because it is infelicitous, and not because it has not been accepted.

When we turn to conditional promises, it makes a difference whether the condition is a condition precedent or one that proposes an exchange. For example, if I say, 'I will take you out to dinner, if it doesn't rain', my duty to perform ripens only if it fails to rain, but once again a response from you is not required in order for my promise to take effect. However, for a conditional promise that proposes an exchange, the situation is quite different. In uttering, 'I will pay you $25, if you wash my car', it is true that I propose to commit myself to a future performance contingent on the prior occurrence of the requested act, and so to that extent, the promise contains a condition precedent. But because control over the act is vested entirely in you – unlike a fortuitous condition, such as whether it will rain – you are free to do or not to do what I have requested. Therefore, a positive or a negative reaction from you will denote your willingness or unwillingness to undertake the requested performance. If you rush outside and begin to wash my car or, alternatively, you promise to do so, you have acquiesced to my condition, which, at the same time, tacitly represents confirmation of your desire to receive $25. Consequently, my commitment takes effect. If, on the other hand, you have no desire to wash my car or to earn $25, and you inform me accordingly, you have rejected my proposal and I am relieved of any further obligation.

Michael Hancher makes a distinction between two kinds of speech acts – 'autonomous' ones, which go into effect immediately upon being uttered, and 'cooperative' ones, which first require a positive response from the hearer before they take full effect.[45] Some examples of autonomous speech acts include requesting, ordering, firing (someone), nominating (someone) and unconditional promising. Some examples of cooperative speech acts are betting, challenging, offering and promising with an exchange. Thus, if I say to you, as your employer, 'I fire you', I have performed autocratically the act of discharging you. Similarly, if I have the authority and I order you to leave the room, even though you refuse to do so, I have succeeded in issuing an order. On the other hand, if I bet you $100 on the outcome of next Sunday's football match, you must accept my proposal – by a handshake or saying something like 'You're on!' – before the bet can take effect. Without your acceptance, I have neither the duty to pay you $100 should my team lose, nor the right to collect that sum should it win.

The distinction between autonomous and cooperative speech acts characterizes the difference between unconditional promises and offers. If we are at a party and I *promise* to drive you home after it is over, I become immediately obligated to drive you, unless of course you explicitly release me from that obligation. On the other hand, if I *offer* to drive you home, I am obliged to do so only after you have accepted my offer. If you neither accept it nor reject it – such as telling me that you want to think about it and will let me know later, then I am free to change my mind and to retract my offer so long as you have not yet responded. Thus, an offeror can withdraw an offer that is not immediately accepted, just as a bettor can call off a bet that is not taken up. However, a promisor cannot renege on a promise.

Unconditional promises and offers differ most dramatically in the degree of certainty attached to the presupposition about the hearer's wanting the speaker to perform the proposed act. For a promise, that presupposition operates as a crucial element of the benefit condition of the preparatory rule and it is the hearer's duty to notify the speaker whenever that presupposition turns out to be erroneous, in which case the promise will become infelicitous. In the case of an offer, the presupposition is weaker. An offer presupposes that the hearer might be reasonably disposed to having the speaker perform the proposed act. Because of this 'inherent incertitude' surrounding an offer, the offeror can express only a willingness that is contingent on receiving a confirmation of the hearer's desire for the offeror to carry out the act. An offer to do X might be paraphrased as: 'I will do X, if you want me to do X', a structure similar to a condition precedent. That is, the promisor makes a commitment to a future act but must perform only if the conditional requirement occurs – namely, that the promisee indicates in some way his or her positive inclination towards the promisor's proposal.

For a conditional promise that proposes an exchange, the uncertainty concerns not just the hearer's willingness for the speaker's act, but also the hearer's willingness to undertake the performance requested of him or her. But precisely because the promisor's commitment is contingent on the promisee's willingness to perform, protocol requires that the promisee communicate his or her desire either by a verbal act of promising or by a non-verbal act of performance. The consequences of positive or negative responses to conditional promises that propose exchanges are exactly analogous to those resulting from offers. Therefore, a promisor who has not received a positive or a negative response – equivalent to an acceptance or a rejection – may subsequently choose to withdraw his proposal. Only a conditional promise that proposes an exchange has the necessary conditions for converting it into the cooperative speech act of an offer. Other kinds of conditions function purely as conditions precedent and are not equivalent to offers.

Now, an offeree can accept an offer by performing an act – either a verbal act or a physical one. For a bilateral agreement, acceptance takes place through a speech act of making a return promise; for a unilateral agreement, acceptance is manifested by undertaking the act requested by the offeror. For the latter situation, the offeree manifests acceptance by *commencing* performance, a view in conformity with the modern rule that an offeror cannot revoke an offer once performance has begun. For example, if I promise to pay you $25 if you wash my car, it seems logical that your starting to wash the car indicates acceptance of my offer, and so from that moment on I am not free to revoke. What happens, though, if you should begin to perform but stop half-way through and never complete the task? Then I need not carry out my end of the bargain. However, this result follows for the other proposals as well. An offeror of a unilateral agreement is not required to perform before completion by the offeree.

Finally, what about an offeree who has expended time or money in preparation for performance? Tiersma's proposal, based on the notion of promise and thereby not ever sanctioning revocation, safeguards the promisee's reliance in this situation. Does my analysis allow an offeror to withdraw the offer at any time prior to the offeree's commencement of performance? To illustrate more concretely how I view this issue, consider again the two conditional promises previously cited.

> 'I will pay you $25, if you wash my car.'
> 'I will pay you $25, if you wash my car this afternoon.'

In the first example, no time period has been specified. Because I am free to revoke an offer prior to commencement of performance, you have no guarantee that the offer will necessarily remain open should you decide to undertake preliminary preparations without notifying me. In this case the standard legal remedies will have to be available to an offeree who has relied on a promise – either reliance damages or promissory estoppel. On the positive side, revocation permits an offeror to withdraw an offer should there be no response forthcoming from the offeree. Tiersma's proposal of a conditional promise requires a promise to remain in effect until it eventually lapses after some arbitrary, but supposedly reasonable, length of time.

The second example is quite different. Where there is a temporal constraint, it serves a dual purpose: it not only stipulates the time frame governing the offeree's performance, but it also ought to represent a commitment by the offeror to keep the offer open for the specified length of time. In the second example I not only inform you that the offer will lapse if you fail to wash my car this afternoon, but I also promise not to revoke it before then. Consequently, you will be protected against revocation prior to your commencement of performance and you can undertake with confidence any necessary preparations. This suggestion that the offer should remain open is not necessarily in accord with a more conservative view that always permits an offeror to withdraw an offer that has not yet been accepted even though he or she might have promised to keep it open for a specified period. The rationale for such a counter-intuitive result rests on the assumption that the parties had never reached a 'meeting of the minds'.[46] It seems to me that such a flagrant disregard of a promise by a promisor completely vitiates the meaning of a commitment, and is totally at odds with a promisee's understanding concerning the time-frame for acceptance.

My analysis of unilateral contracts takes advantage of the dual functions of a promisor's promise. Without a doubt, the promise is a conditional one. But what is so special about the condition is its request of a counter-promise or of a performance by the promisee. It is the unique relationship between the promisee and his or her control over the outcome of the condition that makes these types of promises equivalent to offers. It turns the promise into a cooperative affair requiring a response from the promisee before the promisor's commitment goes into effect. These simultaneous functions – as an offer and as a condition precedent – explain why, for unilateral contracts, the offeree's commencement of performance is sufficient to qualify as an acceptance, whereas completion of the performance will be required before the promisor need make good on the promise. Because an offeree can freely elect whether to carry out the requested act, a positive action will constitute an acceptance, but because the performance is part of a condition precedent, the latter can be satisfied only upon completion of the act. Unilateral contracts then do fit the paradigm of offer and acceptance. The equivalence between 'offers' and 'promises that propose exchanges' is firmly established in legal parlance, and it is no coincidence that the law refers to such promises as offers.

Uncertain acceptance: a return promise or a performance?

Another reason for treating a unilateral contract as an offer – and not simply as conditional promise – has to do with an offeree's possible uncertainty whether a unilateral or a bilateral agreement has been proposed. Suppose I say to you, 'I will pay you $25, if you wash my car this afternoon', and you reply, 'I'll do it'. Assume that I was expecting an acceptance by performance. Instead, you have given me a verbal response. What kind of 'acceptance' is this? Is it an affirmation of your intention to carry out the performance? Or does it count as a commitment equivalent to a fully-fledged promise? The particular reply could be either, for its language is ambiguous. Recall the different roles of the auxiliary 'will' in the absence of an explicit illocutionary verb. Two of those functions are intent and promising. Thus, a reply of 'I'll do it' could be an elliptical expression for either 'I intend to do it' or 'I promise to do it'.

If your reply indicates intent only, then we have a unilateral agreement that ought to take effect with your commencement of performance, but if it constitutes a legitimate promise, then we should have instead a bilateral agreement, providing that I am not adverse to one. The ambiguity inherent in a promisee's response may very well arise from his or her uncertainty as to the type of agreement being proposed. Note what the *Restatement* has to say about this kind of dubious situation.

> In case of doubt an offer is interpreted as inviting the offeree to accept either by promising to perform what the offer requests or by rendering the performance, as the offeree chooses.[47]

Why should the offeree be able to respond with a promise when the offeror intended a performance, and vice versa? The *Restatement* indicates that an offeree has a choice only 'in case of doubt'. One ought to be able to trace 'doubt' to one or more of these factors: (a) misinterpretation by the offeree; (b) ambiguity in the language of the offer; or (c) vague intent on the part of the offeror.

We have advocated that a conditional promise that makes a request is equivalent to an offer and, as such, it will require a response from the offeree. If the latter is agreeable to the terms, he or she may feel compelled to convey immediately that feeling to the promisor. A verbal response is the most natural way to do this. However, by responding verbally to a proposed unilateral agreement, the offeree may have (inadvertently!) converted it into a bilateral one.

A volunteered verbal response from an overenthusiastic offeree is not the only cause of possible ambiguity. The uncertainty may be traceable also to the words of the offer. The conditional clause may be ambiguous or vague, so that the offeree is not sure whether acceptance is by promise or by performance. There are, of course, situations without ambiguity. A promisor who has said, 'I will pay you $25, if you promise to wash my car', unequivocally has asked for an exchange of promises, and nothing short of a promise will satisfy that request. On the other hand, one who has said, 'I offer $200 for the return of my lost dog, Tipsy', wants a performance and not anyone's promise to go looking for the dog. Where there is a misunderstanding, once again it may be due to the auxiliary 'will', but this time to its presence or absence in the conditional clause. Compare the following two sentences.

'I will pay you $25, if you wash my car.'
'I will pay you $25, if you will wash my car.'

Otto Jespersen, the same grammarian who had something to say about the concepts of connotation and denotation in Chapter 1, claimed that these types of sentences make different requests.[48] Because a requested performance must take place in the future, the simple present tense by itself suffices to mark futurity in if-clauses and, therefore, an overt future-marker becomes redundant. Whenever the auxiliary does appear in conditional clauses, it serves to elicit from the hearer an affirmation of 'willingness' to undertake the act. Accordingly, the second sentence would be equivalent to: 'I will pay you $25, if you are willing to wash my car'. It is Jespersen's contention then that a conditional clause with a present tense looks to a future performance, whereas one with a future tense expresses willingness. This subtle linguistic difference, although interesting and perhaps even desirable from the perspective of the law, nonetheless is questionable. I doubt whether speakers of English differentiate conditional sentences in this way. The notions of futurity and willingness cannot always be clearly separated because they overlap to a considerable extent: willingness so often is directed towards future activity. Moreover, even if one were able to distinguish futurity from willingness, there would be the further problem of determining whether the willingness was an expression of intent only or the stronger commitment of a promise. This fusion, or even confusion, of futurity and willingness makes any distinction between the two sentences at best subtle and at worst non-existent. I suspect that speakers treat the two sentences as interchangeable variants. It is no wonder, then, that offerees, confronted with such clauses, may be uncertain about the nature of their responses.

This rejection of Jespersen's claim finds support in the following examples from the *Restatement*. They illustrate that speakers may attribute either interpretation to the same conditional clause.

> A writes B: 'If you will mow my lawn next week, I will pay you $10.' B can accept A's offer either by promptly promising to mow the lawn or by mowing it as requested.
>
> (Sect. 32, 1, 90)

> A says to B: 'If you finish that table you are making and deliver it to my house today, I will give you $100 for it.' B replies, 'I'll do it.' There is a contract. B could also accept by delivering the table as requested.
>
> (Sect. 32, 2, 90)

The conditional clause of the first example contains the auxiliary 'will', whereas that of the second does not. According to Jespersen, the former could request a promise, whereas the latter should request only a performance. Yet, in both cases, the *Restatement* finds either response acceptable.

If the language is imprecise on these points, then why does the offeror not couch the offer in a more precise manner? Herein lies a third reason for misinterpretation. The offeror may not really care which type of response he or she receives. In the car-washing episode, for example, I want my car washed by the afternoon and I may be amenable to waiting until then to see whether you do it. If, instead, you choose to make a promise, I will have no objection. In this instance, the uncertainties of language and those of context tend to reinforce each other: an imprecision of grammar is matched by vagueness in situation.

In this chapter we have sought answers to various questions about contract formation: (a) is a statement a promise or some other kind of speech act?; (b) which modes of acceptance count as promises and which as merely intentions to perform?; (c) does a request constitute consideration or only a condition precedent?; (d) is there a valid exchange making a conditional promise equivalent to an offer?; (e) is a proposal intended to be a unilateral agreement or a bilateral one? Although speech-act theory accommodates admirably the relevant data, it alone cannot provide all the answers. One needs also to take account of ambiguity and context – both verbal and contextual. This dependence should not be too surprising considering what we already know about the role of these linguistic and situational factors in the interpretation of language.

Conclusion

> [Linguistic] research will have to find its way
> into the legal institutions that can make use of it.
> *Lawrence Solan and Peter Tiersma*[1]

The chapters of this book have concentrated on four major areas within the field of linguistics: ambiguity, metaphor, speech acts and promises. I chose those topics not only because of their linguistic relevance, but also because they dovetail with specific issues extensively treated in the field of law: misunderstanding, legal fictions, hearsay and contract formation. It is appropriate now to review briefly and to tie together the main themes from these diverse areas. In particular, I would like to consider the mutual contributions of the two disciplines. What can linguistic research garner from analyses of legal data, and why should a linguistics approach to issues in the law be of concern to lawyers and legal scholars?

Misunderstanding and ambiguity

Without question, a good deal of litigation concerns disputes about language, such as the meaning of a contract, the definition of a term in an insurance policy, the intention of a testator in a will or the interpretation of a statute. Ideally, those responsible for the drafting of a document should endeavour to use language that is clear, unequivocal and expresses to the best of their abilities their intent. Still, no matter how much care has gone into the creation of a document, at times there will be misunderstanding about how words, phrases and even entire sentences and paragraphs are to be interpreted.

A linguistic analysis reveals that problems of misunderstanding do not always arise simply from improper usage, because built into the very structure of language are lexical ambiguity, referential indeterminacy, vagueness and the potential for syntactic ambiguity, and unless one is particularly sensitive to these nuances or has been trained to perceive them, they may go unnoticed. The fact that linguists serve as expert witnesses in disputes having to do with lexical and syntactic ambiguity and with issues about reference and categorization indicates that these subtleties of language are not always so obvious to litigants or to judges and juries. Expert testimony is frequently necessary in order to convince the court of the presence of ambiguity or vagueness. The purpose of the testimony may be to enable a plaintiff to argue for an interpretation that is not so apparent, to permit parties to a dispute to bring in extrinsic evidence in order to show their intentions, to allow a plaintiff's meaning of a term to supersede a drafter's, or even to construe an ambiguous criminal statute in favour of a defendant. I would say that many of the linguists belonging to the International Association of Forensic Linguists (IAFL) have participated in these kinds of legal proceedings. Moreover, whenever linguists serve as consultants to attorneys, not only do they familiarize legal practitioners with the pertinence of linguistic analysis to legal issues, but they also contribute significantly to furthering the dialogue between the two disciplines.

Legal fictions and metaphor

We noted the importance of legal fictions for maintaining the stability and the smooth continuity of the law. In those legal systems where these traits are considered desirable, as they are in the English common law, fiction has flourished. British and American courts will frequently adopt a fiction – by accepting facts often blatantly untrue – in lieu of creating a new law. Although this justification for the fiction is unquestionably of utility to the law, the true genesis of many fictions resides in the realm of metaphor, one of the current 'hot' topics of research in linguistics.

The fiction of 'the corporation as a person' stands out as a prime example of metaphorical underpinnings. In the discussion of this well-known fiction, we pitted against each other the philosopher, John Dewey, and the law professor, Arthur Machen. For Dewey, corporate fiction was a pure invention of the law and its vocabulary was arbitrary; words could mean whatever their proponents chose to have them mean. However, Dewey's claim is not borne out by the use of the word 'person' within the law. It is a well-established fact that corporations can do many of the things that real persons do, and statutes originally intended for the latter to apply to the former as well. Furthermore, the US Supreme Court must have been sufficiently impressed by the striking similarity between the rights and duties of corporations and those of real persons to have pondered painfully, in case after case, over the interpretations of the words 'person' and 'citizen' within the Constitution. In denying that there is any connection between the two senses of 'person' – the ordinary and the legal – Dewey failed to account for why humans and institutions bear so singular a resemblance, and why the law constantly and consistently addresses corporations in language appropriate to persons.

Machen took the opposite position. Corporations do display an uncanny analogy to persons and by calling the corporation a 'person', the resemblance is made explicit. The linguistic evidence is on the side of Machen. Although his suggestion that we can ascribe fraud, malice, and mental states to corporations might at first blush seem outrageous, the proposal appears less so once we understand how the extension of human properties to corporate bodies is woven into the very fabric of language. I demonstrated that it is normal linguistic usage – a part of ordinary language – to speak about institutions as though they are persons, and that this way of talking is independent of the law.

This phenomenon is probably not unique to English. In fact, it may very well turn out to be universal. I would venture to say that any culture with institutions as part of its social and economic structure also has within its language the capacity to talk about those institutions by means of the conceptual metaphor: THE CORPORATION IS A PERSON. Although this way of talking about institutions is clearly convenient for the law, it is significant that the law on its own never invented this linguistic imagery. Rather, it has been able to exploit to its advantage and it has managed to maximize for its needs conceptualizations that were already deeply embedded within language. Here, then, is a stunning example of how contemporary linguistic research, by delving into the cognitive depths of metaphor, has contributed a surprising, and even somewhat atypical, perspective on the anatomy of a crucial legal construct.

Hearsay and speech acts

Legal practice and speech-act theory stand in complete agreement on the kinds of utterances that constitute hearsay. Now, speech-act theory was never conceived with the intention of explaining legal concepts. It is foremost a theory about human language – how utterances are constructed and how they are put to use by speakers. The various illocutions accommodate important semantic and pragmatic principles employed by ordinary speakers speaking ordinary language. The theory deals not only with speakers' illocutions, but also with their states of mind, with the effects that their speech causes on others, and with the structural properties that express their utterances. It is remarkable that this theory, in addition, has provided a novel and elegant account of an intriguing legal topic. Each of the major pieces of speech-act theory finds a logical slot within the hearsay puzzle, so that the desired legal categories automatically fit into place from the various speech-act components.

Perhaps this striking coincidence between the requisite hearsay categories and the elements of speech-act theory should not be so surprising, for, after all, hearsay too is concerned with language, and most decisions about hearsay deal with utterances by ordinary people speaking ordinary language. In any case, the jurists and legal scholars, who, throughout the years, were codifying the principles behind the rule against hearsay, intu-itively arrived at a coherent set of categories, which turn out to have precise correlates in the speech-act analysis. Moreover, speech-act theory offers a resolution to a longstanding dispute within the law about whether state-of-mind statements are exceptions to hearsay or are not hearsay at all. The speech-act approach provides a consistent treatment of this issue. No statement about state of mind is hearsay.

A perusal of any of the casebooks assigned to evidence classes in law-schools reveals a considerable amount of textual space devoted to hearsay. Professors of law allocate several weeks of instruction to the topic, one that their students often find bewildering, arcane, and at times confusing. Questions like those appearing in the Harvard exam further demonstrate that the application of hearsay law to specific issues is not always so trans-parent. Neophyte legal practitioners must not only wrestle with how hearsay applies to courtroom testimony, but they also have to come to grips with myriad exceptions to the hearsay rule. Even trial lawyers and judges on the bench are not immune from the hearsay 'thicket – this incredible mishmash of rules'.[2] I believe that a speech-act approach to hearsay could be a useful implement within the bag of tools for law students and other legal professionals who need to work their way through the intricacies of this 'thicket'. In fact, several of my former students who have gone on to lawschool have reported back to me how their previous experience with the speech-act analysis of hearsay had facilitated their dealing with this topic in the evidence class.

Contract formation and promise

The role of 'promise' has been instrumental within both classical contract law and the philosophy of language. Some legal scholars have been con-cerned entirely with the ethical nature of promise, arguing that a breach of contract constitutes the utmost violation of such a 'sacrosanct' commit-ment. Others deny the continuing relevance of promise to contemporary contract law, advocating that public policy and economic factors have now become the motivating determinants for enforcing agreements. Then there are those scholars that view promise as playing a purely 'formal' role, affirming that a valid agreement must contain at least one promise.

Speech-act theorists, although occasionally acknowledging the special function of legal promises, have by and large concentrated on promises of the everyday, mundane variety. Because of its emphasis on unconditional promises, the standard theory of speech acts could provide at best only a partial characterization of legal promises. It had little to say about condi-tional promises and, in particular, those that propose exchanges. Hence, in order to accommodate the legal data, it became imperative to incorporate into the analysis an aspect of 'consideration'. The proposed criteria for a valid exchange, based on Searle's felicity conditions, serve this function. However, the criteria turn out to be crucial not just for consideration. A promise that proposes an exchange is equivalent to an offer, and it is this special kind of conditional promise that makes a legal offer different from an ordinary, everyday one. This view of 'offer' has the further advantage of providing a unified treatment of unilateral and bilateral agreements. It is of interest to note that we did not formulate the criteria for a valid exchange solely by examining legal data. Rather, we began with the felicity conditions for ordinary promises and then subsequently showed how those linguistic rules could be adapted to the special requirements of contract law.

The two preceding chapters, utilizing the framework of speech acts, provided an in-depth account of hearsay, offer and consideration. It was noted in the Introduction that various researchers have proposed speech-act analyses of other topics relevant to the law, including language crimes, defamation, perjury and statute enactment. These various applications demonstrate the undeniable role of speech acts in the treatment of legal issues, and doubtless there remain still other areas of the law where speech-act theory will continue to function as an effective analytic tool.

In spite of a mutual interest in topics pertaining to language and the law, for the most part, linguists and legal scholars engaged in research have generally worked independently and often in ignorance of achievements from the opposite camp. Yet each side stands to benefit from the accomplishments of the other. The numerous issues arising within the law that are directly concerned with the meanings of words, with the structure of legal discourse or with the interpretation of legal constructs fundamentally are problems having to do with language. By applying linguistic analysis and methodology to these areas of interest, linguists can help legal professionals acquire an additional perspective on the specific kinds of language issues that concern them. In return, the law presents a fascinating challenge for linguists. The vocabulary, the syntax and the pragmatics of legal language often constitute a specialized type of discourse, one that can be quite different from the ordinary variety of language data generally encountered in linguistic research. Linguists ought to welcome from the law this rich source of novel linguistic material. It is relevant for testing their theories and, as a result, it will contribute to advancing our understanding of language and its role in society.

Appendix: Selected Court Cases

FRIGALIMENT IMPORTING CO. v. BNS INTERNATIONAL SALES CORP.
U. S. DISTRICT COURT FOR THE SOUTHERN DISTRICT OF NEW YORK
190 F. Supp. 116 (1960)

OPINION: FRIENDLY

The issue is, what is chicken? Plaintiff says 'chicken' means a young chicken, suitable for broiling and frying. Defendant says 'chicken' means any bird of that genus that meets contract specifications on weight and quality, including what it calls 'stewing chicken' and plaintiff pejoratively terms 'fowl'. Dictionaries give both meanings, as well as some others not relevant here. To support its, plaintiff sends a number of volleys over the net; defendant essays to return them and adds a few serves of its own . . .

The action is for breach of the warranty that goods sold shall correspond to the description, New York Personal Property Law, McKinney's Consol. Laws, c. 41, § 95. Two contracts are in suit. In the first, dated May 2, 1957, defendant, a New York sales corporation, confirmed the sale to plaintiff, a Swiss corporation, of:

> US Fresh Frozen Chicken, Grade A, Government Inspected, Eviscerated, 2½–3 lbs. and 1½–2 lbs. each
> all chicken individually wrapped in cryovac, packed in secured fiber cartons or wooden boxes suitable for export
> 75,000 lbs. 2½–3 lbs . . . @$33.00
> 25,000 lbs. 1½–2 lbs . . . @$36.50
> per 100 lbs. FAS New York scheduled May 10, 1957. . .

The second contract, also dated May 2, 1957, was identical save that only 50,000 lbs. of the heavier 'chicken' were called for, the price of the smaller birds was $37 per 100 lbs., and shipment was scheduled for May 30 . . . When the initial shipment arrived in Switzerland, plaintiff found, on May 28, that the 2½–3 lbs. birds were not young chicken suitable for broiling and frying but stewing chicken or 'fowl'; indeed, many of the cartons and bags plainly so indicated. Protests ensued. Nevertheless, shipment under the second contract was made on May 29, the 2½–3 lbs. birds again being stewing chicken. Defendant stopped the transportation of these at Rotterdam. This action followed . . .

Since the word 'chicken' standing alone is ambiguous, I turn first to see whether the contract itself offers any aid to its interpretation. Plaintiff says the 1½–2 lbs. birds necessarily had to be young chickens since the older birds do not come in that size, hence the 2½–3 lbs. birds must likewise be young. This is unpersuasive – a contract for 'apples' of two different sizes could be filled with different kinds of apples even though only one species came in both sizes. Defendant notes that the contract called not simply for chicken but for 'US Fresh Frozen Chicken, Grade A, Government Inspected'. It says the contract thereby incorporated by reference the Department of Agriculture's regulations, which favor its interpretation; I shall return to this after reviewing plaintiff's other contentions.

The first hinges on an exchange of cablegrams which preceded execution of the formal contracts . . . Plaintiff stresses that, although these and subsequent cables between plaintiff and defendant, which laid the basis for the additional quantities under the first and for all of the second contract, were predominantly in German, they used the English word 'chicken'; it claims this was done because it understood 'chicken' meant young chicken whereas the German word, 'Huhn,' included both 'Brathuhn' (broilers) and 'Suppenhuhn' (stewing chicken), and that defendant, whose officers were thoroughly conversant with German, should have realized this . . .

Plaintiff's next contention is that there was a definite trade usage that 'chicken' meant 'young chicken' . . . Plaintiff endeavored to establish such a usage by the testimony of three witnesses and certain other evidence. Strasser, resident buyer in New York for a large chain of Swiss cooperatives, testified that 'on chicken I would definitely understand a broiler'. However, the force of this testimony was considerably weakened by the fact that in his own transactions the witness, a careful businessman, protected himself by using 'broiler' when that was what he wanted and 'fowl' when he wished older birds . . . Niesielowski, an officer of one of the companies that had furnished the stewing chicken to defendant, testified that 'chicken' meant 'the male species of the poultry industry. That could be a broiler, a fryer or a roaster', but not a stewing chicken; however, he also testified that upon receiving defendant's inquiry for 'chickens', he asked whether the desire was for 'fowl or frying chickens' and, in fact, supplied fowl, although taking the precaution of asking defendant, a day or two after plaintiff's acceptance of the contracts in suit, to change its confirmation of its order from 'chickens', as defendant had originally prepared it, to 'stewing chickens'. Dates, an employee of Urner-Barry Company, which publishes a daily market report on the poultry trade, gave it as his view that the trade meaning of 'chicken' was 'broilers and fryers'. In addition to this opinion testimony, plaintiff relied on the fact that the Urner-Barry service, the Journal of Commerce, and Weinberg Bros. & Co. of Chicago, a large supplier of poultry, published quotations in a manner which, in one way or another, distinguish between 'chicken,' comprising broilers, fryers and certain other categories, and 'fowl', which, Bauer acknowledged, included stewing chickens. This material would be impressive if there were nothing to the contrary. However, there was, as will now be seen.

Defendant's witness Weininger, who operates a chicken eviscerating plant in New Jersey, testified 'Chicken is everything except a goose, a duck, and a turkey. Everything is a chicken, but then you have to say, you have to specify which category you want or that you are talking about'. Its witness Fox said that in the trade 'chicken' would encompass all the various classifications. Sadina, who conducts a food inspection service, testified that he would consider any bird coming within the classes of 'chicken' in the Department of Agriculture's regulations to be a chicken. The specifications approved by the General Services Administration include fowl as well as broilers and fryers under the classification 'chickens'. Statistics of the Institute of American Poultry Industries use the phrases 'Young chickens' and 'Mature chickens,' under the general heading 'Total chickens'. and the Department of Agriculture's daily and weekly price reports avoid use of the word 'chicken' without specification . . . Defendant argues, as previously noted, that the contract incorporated these regulations by reference. Plaintiff answers that the contract provision related simply to grade and Government inspection and did not incorporate the Government definition of 'chicken', and also that the definition in the Regulations is ignored in the trade . . .

Defendant makes a further argument based on the impossibility of its obtaining broilers and fryers at the 33 cents price offered by plaintiff for the 2½–3 lbs. birds. There is no substantial dispute that, in late April, 1957, the price for 2½–3 lbs. broilers was between 35 and 37 cents per pound, and that when defendant entered into the contracts, it was well aware of this and intended to fill them by supplying fowl in these weights . . . It is scarcely an answer to say, as plaintiff does in its brief, that the 33 cents price offered by the 2½–3 lbs. 'chickens' was closer to the prevailing 35 cents price for broilers than to the 30 cents at which defendant procured fowl. Plaintiff must have expected defendant to make some profit – certainly it could not have expected defendant deliberately to incur a loss.

Finally, defendant relies on conduct by the plaintiff after the first shipment had been received . . . Defendant argues that if plaintiff was sincere in thinking it was entitled to young chickens, plaintiff would not have allowed the shipment under the second contract to go forward, since the distinction between broilers and chickens drawn in defendant's cablegram must have made it clear that the larger birds would not be broilers. However, plaintiff answers that the cables show plaintiff was insisting on delivery of young chickens and that defendant shipped old ones at its peril . . . Defendant points out also that plaintiff proceeded to deliver some of the larger birds in Europe, describing them as 'poulets'; defendant argues that it was only when plaintiff's customers complained about this that plaintiff developed the idea that 'chicken' meant 'young chicken'. There is little force in this in view of plaintiff's immediate and consistent protests.

When all the evidence is reviewed, it is clear that defendant believed it could comply with the contracts by delivering stewing chicken in the 2½–3lbs. size. Defendant's subjective intent would not be significant if this did not coincide with an objective meaning of 'chicken'. Here it did coincide with one of the dictionary meanings, with the definition in the Department of Agriculture Regulations to which the contract made at least oblique reference, with at least some usage in the trade, with the realities of the market, and with what plaintiff's spokesman had said. Plaintiff asserts it to be equally plain that plaintiff's own subjective intent was to obtain broilers and fryers; the only evidence against this is the material as to market prices and this may not have been sufficiently brought home. In any event it is unnecessary to determine that issue. For plaintiff has the burden of showing that 'chicken' was used in the narrower rather than in the broader sense, and this it has not sustained.

This opinion constitutes the court's findings of fact and conclusions of law. Judgement shall be entered dismissing the complaint with costs.

RAFFLES v. WICHELHAUS
COURT OF THE EXCHEQUER
2 Hurl. & C. 906 (1864)

Declaration [i.e. Complaint].   For that it was agreed between the plaintiff and the defendants, to wit, at Liverpool, that the plaintiff should sell to the defendants, and the defendants buy of the plaintiff, certain goods, to wit, 125 bales of Surat cotton, guaranteed middling fair merchant's dhollorah, to arrive ex *Peerless* from Bombay; and that the cotton should be taken from the quay, and that the defendants would pay the plaintiff for the same at a certain rate, to wit, at the rate of 17.25 d. per pound, within a certain time then agreed upon after the arrival of said goods in England. Averments: that the said goods did arrive by said ship from Bombay to England, to wit, at Liverpool, and the plaintiff was then and there ready and willing and offered to deliver that said goods to the defendants, etc.

Breach: that the defendants refused to accept the said goods or pay the plaintiff for them.

Plea [i.e. Answer].   That the said ship mentioned in the said agreement was meant and intended by the defendant to be the ship called the *Peerless*, which sailed from Bombay, to wit, in October; and that the plaintiff was not ready and willing, and did not offer to deliver to the defendants any bales of cotton which arrived by the last-mentioned ship, but instead thereof was only ready and willing, and offered to deliver to the defendants 125 bales of Surat cotton which arrived by another and different ship, which was also called the *Peerless*, and which sailed from Bombay, to wit, in December.

Demurrer [to the Plea], and joinder therin. Milward, in support of the demurrer.

The contract was for the sale of a number of bales of cotton of a particular description, which the plaintiff was ready to deliver. It is immaterial by what ship the cotton was to arrive, so that it was a ship called the *Peerless*. The words, 'to arrive ex Peerless,' only mean that if the vessel is lost on the voyage, the contract is to be at an end. [Pollock, C.B. It would be a question for the jury whether both parties meant the same ship to be called the *Peerless*.] That would be so if the contract was for the sale of a ship called the *Peerless*; but it is for the sale of cotton on board a ship of that name. [Pollock, C.B. The defendant only bought that cotton which was to arrive by a particular ship. It may as well be said, that if there is a contract for the purchase of certain goods in a wharehouse A., that is satisfied by the delivery of goods of the same description in wharehouse B.] In that case there would be goods in both wharehouses; here, it does not appear that the plaintiff had any goods on board the other *Peerless*. [Martin, B. It is imposing on the defendant a different contract from that which he entered into. Pollock, C.B. It is like a contract for the purchase of wine coming from a particular estate in Spain or France, where there are two estates of the same name.] The defendant has no right to contradict, by parole evidence, a written contract good upon the face of it. He does not impute mispepresentation or fraud, but only says he fancied the ship a different one. Intention is of no avail, unless stated at the time of contract. [Pollock, C.B. One vessel sailed in October, the other in December.] The time of sailing is no part of the contract.

Mellish (Cohen with him), in support of the plea. There is nothing on the face of the contract to show that any particular ship called the *Peerless* was meant; but the moment it appears that two ships called the *Peerless* were about to sail from Bombay there is a latent ambiguity, and parol evidence may be given for the purpose of showing that the defendant meant one *Peerless* and the plaintiff another. That being so, there was no consensus ad idem, and therefore no binding contract. He was then stopped by the court.

Per Curiam. Judgment for the defendants.

INTERSTATE COMMERCE COMMISSION v. ALLEN E. KROBLIN, Inc.
UNITED STATES DISTRICT COURT FOR THE NORTHERN
DISTRICT OF IOWA
113 F. Supp. 599 (1953)

OPINION: GRAVEN

The issue in this case is whether or not the interstate transportation by truck of New York dressed and eviscerated poultry is within the scope of the so-called 'agricultural' exemption of the Interstate Commerce Act . . .

In this action the Interstate Commerce Commission claims that the defendant is engaged in transporting New York dressed and eviscerated poultry in interstate commerce without a certificate of public convenience and necessity. The Commission asks that the defendant be enjoined from so doing until he obtains such certificate. The defendant admits that it is so engaged and that it does not have a certificate of public convenience and necessity. It claims that under the provisions of Section 203(b)(6) it is not required to have such certificate. The defendant having admitted that it is engaged in interstate transportation of property by motor vehicle, the burden is upon it to establish that its activities come within the exemption.

Section 203(b)(6), above referred to, in its present form exempts from the certificate provisions of the Act:

> (6) motor vehicles used in carrying property consisting of ordinary live-stock, fish (including shell fish), or agricultural (including horticultural) commodities (not including manufactured products thereof), if such motor vehicles are not used in carrying any other property, or passengers, for compensation'.

While Section 203(b)(6) includes fish as well as horticultural commodities, it is commonly and generally referred to as the agricultural exemption.

In the present case the defendant is a corporation that owns and operates a number of trucks which are used to haul New York dressed and eviscerated poultry from points in Iowa to Chicago, Illinois, and other points in other states. New York dressed poultry is defined by those engaged in the poultry trade as being poultry with the head and feathers removed and in some instances with the feet also removed. Eviscerated poultry is defined by those engaged in the poultry trade as poultry with the head, feet, feathers, and entrails removed and with the liver, heart, and gizzard cleaned, wrapped, and replaced in the carcass . . .

The parties are in agreement that live poultry is an agricultural commodity. They are in disagreement as to whether New York dressed and eviscerated poultry is an 'agricultural commodity' or a 'manufactured product'. While eviscerated poultry is somewhat more extensively processed than is New York dressed poultry, yet counsel in argument stated that no distinction is claimed as between the two so far as the agricultural exemption is concerned. Since the parties are in agreement that live fowls as they leave the farm are an 'agricultural commodity', the real disagreement between the parties is as to when they become a 'manufactured product'. It is the claim of the Interstate Commerce Commission that they probably become such upon being killed and in all events after they have been New York dressed or eviscerated. It is the claim of the defendant and the Secretary of Agriculture that by such dressing or eviscerating the fowls have not as yet reached the point where they can be properly and legally classified as a 'manufactured product' and that something further or other is required before they have that status . . .

The defendant and the Secretary of Agriculture particularly rely upon the definition of the word 'manufacture' approved in the case of American

Fruit Growers, Inc., v. Brogdex Co., 1931, 283 U.S. 1, 51 S.Ct. 328, 75 L.Ed. 801 . . . [The Interstate Commerce Commission] stated that the definition which was approved in the Fruit Growers case was the appropriate and applicable definition to be used in connection with the determination of whether a commodity is or is not a 'manufactured product' under the agricultural exemption. The definition referred to is as follows, at page 11 of 283 U.S., at page 330 of 51 S.C t.:

> ' "Manufacture", as well defined by the Century Dictionary, is "the production of articles for use from raw or prepared materials by giving to these materials new forms, qualities, properties, or combinations, whether by hand-labor or by machinery"; also "anything made for use from raw or prepared materials" '.

It is the claim of the defendant and the Secretary of Agriculture that under the latter definition dressed poultry is not a manufactured product. The Interstate Commerce Commission making use of the same definition concluded that dressed poultry is a manufactured product . . .

The definitions relied upon by the parties are broad, general definitions . . . This Court is of the view that the tracing out of the meaning of 'manufactured products' in the agricultural exemption by means of general definitions and the attempted definitions of those definitions would only lead into a semantic wilderness. All of the parties are agreed that the words 'agricultural commodities' and 'manufactured products thereof' used in the agricultural exemption are ambiguous words. They are not defined in the Act. Therefore, it is necessary that resort be made to decisions construing the provisions of the agricultural exemption and to the extrinsic aids of legislative history and administrative interpretation . . .

In the present case, the only relevancy of administrative construction or interpretation is to the matter of Congressional intent. The question is whether or not the agency making the particular contention or interpretation has correctly ascertained the intent of Congress. Administrative construction or interpretation is but one of several extrinsic aids in the interpretation of statutes. Another extrinsic aid is legislative history. Where the provisions of a statute are ambiguous, the legislative history may often be revealing on the matter of legislative intent and may be more satisfactory evidence of legislative intent than administrative construction or interpretation. In the present case the parties are in controversy as to whether the administrative constructions or interpretations advanced are in accord with the intent of Congress as revealed by the legislative history of the Act. All of the parties contend that the legislative history of the Act supports their respective claims as to the intent of Congress. It would then seem desirable to next give consideration to the legislative history of the Act before proceeding any further with the matter of administrative construction or interpretation.

In the present case, the matters of importance are what was the purpose of Congress in enacting Section 203(b)(6), and what commodities did it intend to include within its provisions? The parties are agreed that the purpose of Section 203(b)(6) was to benefit the farmers . . . In the present case it was claimed in oral argument by counsel for the defendant and the Secretary of Agriculture that the biggest benefit to the farmers of exempting commercial truckers engaged in hauling farm commodities from the certificate provisions of the Act was the flexibility of operations permitted such carriers. It was stated by them that poultry is a commodity as to which the market is variable and shifting and that it is frequently necessary to be able to make shifts and changes in marketing arrangements on short notice and, in some cases, even when the commodities are en route . . .

An unusually large number of amendments have been proposed to Section 203(b)(6) and there is an unusually large amount of legislative history material available in connection therewith. The action and attitude of Congress as to proposed amendments could be indicative of Congressional intent as to the scope and coverage of that subparagraph . . .

There are two features that stand out most predominantly in the voluminous legislative history relating to amendments made or proposed to Section 203(b)(6). One feature is that every amendment that Congress has made to it has broadened and liberalized its provisions in favor of exemption and the other feature is that although often importuned to do so, Congress has uniformly and steadfastly refused or rejected amendments which would either directly or indirectly have denied the benefits of the exemptions contained therein to truckers who are engaged in operations similar to that of the defendant herein. It is believed that the actions and attitude of Congress as manifested in connection with amendments to Section 203(b)(6) are preponderantly indicative of an intent on the part of Congress that the words 'manufactured products' used in that subparagraph are not to be given the restricted meaning contended for by the Interstate Commerce Commission herein.

It is the holding of the court that New York dressed poultry or eviscerated poultry do not constitute 'manufactured' products within the intent and meaning of Section 203(b)(6). It is the feeling of the court that an opposite holding would in reality constitute an attempt to accomplish by means of judicial construction that which Congress has steadfastly refused to allow to be accomplished by legislation.

Judgment will be entered in accord with this opinion.

CALIFORNIA v. BROWN
SUPREME COURT OF THE UNITED STATES
479 U.S. 538; Argued December 2, 1986, Decided January 27, 1987

OPINION: CHIEF JUSTICE REHNQUIST delivered the opinion of the court.

The question presented for review in this case is whether an instruction informing jurors that they 'must not be swayed by mere sentiment, conjecture, sympathy, passion, prejudice, public opinion or public feeling' during the penalty phase of a capital murder trial violates the Eighth and Fourteenth Amendments to the United States Constitution. We hold that it does not.

Respondent Albert Brown was found guilty by a jury of forcible rape and first-degree murder in the death of 15-year-old Susan J. At the penalty phase, the State presented evidence that respondent had raped another young girl some years prior to his attack on Susan J. Respondent presented the testimony of several family members, who recounted respondent's peaceful nature and expressed disbelief that respondent was capable of such a brutal crime. Respondent also presented the testimony of a psychiatrist, who stated that Brown killed his victim because of his shame and fear over sexual dysfunction. Brown himself testified, stating that he was ashamed of his prior criminal conduct and asking for mercy from the jury.

California Penal Code Ann. § 190.3 (West Supp. 1987) provides that capital defendants may introduce at the penalty phase any evidence 'as to any matter relevant to . . . mitigation . . . including, but not limited to, the nature and circumstances of the present offense . . . and the defendant's character, background, history, mental condition and physical condition'. The trial court instructed the jury to consider the aggravating and mitigating circumstances and to weigh them in determining the appropriate penalty. But the court cautioned the jury that it 'must not be swayed by mere sentiment, conjecture, sympathy, passion, prejudice, public opinion or public feeling'. Respondent was sentenced to death.

On automatic appeal, the Supreme Court of California reversed the sentence of death. Over two dissents on this point, the majority opinion found that the instruction at issue here violates the Federal Constitution: 'federal constitutional law forbids an instruction which denies a capital defendant the right to have the jury consider any "sympathy factor"' raised by the evidence when determining the appropriate penalty . . . We granted certiorari to resolve whether such an instruction violates the United States Constitution.

We think that the California Supreme Court improperly focused solely on the word 'sympathy' to determine that the instruction interferes with the jury's consideration of mitigating evidence. 'The question, however, is not what the State Supreme Court declares the meaning of the charge to be, but rather what a reasonable juror could have understood the charge as meaning.' *Francis* v. *Franklin*, 471 U.S. 307, 315–316 (1985); see *Sandstrom* v. *Montana*, 442 U.S. 510, 516–517 (1979) . . .

The jury was told not to be swayed by 'mere sentiment, conjecture, sympathy, passion, prejudice, public opinion or public feeling'. Respondent does not contend, and the Supreme Court of California did not hold, that conjecture, passion, prejudice, public opinion, or public feeling should properly play any role in the jury's sentencing determination, even if such factors might weigh in the defendant's favor. Rather, respondent reads the instruction as if it solely cautioned the jury not to be swayed by 'sympathy'. Even if we were to agree that a rational juror could parse the instruction in such a hypertechnical manner, we would disagree with both respondent's interpretation of the instruction and his conclusion that the instruction is unconstitutional.

By concentrating on the noun 'sympathy', respondent ignores the crucial fact that the jury was instructed to avoid basing its decision on mere sympathy. Even a juror who insisted on focusing on this one phrase in the instruction would likely interpret the phrase as an admonition to ignore emotional responses that are not rooted in the aggravating and mitigating evidence introduced during the penalty phase. While strained in the abstract, respondent's interpretation is simply untenable when viewed in light of the surrounding circumstances. This instruction was given at the end of the penalty phase, only after respondent had produced 13 witnesses in his favor. Yet respondent's interpretation would have these two words transform three days of favorable testimony into a virtual charade. We think a reasonable juror would reject that interpretation, and instead understand the instruction not to rely on 'mere sympathy' as a directive to ignore only the sort of sympathy that would be totally divorced from the evidence adduced during the penalty phase.

We also think it highly unlikely that any reasonable juror would almost perversely single out the word 'sympathy' from the other nouns which accompany it in the instruction conjecture, passion, prejudice, public opinion, and public feeling. Reading the instruction as a whole, as we must, it is no more than a catalog of the kind of factors that could improperly influence a juror's decision to vote for or against the death penalty . . .

We hold that the instruction challenged in this case does not violate the provisions of the Eighth and Fourteenth Amendments to the United States Constitution. The judgement of the Supreme Court of California is therefore reversed, and the cause is remanded for further proceedings not inconsistent with this opinion.

It is so ordered.

DISSENT: JUSTICE BRENNAN

Adhering to my view that the death penalty is in all circumstances cruel and unusual punishment forbidden by the Eighth and Fourteenth Amendments, I dissent from the court's opinion to the extent that it would result in the imposition of the death penalty upon respondent. *Gregg* v. *Georgia*, 428 U.S. 153, 227 (1976). However, even if I believed that the death penalty could be imposed constitutionally under certain circumstances, I would affirm the California Supreme Court, for that court has reasonably interpreted the jury instruction at issue to divert the jury from its constitutional duty to consider all mitigating evidence introduced by a defendant at the sentencing phase of trial . . .

The instruction at issue informed the jury: 'You must not be swayed by mere sentiment, conjecture, sympathy, passion, prejudice, public opinion or public feeling . . .'. The State acknowledges that sympathy for the defendant is appropriate, but contends that the antisympathy instruction simply prevents the jury from relying on 'untethered sympathy' unrelated to the circumstances of the offense or the defendant. [T]he instruction gives no indication whatsoever that the jury is to distinguish between 'tethered' and 'untethered' sympathy. The Court nonetheless accepts the notion that a jury would interpret the instruction to require such a distinction. None of the reasons it offers for accepting this implausible construction are persuasive.

First, the Court finds it significant that the jury was instructed not simply to avoid sympathy, but to avoid 'mere' sympathy. This word, contends the Court, would likely lead a juror to interpret the instruction 'as an admonition to ignore emotional responses that are not rooted in the aggravating and mitigating evidence introduced during the penalty phase'. The instruction, however, counsels the jury not to be swayed by 'mere sentiment, conjecture, sympathy, passion, prejudice, public opinion or public feeling'. A juror could logically conclude that 'mere' modified only 'sentiment', so it is by no means clear that the instruction would likely be construed to preclude reliance on 'mere sympathy'. In order for 'mere' to be regarded as modifying 'sympathy', as the Court contends, 'mere' must be read to modify all the other terms in the instruction as well: conjecture, passion, prejudice, public opinion, or public feeling. By the Court's own logic, since 'mere' serves to distinguish 'tethered' from 'untethered' sympathy, it also serves to distinguish 'tethered' from 'untethered' versions of all the other emotions listed. Yet surely no one could maintain, for instance, that some 'tethered' form of prejudice relating to the case at hand could ever be appropriate in capital sentencing deliberations. Indeed, the Court describes the nouns accompanying 'sympathy' in the instructions as 'no more than a catalog of the kind of factors that could improperly influence a juror's decision to vote for or against the death penalty'. The single word 'mere' therefore cannot shoulder the burden of validating this antisympathy instruction.

Second, the Court argues that jurors must assume that the defendant would not introduce evidence of character and background if the jury could not consider such information. It is equally likely, however, that jurors instructed not to rely on sympathy would conclude that the defendant had simply gone too far in his presentation, and that, as in other trial contexts, the jury must look to the judge for guidance as to that portion of the evidence that appropriately could be considered. Instructions are commonly given at the end of trial which clarify the significance of evidence and of events at trial, since the jury is not at liberty to assume that everything that occurs at trial is automatically or equally relevant to its deliberations.

Finally, the Court says that, since 'sympathy' is accompanied in the instruction by a list of obviously impermissible factors, a juror would naturally assume that the instruction 'was meant to confine the jury's deliberations to considerations arising from the evidence presented, both aggravating and mitigating'. How a juror would be expected to make this leap is unclear. The inclusion of 'sympathy' in an expansive list of impermissible emotions would logically lead a juror to conclude that any response rooted in emotion was inappropriate. An average juror is likely to possess the common understanding that law and emotion are antithetical, and an instruction that a wide range of emotional factors are irrelevant to his or her deliberation reinforces that notion. It is simply unrealistic to assume that an instruction ruling out several emotions in unqualified language would be construed as a directive that certain forms of emotion are permissible while others are not. While we generally assume that jurors are rational, they are not telepathic.

The vast majority of jurors thus can be expected to interpret 'sympathy' to mean 'sympathy', not to engage in the tortuous reasoning process necessary to construe it as 'untethered sympathy'. We would be far more likely in fact to call into question the fidelity to duty of a juror who did the latter. The assertion that the instruction in question serves the purpose of channeling the jury's sympathy in a legitimate direction is therefore completely unfounded.

SIOUX CITY & P. R. CO. v. STOUT
UNITED STATES SUPREME COURT
84 U.S. 657 (1873)

ERROR to the Circuit Court for the District of Nebraska.

Henry Stout, a child six years of age and living with his parents, sued, by his next friend, the Sioux City and Pacific Railroad Company, in the Court below, to recover damages for an injury sustained upon a turntable belonging to the said company. The turntable was in an open space, about eighty rods from the company's depot, in a hamlet or settlement of one hundred to one hundred and fifty persons . . . The child, without the knowledge of his parents, set off with two other boys, the one nine and the other ten years of age, to go to the depot, with no definite purpose in view. When the boys arrived there, it was proposed by some of them to go to the turntable to play. The turntable was not attended or guarded by any servant of the company, was not fastened or locked, and revolved easily on its axis. Two of the boys began to turn it, and in attempting to get upon it, the foot of the child (he being at the time upon the railroad track) was caught between the end of the rail on the turntable as it was revolving, and the end of the iron rail on the main track of the road, and was crushed.

The table was constructed on the railroad company's own land, and, the testimony tended to show, in the ordinary way. It was a skeleton turntable, that is to say, it was not planked between the rails, though it had one or two loose boards upon the ties. There was an iron latch fastened to it which turned on a hinge, and, when in order, dropped into an iron socket on the track, and held the table in position while using. The catch of this latch was broken at the time of the accident. The latch, which weighed eight or ten pounds, could be easily lifted out of the catch and thrown back on the table, and the table was allowed to be moved about. This latch was not locked, or in any way fastened down before it was broken, and all the testimony on that subject tended to show that it was not usual for railroad companies to lock or guard turntables, but that it was usual to have a latch with a catch, or a draw-bolt, to keep them in position when used.

The record stated that 'the counsel for the defendant disclaimed resting their defence on the ground that the plaintiff's parents were negligent, or that the plaintiff (considering his tender age) was negligent, but rested their defence on the ground that the company was not negligent, and asserted that the injury to the plaintiff was accidental or brought upon himself . . .'.

The jury found a verdict of $7500 for the plaintiff, from the judgement upon which this writ of error was brought.

Mr. Isaac Cook, for the plaintiff in error, insisted –
1st. That the party injured was himself in fault, that his own negligence produced the result, and that upon well-settled principles, a party thus situated is not entitled to recover.

2d. That there was no negligence proved on the part of the defendant in the condition or management of the table.

Mr. Justice HUNT delivered the opinion of the Court.

1st. It is well settled that the conduct of an infant of tender years is not to be judged by the same rule which governs that of an adult. While it is the general rule in regard to an adult, that to entitle him to recover damages for an injury resulting from the fault or negligence of another, he must himself have been free from fault, such is not the rule in regard to an infant of tender years. The care and caution required of a child is according to his maturity and capacity only, and this is to be determined in each case by the circumstances of that case.

But it is not necessary to pursue this subject. The record expressly states that 'the counsel for the defendant disclaim resting their defence on the ground that the plaintiff's parents were negligent, or that the plaintiff (considering his tender age) was negligent, but rest their defence on the ground that the company was not negligent, and claim that the injury to the plaintiff was accidental or brought upon himself . . .'.

2d. Was there negligence on the part of the railway company in the management or condition of its turntable?

That the turntable was a dangerous machine, which would be likely to cause injury to children who resorted to it, might fairly be inferred from the injury which actually occurred to the plaintiff. There was the same liability to injury to him, and no greater, that existed with reference to all children. When the jury learned from the evidence that he had suffered a serious injury, by his foot being caught between the fixed rail of the road-bed and the turning rail of the table they were justified in believing that there was a probability of the occurrence of such accidents.

So, in looking at the remoteness of the machine from inhabited dwellings, when it was proved to the jury that several boys from the hamlet were at play there on this occasion, and that they had been at play upon the turntable on other occasions, and within the observation and to the knowledge of the employees of the defendant, the jury were justified in believing that children would probably resort to it, and that the defendant should have anticipated that such would be the case.

As it was in fact, on this occasion, so it was to be expected that the amusement of the boys would have been found in turning this table while they were on it or about it. This could certainly have been prevented by locking the turntable when not in use by the company. It was not shown that this would cause any considerable expense or inconvenience to the defendant. It could probably have been prevented by the repair of the broken latch. This was a heavy catch which, by dropping into a socket, prevented the revolution of the table. There had been one on this table weighing some eight or ten pounds, but it had been broken off and had not been replaced. It was proved to have been usual with railroad companies to have upon their turntables a latch or bolt, or some similar instrument. The jury may well have believed that if the defendant had incurred the trifling expense of replacing this latch, and had taken the slight trouble of putting it in its place, these very small boys would not have taken the pains to lift it out, and thus the whole difficulty have been avoided. Thus reasoning, the jury would have reached the conclusion that the defendant had omitted the care and attention it ought to have given, that it was negligent, and that its negligence caused the injury to the plaintiff. The evidence is not strong and the negligence is slight, but we are not able to say that there is not evidence sufficient to justify the verdict. We are not called upon to weigh, to measure, to balance the evidence, or to ascertain how we should have decided if acting as jurors. The charge was in all respects sound and judicious, and there being sufficient evidence to justify the finding, we are not authorized to disturb it . . .

It has been already shown that the facts proved justified the jury in finding that the defendant was guilty of negligence, and we are of the opinion that it was properly left to the jury to determine that point.

Upon the whole case, the judgment must be
AFFIRMED.

THE BANK OF THE UNITED STATES v. DEVEAUX
UNITED STATES SUPREME COURT
9 U.S. 61 (1809)

ERROR to the circuit Court for the district of Georgia.

In the year 1805 the State of Georgia passed a law to tax the Branch Bank of the United States, at Savannah. The bank having refused to pay the tax, the state officers entered their office of discount and deposit, and took and carried away two thousand dollars, for which the bank of the United States brought their action of trespass in the circuit Court of the United States for the district of Georgia. The plea to the jurisdiction does not deny that the plaintiffs were citizens of the State of Pennsylvania, but relies upon the fact that the plaintiffs sue as a body corporate.

OPINION: MARSHALL, Ch. J. delivered the opinion of the Court as follows:

Two points have been made in this cause.

1. That a corporation, composed of citizens of one state, may sue a citizen of another state, in the federal Courts.
2. That a right to sue in those Courts is conferred on this bank by the law which incorporates it.

The last point will be first considered.

The plaintiffs contend that the incorporating act confers this jurisdiction. That act creates the corporation, gives it a capacity to make contracts and to acquire property, and enables it 'to sue and be sued, plead and be impleaded, answer and be answered, defend and be defended, in Courts of record, or any other place whatsoever . . .'.

This evinces the opinion of congress, that the right to sue does not imply a right to sue in the Courts of the union, unless it be expressed. The Court, then, is of opinion, that no right is conferred on the bank, by the act of incorporation, to sue in the federal Courts.

The other point is one of much more difficulty. The jurisdiction of this Court being limited, so far as respects the character of the parties in this particular case, 'to controversies between citizens of different states', both parties must be citizens, to come within the description.

That invisible, intangible, and artificial being, that mere legal entity, a corporation aggregate, is certainly not a citizen; and, consequently, cannot sue or be sued in the Courts of the United States, unless the rights of the members, in this respect, can be exercised in their corporate name. If the corporation be considered as a mere faculty, and not as a company of individuals, who, in transacting their joint concerns, may use a legal name, they must be excluded from the Courts of the union.

The duties of this Court, to exercise jurisdiction where it is conferred, and not to usurp it where it is not conferred, are of equal obligation. The constitution, therefore, and the law, are to be expounded, without a leaning the one way or the other, according to those general principles which usually govern in the construction of fundamental or other laws . . .

As our ideas of a corporation, its privileges and its disabilities, are derived entirely from the English books, we resort to them for aid, in ascertaining its character. It is defined as a mere creature of the law, invisible, intangible, and incorporeal. Yet, when we examine the subject further, we find that corporations have been included within terms of description appropriated to real persons . . .

If, then, the congress of the United States had, in terms, enacted that incorporated aliens might sue a citizen, or that the incorporated citizens of one state might sue a citizen of another state, in the federal Courts, by its corporate name, this Court would not have felt itself justified in declaring that such a law transcended the constitution.

If the constitution would authorize congress to give the Courts of the union jurisdiction in this case, in consequence of the character of the members of the corporation, then the judicial act ought to be construed to give it. For the term citizen ought to be understood as it is used in the constitution, and as it is used in other laws. That is, to describe the real persons who come into Court, in this case, under their corporate name.

That corporations composed of citizens are considered by the legislature as citizens, under certain circumstances, is to be strongly inferred from the registering act. It never could be intended that an American registered vessel, abandoned to an insurance company composed of citizens, should lose her character as an American vessel; and yet this would be the consequence of declaring that the members of the corporation were, to every intent and purpose, out of view, and merged in the corporation.

The Court feels itself authorized . . . to look to the character of the individuals who compose the corporation, and they think that the precedents of this Court, though they were not decisions on argument, ought not to be absolutely disregarded.

If a corporation may sue in the Courts of the union, the Court is of opinion that the averment in this case is sufficient. Being authorized to sue in their corporate name, they could make the averment, and it must apply to the plaintiffs as individuals, because it could not be true as applied to the corporation.

Judgment reversed; plea in abatement overruled, and cause remanded.

MARSHALL v. BALTIMORE & OHIO R.R. CO.
UNITED STATES SUPREME COURT
57 U.S. 314 (1853)

THIS case was brought up, by writ of error, from the Circuit Court of the United States for the District of Maryland.

Marshall, a citizen of Virginia, sued the Railroad Company, to recover the sum of fifty thousand dollars, which he alleged that they owed him under a special contract, for his services in obtaining a law from the Legislature of Virginia, granting to the company a right of way through Virginia to the Ohio River.

Mr Justice GRIER delivered the opinion of the Court.

The plaintiff in error, who was also plaintiff below, avers in his declaration that he is a citizen of Virginia, and that 'The Baltimore and Ohio Railroad Company, the defendant, is a body corporate by an act of the General Assembly of Maryland'. It has been objected, that this averment is insufficient to show jurisdiction in the Courts of the United States over the 'suit' or 'controversy . . .'.

By the Constitution, the jurisdiction of the Courts of the United States is declared to extend, inter alia, to 'controversies between citizens of different States'. The Judiciary Act confers on the circuit Courts jurisdiction 'in suits between a citizen of the State where the suit is brought and a citizen of another State . . .'.

Now, if this be a right, or privilege guaranteed by the Constitution to citizens of one State in their controversies with citizens of another, it is plain that it cannot be taken away from the plaintiff by any legislation of the State in which the defendant resides. If A, B, and C, with other dormant or secret partners, be empowered to act by their representatives, to sue or to be sued in a collective or corporate name, their enjoyment of these privileges, granted by State authority, cannot nullify this important right conferred on those who contract with them . . .

Let us now examine the reasons which are considered so conclusive and imperative, that they should compel the Court to give a construction to this clause of the Constitution, practically destructive of the privilege so clearly intended to be conferred by it.

'A corporation, it is said, is an artificial person, a mere legal entity, invisible and intangible.'

This is no doubt metaphysically true in a certain sense. The inference, also, that such an artificial entity 'cannot be a citizen' is a logical conclusion from the premises which cannot be denied.

But a citizen who has made a contract, and has a 'controversy' with a corporation, may also say, with equal truth, that he did not deal with a mere metaphysical abstraction, but with natural persons; that his writ has not been served on an imaginary entity, but on men and citizens; and that his contract was made with them as the legal representatives of numerous unknown associates, or secret and dormant partners.

The necessities and conveniences of trade and business require that such numerous associates and stockholders should act by representation, and have the faculty of contracting, suing, and being sued in a factitious or collective name. But these important faculties, conferred on them by State legislation, for their own convenience, cannot be wielded to deprive others of acknowledged rights. It is not reasonable that those who deal with such persons should be deprived of a valuable privilege by a syllogism, or rather sophism, which deals subtly with words and names, without regard to the things or persons they are used to represent . . .

In Courts of law, an act of incorporation and a corporate name are necessary to enable the representatives of a numerous association to sue and be sued . . . The persons who act under these faculties, and use this corporate name, may be justly presumed to be resident in the State which is the necessary habitat of the corporation, and where alone they can be made subject to suit; and should be estopped in equity from averring a different domicil as against those who are compelled to seek them there, and can find them there and nowhere else. If it were otherwise it would be in the power of every corporation, by electing a single director residing in a different State, to deprive citizens of other States with whom they have controversies, of this constitutional privilege, and compel them to resort to State tribunals in cases in which, of all others, such privilege may be considered most valuable . . .

The presumption arising from the habitat of a corporation in the place of its creation being conclusive as to the residence or citizenship of those who use the corporate name and exercise the faculties conferred by it, the allegation that the 'defendants are a body corporate by the act of the General Assembly of Maryland', is a sufficient averment that the real defendants are citizens of that State. This form of averment has been used for many years . . . The right of choosing an impartial tribunal is a privilege of no small practical importance, and more especially in cases where a distant plaintiff has to contend with the power and influence of great numbers and the combined wealth wielded by corporations in almost every State. It is of importance also to corporations themselves that they should enjoy the same privileges, in other States, where local prejudices or jealousy might injuriously affect them . . .

The judgment of the Circuit Court is therefore affirmed, with costs.

STATE v. HARGRAVE
SUPREME COURT OF NORTH CAROLINA
97 N.C. 457 (1887)

PRIOR HISTORY: INDICTMENT for larceny

The defendant was charged with stealing a bay mare, the property of W. P. Brown, and the following is the case on appeal.

There was evidence that immediately after the larceny the owner's son was sent in search of the stolen mare by his father. The mare was found in Tazewell County, Virginia, in the possession of one Buchanan, who had testified that he obtained the mare from the defendant. The defendant denied that the mare he traded to Buchanan was the property of Brown, the person in whom the property was laid in the bill. The State insisted that the mare was the property of Brown, and that the defendant knew it, having been heard to admit as much on a certain occasion. The State was permitted to prove, under objection of the defendant, that upon seeing the mare in the possession of Buchanan, in Virginia, the owner's son exclaimed: 'That's father's mare!' as tending to establish the identity of the mare.

There was a verdict of guilty, and judgement, from which the defendant appealed.

DISPOSITION: New trial.

OPINION: DAVIS, J. (after stating the facts).

There was error in admitting the exclamation, which was but the declaration of a person who was not put upon the stand as a witness, who was not sworn, and whom the accused had no opportunity to cross-examine. Every person accused of a crime has a right to confront the accusers and witnesses against him, and there is no surer safeguard thrown around the person of the citizen than this guarantee contained in the Declaration of Rights. We are unable to perceive any ground upon which the exclamation, 'that's father's mare', can be admitted as evidence against the accused, to show the identity of the mare. If any number of persons of the most undoubted credit had seen the mare in the State of Virginia, in the possession of Buchanan, and had made affidavits as to its identity as the property of W. P. Brown, they would have been inadmissible as evidence; certainly the exclamation of the son would be equally as inadmissible. It can come under no one of the classes of exceptions to the general rule of evidence that excludes hearsay.

There is error, and the prisoner is entitled to a new trial.

SAFEWAY STORES, INC. v. COMBS
UNITED STATES COURT OF APPEALS FIFTH CIRCUIT
273 F.2d 295 (1960)

OPINION: WISDOM

This is a slip-and-fall case.

Mrs Louella Combs was shopping in a Safeway Store in El Paso, Texas, when she stepped into a puddle of ketchup that had spilled on the floor from a broken bottle. Mr and Mrs Combs sued Safeway Stores, Inc., alleging that the defendant was negligent in creating a hazardous condition; in failing to remove the ketchup or in failing to isolate the hazardous condition by placing a barrier around the ketchup; in failing to warn Mrs Combs of the presence of the ketchup; and in allowing the ketchup to remain on the floor in the immediate vicinity of an eye-catching advertizing display that would divert one's attention from the ketchup puddle. Safeway Stores relies upon Mrs Combs' alleged failure to keep a proper lookout, failure to heed an alleged warning, and on the contention that the hazard, such as it was, was open and obvious . . .

Safeway contended that Mrs Combs failed to heed timely warnings. In support of this contention, Kenneth Tunnell, the Safeway Manager, testified that he saw Mrs Combs walking toward the ketchup and that he called out to her, 'Please don't step in that ketchup'. At that time he was about ten feet from her. Mrs Tunnell, the manager's wife, was in the store at the time of the accident. She testified that she saw the broken bottle, left her shopping buggy, and told her husband that there was a broken bottle of ketchup in the frozen-food aisle. He stopped what he was doing, hurried toward the ketchup bottle, picked up the glass, then started toward the back to get a mop. As he came out with a mop she heard him call out. She understood what he said. When she was asked what he had said, plaintiff's counsel objected that the question called for hearsay. The trial judge sustained the objection and refused to permit the question to be answered. Had she been permitted to answer – it was stipulated – she would have testified that Tunnell said, 'Lady, please don't step in that ketchup'.

The hearsay rule is inapplicable to an utterance proved as an operative fact. Tunnell's utterance was a probative verbal act bearing on the critical objective fact whether there was a warning from the defendant, bearing on the plaintiff's state of mind as to notice and knowledge at the danger. The witness testified from her personal knowledge.

Tunnell's warning – if he gave a warning – was a prime element in the defense. The jury was entitled to know if he gave it, and to weigh it with the other evidence. Failure to permit Mrs Tunnell to testify as to the fact of the warning deprived the defendant of the opportunity of showing whether the plaintiff exercised due care. The trial judge's ruling on this point is sufficient in itself to require the Court to reverse and remand.

In view of these errors below, we reverse the judgement and remand the case for a new trial.

JOHN H. HANSON v. ED. JOHNSON AND ANOTHER
SUPREME COURT OF MINNESOTA
161 Minn. 229 (1924)

OPINION: WILSON, C.J.

Action in conversion. Appeal from judgment by defendants. Case was tried to the Court without a jury. It is claimed that the Court erred in the reception of evidence.

Plaintiff owned and leased a farm to one Schrik under a written lease, the terms of which gave plaintiff 2/5 of the corn grown. The tenant gave a mortgage to defendant bank on his share of the crops. The tenant's mortgaged property was sold at auction by the bank with his permission. At this sale a crib of corn containing 393 bushels was sold by the bank to defendant Johnson. If plaintiff owned the corn it was converted by defendants.

In an effort to prove that the corn was owned by plaintiff and that it was a part of his share, he testified, over the objection of hearsay and self-serving, that when the tenant was about through husking corn he was on the farm and the tenant pointed out the corn in question (and a double crib of corn) and said: 'Mr Hanson, here is your corn for this year, this double crib here and this single crib here is your share for this year's corn; this belongs to you, Mr Hanson'. A bystander was called and against the same objection testified to having heard the talk in substantially the same language.

There is no question but that plaintiff owned some corn. It was necessary to identify it. The division made his share definite. This division and identity was made by the acts of tenant in husking the corn and putting it in separate cribs and then his telling Hanson which was his share and the latter's acquiescence therein. The language of the tenant was the very fact necessary to be proved. The verbal part of the transaction between plaintiff and the tenant was necessary to prove the fact. The words were the verbal acts. They aid in giving legal significance to the conduct of the parties. They accompanied the conduct. There could be no division without words or gestures identifying the respective shares. This was a fact to be shown in the chain of proof of title. It was competent evidence. It was not hearsay nor self-serving. As between plaintiff and the tenant this evidence would be admissible. It was original evidence. The issues here being between different persons does not change the rule.

There is evidence to sustain the findings of the Court, and the record is free from error.

Affirmed.

HAMER v. SIDWAY
COURT OF APPEALS OF NEW YORK
124 N.Y. 538 (1891)

OPINION: PARKER, J.

The question which provoked the most discussion by counsel on this appeal, and which lies at the foundation of plaintiff's asserted right of recovery, is whether by virtue of a contract defendant's testator William E. Story became indebted to his nephew William E. Story, 2d, on his twenty-first birthday in the sum of five thousand dollars. The trial Court found as a fact that 'on the 20th day of March, 1869, William E. Story agreed to and with William E. Story, 2d, that if he would refrain from drinking liquor, using tobacco, swearing, and playing cards or billiards for money until he should become 21 years of age then he, the said William E. Story, would at that time pay him, the said William E. Story, 2d, the sum of $ 5,000 for such refraining, to which the said William E. Story, 2d, agreed,' and that he 'in all things fully performed his part of said agreement'.

The defendant contends that the contract was without consideration to support it, and, therefore, invalid. He asserts that the promisee by refraining from the use of liquor and tobacco was not harmed but benefited; that that which he did was best for him to do independently of his uncle's promise, and insists that it follows that unless the promisor was benefited, the contract was without consideration. A contention, which if well founded, would seem to leave open for controversy in many cases whether that which the promisee did or omitted to do was, in fact, of such benefit to him as to leave no consideration to support the enforcement of the promisor's agreement. Such a rule could not be tolerated, and is without foundation in the law. The Exchequer Chamber, in 1875, defined consideration as follows: 'A valuable consideration in the sense of the law may consist either in some right, interest, profit or benefit accruing to the one party, or some forbearance, detriment, loss or responsibility given, suffered or undertaken by the other'. Courts 'will not ask whether the thing which forms the consideration does in fact benefit the promisee or a third party, or is of any substantial value to anyone. It is enough that something is promised, done, forborne or suffered by the party to whom the promise is made as consideration for the promise made to him'. (Anson's Prin. of Con. 63.)

Now, applying this rule to the facts before us, the promisee used tobacco, occasionally drank liquor, and he had a legal right to do so. That right he abandoned for a period of years upon the strength of the promise of the testator that for such forbearance he would give him $ 5,000. We need not speculate on the effort which may have been required to give up the use of those stimulants. It is sufficient that he restricted his lawful freedom of action within certain prescribed limits upon the faith of his uncle's agreement, and now having fully performed the conditions imposed, it is of no moment whether such performance actually proved a benefit to the promisor, and the Court will not inquire into it, but were it a proper subject of inquiry, we see nothing in this record that would permit a determination that the uncle was not benefited in a legal sense. Few cases have been found which may be said to be precisely in point, but such as have been support the position we have taken . . .

The order appealed from should be reversed and the judgment of the Special Term affirmed, with costs payable out of the estate.

STILK v. MYRICK
COURT OF COMMON PLEAS
2 Camp 317 (1809)

This was an action for seaman's wages, on a voyage from London to the Baltic and back.

By the ship's articles, executed before the commencement of the voyage, the plaintiff was to be paid at the rate of £5 a month; and the principal question in the cause was, whether he was entitled to a higher rate of wages? In the course of the voyage two of the seamen deserted; and the captain having in vain attempted to supply their places at Cronstadt, there entered into an agreement with the rest of the Crew, that they should have the Wages of the two who had deserted equally divided among them, if he could not procure two other hands at Gottenburgh. This was found impossible; and the ship was worked back to London by the plaintiff and eight more of the original crew, with whom the agreement had been made at Cronstadt.

Garrow for the defendant insisted, that this agreement was contrary to public policy, and utterly void. In West India voyages, crews are often thinned greatly by death and desertion; and if a promise of advanced wages were valid, exorbitant claims would be set up on all such occasions. This ground was strongly taken by Lord Kenyon in *Harris* v. *Watson*, Peak. Cas. 72, where that learned Judge held, that no action would lie at the suit of a sailor on a promise of a captain to pay him extra wages, in consideration of his doing more than the ordinary share of duty in navigating the ship; and his Lordship said, that if such a promise could be enforced, sailors would in many cases suffer a ship to sink unless the captain would accede to any extravagant demand they might think proper to make.

[. . .]

Lord Ellenborough: I think *Harris* v. *Watson* was rightly decided; but I doubt whether the ground of public policy, upon which Lord Kenyon is stated to have proceeded, be the true principle on which the decision is to be supported. Here, I say, the agreement is void for want of consideration. There was no consideration for the ulterior pay promised to the mariners who remained with the ship. Before they sailed from London they had undertaken to do all that they could under all the emergencies of the voyage. They had sold all their services till the voyages would be completed. If they had been at liberty to quit the vessel at Cronstadt, the case would have been quite different; or if the captain had capriciously discharged the two men who were wanting, the others might not have been compellable to take the whole duty upon themselves, and their agreeing to do so might have been a sufficient consideration for the promise of an advance of wages. But the desertion of a part of the crew is to be considered an emergency of the voyage as much as their death; and those who remain are bound by the terms of their original contract to exert themselves to the utmost to bring the ship in safety to her destined port. Therefore, without looking to the policy of this agreement, I think it is void for want of consideration, and that the plaintiff can only recover at the rate of £5 a month.

Verdict accordingly.

References

Akmajian, Adrian, Richard A. Demers, Ann K. Farmer and Robert M. Harnish, *Linguistics: an Introduction to Language and Communication*, 4th edn, Cambridge, Mass.: MIT Press, 1995.

Ashley, Clarence D., 'Offers calling for a consideration other than a counter promise', *Harvard Law Review* 1910: 160–1.

Atiyah, P. S., *The Rise and Fall of Freedom of Contract*, Oxford, Oxford University Press, 1979.

——*An Introduction to the Law of Contract*, 3rd edn, Oxford: Clarendon Press, 1981.

Austin, John. *How to do Things with Words*, 2nd edn, Cambridge, Mass.: Harvard University Press, 1962.

——'Performative–constative' in *The Philosophy of Language*, ed. by J. Searle, Oxford: Oxford University Press, 1971.

Black's Law Dictionary, 6th edn, St Paul, Minn.: West Publishing Co., 1990.

Charrow, Robert P. and Veda R. Charrow, 'Making legal language understandable: a psycholinguistic study of jury instructions', 79 *Columbia Law Review*, 1979.

Cohen, 'Transcendental nonsense and the functional approach, 35 *Columbia Law Review*, 1935.

Conley John M. and William M. O'Barr, *Just Words: Law, Language and Power*, 2nd edn, Chicago: University of Chicago Press, 2005.

Corbin, Arthur L., 'Offer and acceptance, and some of the resulting legal relations', 26 *Yale Law Journal*, 1917.

——*Corbin on Contracts*, one-volume edition, St Paul, Minn.: West Publishing Co., 1952.

——'The interpretation of words and the parol evidence rule', 50 *Cornell Law Quarterly*, 1965.

'Death penalty: factors to consider – identified as aggravating or mitigating', Judicial Council of California, Sect. 702 ADP. Draft circulated for comment only, (criminst6.pdf), 2005.

Dewey, John, 'The historic background of corporate legal personality', 35 *Yale Law Journal*, 1926.

Elwork, Amiram, B. D. Sales and J. J. Alfini, *Making Jury Instructions Understandable*, Charlottesville, Virginia: Michie/Bobss-Merrill, 1982.

Farnsworth, E. Allen, *Farnsworth on Contracts*, New York: Aspen Publishers, Inc., 1990.

Federal Rules of Evidence, Committee on the Judiciary, House of Representatives. Washington: U.S. Government Printing Office, 401, 2004–05.

Fenner, G. Michael, *Practical Trial Evidence: a Video Handbook*, New York: Joseph M. McLauglin, Fordham University School of Law, Practising Law Institute, 1977.

——*The Hearsay Rule*, Durham, NC: Carolina Academic Press, 2003.

Finegan, Edward, *Language: Its Structure and Use*, 4th edn, Florence, Kentucky: Heinle, 2003.

Fried, Charles, *Contract as Promise*, Cambridge, Mass.: Harvard University Press, 1981.

Fuller, Lon L., *Legal Fictions*, Stanford California: Stanford University Press, 1967.

Gibbons, John, *Forensic Linguistics: an Introduction to Language in the Justice System*, Oxford: Blackwell Publishing, 2003.

Gierke, Otto, *Political Theories of The Middle Ages*, translated by F. M. Maitland, New York: Cambridge University Press, 1987.

Gilmore, Grant, *The Death of Contract*, Columbus, Ohio: Ohio State University Press, 1974.

Greene, Brian, *The Elegant Universe*, New York: Random House, 1999.

Haiman, Franklyn S., *Speech and Law in a Free Society*, Chicago: University of Chicago Press, 1970.

Hancher, Michael, 'The classification of cooperative illocutionary acts', 5 *Language in Society*, 1979.

Hart, H. L. A., *The Concept of Law*, 2nd edn, Oxford: Oxford University Press, 1944.

Heiman, G., *Otto Gierke: Association and Law*, 1977.

Henderson, 'The position of foreign corporations in American constitutional law', 2 *Harvard Studies in Jurisprudence*, 1918.

Holmes, Oliver W., *The Path of the Law: Collected Legal Papers*, New York: Harcourt-Brace, 1920.

Horwitz, Morton, *The Transformation of American Law, 1780–1860*, Oxford University Press, 1977.

——'Santa Clara revisited: the development of corporate theory', 88 *West Virginia Law Review*, 1985.

Jespersen, Otto, *A Modern English Grammar on Historical Principles*, Copenhagen: E. Munksgaard, 1961.

——*The Philosophy of Grammar*, New York: W.W. Norton and Co., 1965.

Kövecses, Zoltán, *Metaphor: a Practical Introduction*, Oxford: Oxford University Press, 2002.

Kuntz, Phil (ed.), *The Evidence: the Star Report*, New York: Pocket Books, 1998.

Kurzon, Dennis, *It is Hereby Performed: Explorations in Legal Speech Acts*, Amsterdam: John Benjamins, 1986.

Lakoff, George, *Women, Fire, and Dangerous Things: What Categories Reveal about the Mind*, Chicago: University of Chicago Press, 1987.

——and Mark Johnson, *Metaphors we Live by*, Chicago: University of Chicago Press, 1980.

Levi, Judith N., 'The study of language in the judicial process' in *Language in the Judicial Process*, Judith N. Levi and Ann Graffam Walker (eds), New York: Plenum Press, 1990: 3–35.

Lily, Graham C., *An Introduction to the Law of Evidence* 2nd edn, St Paul, Minn: West Publishing Co., 1987.

Louisell, David W., John Kaplan and Jon R. Waltz. *Evidence: Cases and Materials*, 3rd edn, Mineola, N Y: Foundation Press, Inc., 1976.

Machen, Arthur, 'Corporate personality' 24 *Harvard Law Review*, 1911.

Mellinkoff, David, *The Language of the Law*, Boston: Little, Brown & Co., 1963.

——*Legal Writing: Sense and Nonsense*, New York: Scribner, 1982.

Mill, John Stuart, *A System of Logic*, 8th edn, London: Longmans, 1961.

Mueller, Christopher B. and Laird C. Kirkpatrick, *Federal Evidence* 2nd edn, vol. 4, Rochester, NY: Lawyer's Cooperative Pub., 1994.

Olivier, Pierre J., *Legal Fictions in Practice and Legal Science*, Rotterdam: Rotterdam University Press, 1975.

Olsson, John, *Forensic Lingusitics: an Introduction to Language, Crime and the Law*, London: Continuum, 2004.

Oxford American Dictionary and Thesaurus, Oxford: Oxford University Press, 2003.

Oxford English Dictionary, Oxford: Oxford University Press, 1961.

Pupier, Paul and J. Woehrling (eds), *Language and Law*, Montreal: Wilson & Lafleur, 1989.

Restatement of the Law Second, Contracts 2d, St Paul, MN American Law Institute Publishers, 1981.

Rosch, Eleanor, 'Principles of categorization', in E. Rosch and Lloyd (eds), *Cognition and Categorization*, Hillsdale, NJ: Lawrence Erlbaum Associates, 1978.

Rothstein, Paul F., Myrna S. Raeder and David Crump, *Evidence in a Nutshell: State and Federal Rules*, 3rd edn, St Paul, Minn.: West Publishing Co., 1997.

Sapir, Edward, *Language*, New York: Harcourt, Brace, 1921.

Schane, Sanford A., 'The corporation is a person: the language of a legal fiction', 61 *Tulane Law Review*, 1987.

——'A speech act analysis of consideration in contract law', Paul Pupier and J. Woehrling (eds), *Language and Law*, Montreal: Wilson & Lafleur, 1989: 581–90.

——'Ambiguity and misunderstanding in the law', 25 *Thomas Jefferson Law Review*, 2002.

Searle, John, *Speech Acts: an Essay in the Philosophy of Language*, Cambridge: Cambridge University Press, 1969.

——and Daniel Vanderveken, *Foundations of Illocutionary Logic*, Cambridge: Cambridge University Press, 1985.

Shakespeare, William, *As You Like It*, Act II, Scene VII.

Shuy, Roger W., *Language Crimes: the Use and Abuse of Language Evidence in the Courtroom*, Cambridge, Mass.: Blackwell Publishers, 1993.

——*The Language of Confession, Interrogation and Deception*, Thousand Oaks, CA: Sage, 1998.

——*Linguistic Battles in Trademark Disputes*, New York: Palgrave Macmillan, 2002.

——*Creating Language Crimes: How Law Enforcement Uses (and Misuses) Language*, Oxford: Oxford University Press, 2005.

Singer, Norman J., *Statutes and Statutory Construction*, 5th edn, New York: Clark Boardman Callaghan, 1992.

Solan, Lawrence, M., *The Language of Judges*, Chicago, IL: University of Chicago Press, 1993.

——and Peter M. Tiersma, *Speaking of Crime: the Language of Criminal Justice*, Chicago: University of Chicago Press, 2005.

Tiersma, Peter, 'The language of offer and acceptance: speech acts and the question of intent', 74 *California Law Review*, 1986.

——'The language of defamation', 66 *Texas Law Review*, 1987.

Tiersma, Peter, 'The language of perjury: "literal truth," ambiguity, and the false statement requirement', 63 *Southern California Law Review*, 1990.

——'Reassessing unilateral contracts: the role of offer, acceptance and promise', 26 *UC Davis Law Review*, 1992.

——*Legal Language*, Chicago: University of Chicago Press, 1999.

——'A message in a bottle: text, autonomy and statutory interpretation', *Tulane Law Review*, 2001.

Tribe, Lawrence, 'Triangulating hearsay', 87 *Harvard Law Review*, 1974.

Webster's New Twentieth Century Dictionary, 2nd edn, New York: Dorset & Baber, 1964.

Webster's Third New International Dictionary (unabridged), Springfield, Mass.: Merriam-Webster, 1964.

Winter, Steven L., *A Clearing in the Forest: Law, Life and Mind*, Chicago: University of Chicago Press, 2001.

Words and Phrases, vol. 3, St Paul, Minn.: Westfield Publishing, 1953.

Wydick, Richard C., *Plain English for Lawyers*, 4th edn, Durham: North Carolina: Carolina Academic Press, 1998.

Younger, Irving, *Hearsay: a Practical Guide through the Thicket*, Clifton, New Jersey: Prentice-Hall, 1988.

Court Cases Cited in Text

The page number and accompanying endnote number refer to the line in the main text where the case is cited.

194th St Hotel Corp. v. *Hopf*, 383 So. 2d 739 (Fla. App. 1980). 120 n. 30

American Fruit Growers, Inc., v. *Brogdex Co.*, 1931, 283 US 1, 51 S. Ct. 328, 75 23 n. 15

Bank of Augusta v. *Earle*, 38 US (13 Pet.) 519 (1839). 69 n. 37

Bank of the United States v. *Deveaux*, 9 US (5 Cranch) 61, 87 (1809). 61 n. 14, 62 n. 17

Betts v. *Betts*, 473 P.2d 403 (Wash. Ct. App. 1970). 125 n. 34

California v. *Brown*, 479 US 538; 107 S. Ct. 1987. 13 n. 3, 43 n. 53

Commonwealth Communications, Inc. v. *National Labor Relations Board*, 354 US App. D.C. 96; 312 F.3d 465; 2002 US App. LEXIS 25651; 171 LRRM 2513. 36 n. 40

Dickenson v. *Dodds*, 2 Ch. D. 463 (CA 1876). 176 n. 46

Donald E. Cleveland and Enrique Gray-Santana v. *US*, 524 US 125; 118 S. Ct. 1911; 141 L. Ed. 2d 111; 1998 US LEXIS 3879. 30 n. 28

First National Bank v. *Bellotti*, 435 US 765 (1978). 71 n. 44

Frank J. Muscarello v. *US* 524 US 125; 118 S. Ct. 1911; 141 L. Ed. 2d 111; 1998 US LEXIS 3879. 30 n. 28

Freeman v. *Metropolitan Life Insurance. Co.* 468 F. Supp. 1269, 1271 (W.D. Va. 1970). 118 n. 27

Frigaliment Importing Co. v. *B.N.S. International Sales Corp.*, 190 F.Supp.116 (SDNY 1960). 12 n. 2, 27 n. 22

Hale v. *Henkel*, 201 US 43 (1906). 71 n. 43

Hamer v. *Sidway*, Court of Appeals of New York, 1891. 124 NY 538, 27 NE 256. 144 n. 14

Hanson v. *Johnson et al.*, Supreme Court of Minnesota, 1924. 161 Minn. 229, 201 NW 322. 119 n. 29

Hardy and Hardy, Cal. App, 135 P. 2d, 615, 619. (*Words and Phrases*, 438). 17 n. 9

Hope Insurance Co. v. *Boardman*, 9 US (5 Cranch) 57 (1809). 62 n. 17

Interstate Commerce Commission v. *Kroblin*, 113 F. Supp. 599 (ND Iowa, ED 1953). 12 n. 2, 36 n. 42

Jones v. *Clinton*, 990 F. Supp. 1217 (E.D. Ark. 1998) 24 n. 16

Keffe v. *Milwaukee & St. Paul Railroad Co.*, 21 Minn. 207 (1875). 56 n. 4

Kirsky v. *Kirksy*, 8 Ala. 131 (1845). 143 n. 12

Kyle v. *Kavanagh.* Mass. 356. 4 Am. Rep. 560 (1869). [103 Mass. 356; 1869 Mass. LEXIS 88] 35 n. 38

Liparota v. *United States*, 471 US 419 (1985). 47 n. 56

Louis B. Weinberg v. *Mark Edelstein*, Supreme Court of New York, 201 Misc. 343, 110 NYS 2d 806; 1952 NY Misc. LEXIS 2459. 38 n. 48

Notes

Introduction

1. David Mellinkoff, *The Language of the Law*, Boston: Little, Brown & Co., 1963: vi.
2. For a review and an excellent bibliography of the law and language research in the social sciences up to 1990, see Judith N. Levi, 'The study of language in the judicial process' in *Language in the Judicial Process*, Judith N. Levi and Ann Graffam Walker (eds). New York: Plenum Press, 1990: 3–35; see also Peter Tiersma's online bibliography that includes more recent works at: www.languageandlaw.org/BIBLIO.HTM.
3. Levi, pp. 3–4.
4. For the language-oriented approach, see Peter Tiersma, *Legal Language*, Chicago: University of Chicago Press, 1999; Lawrence M. Solan, *The Language of Judges*, Chicago: University of Chicago Press, 1993; and Lawrence M. Solan and Peter M. Tiersma, *Speaking of Crime: The Language of Criminal Justice*, Chicago: University of Chicago Press, 2005. For the law-oriented approach, see John Gibbons, *Forensic Linguistics: an Introduction to Language in the Justice System*, Oxford: Blackwell Publishing, 2003. For the social sciences approach, see John M. Conley and William M. O'Barr, *Just Words: Law, Language and Power*, 2nd edn, Chicago: University of Chicago Press, 2005.
5. David Mellinkoff, *The Language of the Law*, Boston: Little, Brown & Co., 1963.
6. Peter Tiersma, *Legal Language*, Chicago: University of Chicago Press, 1999.
7. Robert P. Charrow and Veda R. Charrow, 'Making legal language understandable: a psycholinguistic study of jury instructions', 79 *Columbia Law Review*, 1979.
8. Amiram Elwork *et al.*, *Making Jury Instructions Understandable*, Charlottesville, Virginia: Michie/Bobbs-Merrill, 1982: 438.
9. Tiersma has been a member on a California taskforce for revising jury instructions; the examples of jury instructions cited in the text are from his website: www.languageandlaw.org/JURYINST/COMPARE2.HTM.
10. Richard C. Wydick, *Plain English for Lawyers*, 4th edn, Durham, North Carolina: Carolina Academic Press, 1998: 3.
11. See the website: www.law.ucla.edu/home/index.asp?page=835; also David Mellinkoff, *Legal Writing: Sense and Nonsense*, New York: Scribner, 1982.

12. Lon L. Fuller, *Legal Fictions*, Stanford, CA: Stanford University Press, 1967.
13. *Ibid.*, p. 11.
14. George Lakoff and Mark Johnson, *Metaphors we Live By*, Chicago, IL: University of Chicago Press, 1980.
15. *Ibid.*, p. 3.
16. John Austin, *How to do Things with Words*, 2nd edn, Cambridge, MA: Harvard University Press, 1962; John Searle, *Speech Acts: an Essay in the Philosophy of Language*, Cambridge: Cambridge University Press, 1969.
17. Searle, p. 3.
18. Roger W. Shuy, *Language Crimes: the Use and Abuse of Language Evidence in the Courtroom*, Cambridge, MA: Blackwell Publishers, 1993; see also Shuy, *The Language of Confession, Interrogation and Deception*, Thousand Oaks, CA: Sage, 1998; and Shuy, *Creating Language Crimes: How Law Enforcement Uses (and Misuses) Language*, Oxford: Oxford University Press, 2005.
19. Solan 1993, pp. 155–63.
20. Peter Tiersma, 'The language of defamation', 66 *Texas Law Review*, 1987; 'The language of perjury: "literal truth", ambiguity and the false statement requirement', 63 *Southern California Law Review*, 1990.
21. Solan and Tiersma, pp. 221–33.
22. Dennis Kurzon, *It is Hereby Performed: Explorations in Legal Speech Acts*, Amsterdam: John Benjamins, 1986.
23. John R. Searle and Daniel Vanderveken, *Foundations of Illocutionary Logic*, Cambridge: Cambridge University Press, 1985: 57–61.
24. My course website can be found at: http://ling.ucsd.edu/courses/lign105.

Chapter 1   Ambiguity in Language and Misunderstanding in Law

Parts of Chapter 1, in particular the analyses of the *Frigaliment, Raffles* and *ICC* cases, were originally published in Sanford Schane, 'Ambiguity and misunderstanding in the law', *Thomas Jefferson Law Review*, 25(1): 167–93 (2002). Those passages are reprinted with permission of the Thomas Jefferson School of Law, which holds the copyright.

1. Clinton deposition quoted in Phil Kuntz (ed.), *The Evidence: the Star Report*, New York: Pocket Books, 1998: 373.
2. *Frigaliment Importing Co.* v. *BNS International Sales Corp.*, 190 F. Supp. 116 (SDNY 1960); *Raffles* v. *Wichelhaus*, 2 Hurl. & C. 906, 159 Eng. rep. 375 (Ex.1864); *Interstate Commerce Commission* v. *Allen E. Kroblin, Inc.*, 113 F. Supp. 599 (ND Iowa, ED 1953).
3. *California* v. *Brown*, 479 US 538; 107 S. Ct. 1987.
4. *Words and Phrases*, vol. 3, St Paul, MN: Westfield Publishing, 1953.
5. *Universal CIT Credit Corp.* v. *Daniel*, 243 S.W. 2d 154, 157, 150 Tex. 513. (*Words and Phrases*, 440).
6. *Osterholm* v. *Boston and Montana Consol. Copper and Silver Mining Co.*, 107 P.499, 502, 40 Mont. 508 (*Words and Phrases*, 440).
7. *Simpkin's* v. *Business Men's Assur. Co. of America*, 215 S.W. 2d 1, 3, 31 Tenn. App. 306. (*Words and Phrases*, 440).
8. For a general discussion of the linguistic notions of ambiguity, see Adrian Akmajian *et al.*, *Linguistics: an Introduction to Language and Communication*, 4th edn, Cambridge, MA: M.I.T. Press, 1995; also Edward Finegan, *Language: Its Structure and Use*, 4th edn, Florence, Kentucky: Heinle, 2003. For some law

cases exemplifying syntactic ambiguity, see Lawrence Solan, *The Language of Judges*, Chicago, IL: University of Chicago Press, 1993 (in particular, Chs 2 and 3); also Peter M. Tiersma, *Legal Language*, Chicago, IL: University of Chicago Press, 1999.

9. *Hardy and Hardy*, Cal. App, 135 P. 2d, 615, 619. (*Words and Phrases*, 438).
10. *Webster's New Twentieth Century Dictionary*, 2nd edn, New York: Dorset & Baber, 1964: 146
11. *Webster's Third New International Dictionary* (unabridged), Springfield, MA: Merriam-Webster, 1964: 387.
12. John Stuart Mill, *A System of Logic*, 8th edn, London: Longmans (1961: I, Ch. II).
13. Otto Jespersen, *The Philosophy of Grammar*, New York: W.W. Norton and Co., 1965: 64–71.
14. For an overview of trademark disputes, see Roger Shuy, *Linguistic Battles in Trademark Disputes*, New York: Palgrave Macmillan, 2002.
15. *American Fruit Growers, Inc.,* v. *Brogdex Co.*, 1931, 283 US 1, 51 S. Ct. 328, 75 L.Ed. 801. The definition is found on page 11 of 283 US and on page 330 of 51 S.Ct.
16. *Jones* v. *Clinton*, 990 F. Supp. 1217 (E.D. Ark. 1998); for a linguistic analysis of the Clinton impeachment trial, see Lawrence M. Solan and Peter M. Tiersma, *Speaking of Crime: the Language of Criminal Justice*, Chicago, IL: University of Chicago Press, 2005: 221–33.
17. For an overview of the history and problems of categorization as well as a cognitive linguistic approach, see George Lakoff, *Women, Fire, and Dangerous Things: What Categories Reveal about the Mind*, Chicago, IL: University of Chicago Press, 1987.
18. For an overview of prototype theory in cognitive psychology, see Eleanor Rosch, 'Principles of categorization', in E. Rosch and Lloyd (eds), *Cognition and Categorization*, Hillsdale, NJ: Lawrence Erlbaum Associates, 1978: 27–48.
19. Arthur L. Corbin, *Corbin on Contracts*, one-volume edition, St Paul, MN: West Publishing Co., 1952: 156–7.
20. Arthur L. Corbin, 'The Interpretation of Words and the Parol Evidence Rule', *Cornell Law Quarterly* 1965, 50: 161. In this article Corbin analyses the *Frigaliment* case, for which he justifies the introduction of extrinsic evidence.
21. E. Allen Farnsworth, *Farnsworth on Contracts*, New York: Aspen Publishers, Inc, 1990.
22. *Frigaliment*. The quote from Holmes is from *The Path of the Law: Collected Legal Papers*, New York: Harcourt-Brace, 1920: 178.
23. *Frigaliment*.
24. *Frigaliment*.
25. *Frigaliment*.
26. *Shrum* v. *Zeltwanger*, 559 P.2d. 1384; 1977 Wyo.
27. *Webster's*, 3rd edn, 525.
28. *Frank J. Muscarello* v. *USA; Donald E. Cleveland and Enrique Gray-Santana* v. *USA*, 524 US 125; 118 S. Ct. 1911; 141 L. Ed. 2d 111; 1998 US LEXIS 3879.
29. Reference to page in *Muscarello*.
30. Reference to *Muscarello*.
31. *Black's Law Dictionary*, 6th edn, St Paul, MN: West Publishing Co., 1990: 214.

32. *Michael Viviano* v. *Jewelers Mutual Insurance Company*, District Court of New York, 115 Misc. 2d 518; 454 N.Y.S. 2d 404; 1982.
33. *Webster's*, 2nd edn, 274.
34. *Viviano*.
35. *Raffles*.
36. *Raffles*.
37. The analysis by Holmes is found in Grant Gilmore, *The Death of Contract*, Columbus, OH: University of Ohio Press, 1974: 41–2.
38. *Kyle* v. *Kavanagh*. Mass. 356. 4 Am. Rep. 560 (1869). [103 Mass. 356; 1869 Mass. LEXIS 88]
39. *Oswald* v. *Allen*, 417 F.2d 43 (2d Cir. 1969).
40. *Commonwealth Communications, Inc.* v. *National Labor Relations Board*, 354 US App. D.C. 96; 312 F.3d 465; 2002 US App. LEXIS 25651; 171 L.R.R.M. 2513; 147 Lab.Cas (CCH) P10, 151.
41. *Commonwealth Communications, Inc.* v. *National Labor Relations Board*, 354 US App. D.C. 96; 312 F.3d 465; 2002 US App. LEXIS 25651; 171 LRRM 2513; 147 Lab. Cas (CCH) P10, 151.
42. *ICC* 113 F.Supp. 599 (ND Iowa, ED 1953).
43. *ICC*.
44. No. MC-C-968, Determination of Exempted Agricultural Products, (52 MCC 511)
45. No. MC-C-968, Determination of Exempted Agricultural Products, (52 MCC 511)
46. No. MC-C-968, Determination of Exempted Agricultural Products, (52 MCC 511)
47. *ICC*.
48. *Louis B. Weinberg* v. *Mark Edelstein*, Supreme Court of New York, 201 Misc. 343, 110 NYS 2d 806; 1952 NY Misc. LEXIS 2459.
49. *Mack Oil Company* v. *Mamie Lee Laurence*, Supreme Court of Okolahoma, 1964 OK 39; 389 P.2d 955; 1964 Okla. LEXIS 270.
50. *Watt* v. *Western Nuclear, Inc.*, 462 US 36 (1983).
51. *Watt*.
52. Norman J. Singer, *Statutes and Statutory Construction*, 5th edn, New York: Clark Boardman Callaghan, 1992: 59.
53. *California* v. *Brown* 107 S.ct.837 (1987).
54. Lawrence M. Solan, *The Language of Judges*, Chicago, IL: University of Chicago Press, 1993: 55–61.
55. 'Death Penalty: factors to consider – identified as Aggravating or Mitigating', Judicial Council of California, Sect. 702 ADP. Draft circulated for comment only, (criminst6.pdf) 2005.
56. *Liparota* v. *USA*, 471 US 419 (1985).
57. *Rewis* v. *USA*, 401 US 808, 812 (1971).
58. *Restatement of the Law of Contracts*, 2d, §201, Illustration 4. St. Paul, Minn.: American Law Institute Publishers, 1981.
59. See H. L. A. Hart, *The Concept of Law*, 2nd edn, Oxford: Oxford University Press, 1944: 128–9.
60. Peter M. Tiersma, 'A message in a bottle: text, autonomy and statutory interpretation', *Tulane Law Review*, 2001: 76:2.
61. No. MC-C-968, 'Determination of Exempted Agricultural Products', (52 MCC 511).

Chapter 2 Linguistic Metaphor and Legal Fiction

Parts of this chapter, in particular some of the material about corporate personality, the Supreme Court cases on diversity and the analysis of the corporation as a person, were originally published in Sanford A. Schane, 'The corporation is a person: the language of a legal fiction', 61 *Tulane Law Review*, 1987: 563–609. Reprinted with the permission of the Tulane Law Review Association, which holds the copyright.

In this chapter I provide an analysis of the poem, 'Trees', by Joyce Kilmer, which first appeared in *Modern American Poetry: an Introduction*, ed. by Louis Untermeyer. New York: Harcourt, Brace and Howe, 1919.

1. Lon L. Fuller, *Legal Fictions*. Stanford, CA: Stanford University Press, 1967: 10.
2. For a fascinating account of the implications of recent work in cognitive linguistics and metaphor for the law, see Steven L. Winter, *A Clearing in the Forest: Law, Life and Mind*, Chicago, IL: University of Chicago Press, 2001.
3. *Sioux City & Pennyslvania Railroad Co.* v. *Stout*, 84 US 657 (1873).
4. *Keffe* v. *Milwaukee & St. Paul Railroad Co.*, 21 Minn. 207 (1875).
5. Fuller, 22.
6. Fuller, 69, note 32.
7. The citation from the Rolls of Parliament appears under the entry 'person' (IV.6) in the *Oxford English Dictionary*, Oxford: Oxford University Press, 1961: 724.
8. *Commentaries on the Laws of England 1765–9*, cited in the *Oxford English Dictionary* under the entry 'person' (IV.6), 724.
9. A summary of Savigny's views is found in G. Heiman, *Otto Gierke: Association and Law*, 27–33 (1977).
10. *Trustees of Dartmouth College* v. *Woodward*, 17 US (4 Wheat.) 518, 636 (1819).
11. Arthur Machen, 'Corporate personality' 24 *Harvard Law Review* (1911: 257–8, note 5).
12. Otto Gierke, *Political Theories of the Middle Ages*, introduction and translation by F. M. Maitland, New York: Cambridge University Press (1987: xviii–xliii).
13. The discussion of the evolution of US corporations within the context of the three theories of corporate personality is a summary of the views of Morton Horwitz, 'Santa Clara revisited: the development of corporate theory', 88 *West Virginia Law Review*, 1985: 173.
14. *Bank of the United States* v. *Deveaux*, 9 US (5 Cranch) 61, 87 (1809).
15. United States Constitution, Art. III, § 2, cl.1.
16. For a survey of the nature and kinds of colonial corporations, see Henderson, 'The position of foreign corporations in American constitutional law', 2 *Harvard Studies in Jurisprudence* 1, 1918.
17. 9 US (5 Cranch) 61 (1809). The Supreme Court reviewed three different cases having to do with corporations and their admission into federal courts. The cases were argued and considered together: *Deveaux* 9 US (5 Cranch) 61; *Hope Insurance Co.* v. *Boardman*, 9 US (5 Cranch) 57 (1809); and *Maryland Insurance Co.* v. *Woods*, 10 US (6 Cranch) 29 (1809).
18. *Deveaux*, 88.
19. *Deveaux*, 88–9.
20. *Deveaux*, 86–7.
21. *Deveaux*, 87.

22. *Deveaux*, 91.
23. *Strawbridge* 7 US (3 Cranch) 267 (1806).
24. *Letson* 43 US (2 How.) 497 (1844).
25. *Letson* 554.
26. *Letson* 555.
27. *Letson* 558.
28. *Rundle* v. *Delaware & Raritan Canal Co.*, 55 US (14 How.) SO, 109 (1852) (Daniel, J., dissenting).
29. *Rundle*, 101.
30. *Marshall*, US (16 How.) 314 (1853).
31. *Marshall*, 327 (citation omitted).
32. *Marshall*, 327–8.
33. *Marshall*, 325.
34. *Marshall*, 328.
35. 28 *USC* § 1332(c) (1982).
36. For a fuller treatment of the rights of foreign corporations, see Schane, 'The corporation is a person: the language of a legal fiction', *Tulane Law Review*, 61:3, 1987: 584–92.
37. *Bank of Augusta* v. *Earle*, 38 US (13 Pet.) 519 (1839).
38. US Constitution, amendment XIV, §1.
39. *Pembina Mining Co.* v. *Pennsylvania*, 125 US 181 (1888: 187–8).
40. *Pembina*, 189.
41. *Southern Railway Co.* v. *Greene*, 216 US 400 (1910).
42. *Greene*, 412.
43. *Hale* v. *Henkel*, 201 US 43 (1906).
44. *First National Bank* v. *Bellotti*, 435 US 765 (1978).
45. George Lakoff and Mark Johnson, *Metaphors We Live by*, Chicago, IL: University of Chicago Press (1980: 159).
46. Brian Greene, *The Elegant Universe*, New York: Random House, 1999: 135, 146.
47. Lakoff and Johnson 5.
48. *Webster's New Twentieth Century Dictionary*, 2nd edn, New York: Dorset & Baber, 1964: 1132.
49. *Oxford English Dictionary*, 384
50. William Shakespeare, *As You Like It*, Act II, Scene VII.
51. Zoltán Kövecses, *Metaphor: a Practical Introduction*, Oxford: Oxford University Press, 2002: 3.
52. Kövecses, 70–1.
53. Lakoff and Johnson, 51.
54. *Webster's New Universal Unabridged Dictionary*, 2nd edn, New York: Simon & Schuster, 1983.
55. *Oxford American Dictionary and Thesaurus*, Oxford: Oxford University Press, 2003.
56. *Black's Law Dictionary*, 4th edn, St Paul, MN: West Publishing Co. 1968: 165.
57. Cohen, 'Transcendental nonsense and the functional approach', 35 *Columbia Law Review*, 1935: 811.
58. Fuller, 10.
59. Pierre J. Olivier, *Legal Fictions in Practice and Legal Science*, Rotterdam: Rotterdam University Press, 1975: 91.
60. Fuller, 66–8.
61. Fuller, 68.

62. Fuller, 66.

63. Edward Sapir, *Language*. New York: Harcourt, Brace, 1921: 16.

64. *Webster's Third New International Dictionary* (unabridged), Springfield, MA: Merriam-Webster, 1964: 223.

65. John Dewey, 'The historic background of corporate legal personality', 35 *Yale Law Journal*, 1926: 656.

66. Machen, 263.

67. Machen, 348.

68. www.irs.gov/compliance/enforcement/

Chapter 3   Speech Acts and Legal Hearsay

1. G. Michael Fenner, *Practical Trial Evidence: a Video Handbook*, New York: Joseph M. McLauglin, Fordham University School of Law, Practising Law Institute, 1977: 51.

2. *Federal Rules of Evidence*, Committee on the Judiciary, House of Representatives. Washington: US Government Printing Office, 2003: 401.

3. G. Michael Fenner, *The Hearsay Rule*, Durham, N. Carolina: Carolina Academic Press, 2003: 4.

4. *FRE* 801(c).

5. *FRE* 801(a).

6. *FRE* 801(b).

7. *FRE* 82.

8. *Subramaniam* v. *Public Prosecutor* [1956] 1 WLR 956 at 969, PC; and *Ratten* v. *R.*, *ante*.

9. 'Morgan, Evidence exam, summer term, 1946', Harvard Law School in *Evidence: Cases and Materials*, 3rd edn, David W. Louisell, John Kaplan and Jon R. Waltz. Mineola, NY: Foundation Press, Inc, 1976: 126–30.

10. 5 *California Real Estate* 2nd 629, *et seq.*, Miller & Starr, 1989.

11. *California Code of Civil Procedure*, Sections 318 *et seq.*

12. *FRE*, art VII, advisory committee note.

13. *FRE* 803, 804.

14. *FRE* 801(d).

15. *FRE* 804 (b) (2).

16. *FRE* 803.

17. John Searle, *Speech Acts: an Essay in the Philosophy of Language*, Cambridge: Cambridge University Press, 1969: 3.

18. John Austin, *How to do Things with Words*, 2nd edn, Cambridge, MA: Harvard University Press, 1962.

19. Austin, p. 8; also Austin, 'Performative–constative' in *The Philosophy of Language*, ed. by J. Searle, Oxford: Oxford University Press, 1971: 13.

20. John Olsson, *Forensic Lingusitics: an Introduction to Language, Crime and the Law*, London: Continuum, 2004: 25.

21. John Searle and Daniel Vanderveken, *Foundations of Illocutionary Logic*, Cambridge: Cambridge University Press, 1985: Ch. 9.

22. Peter Tiersma, 'The language of perjury: "Literal truth," ambiguity, and the false statement requirement', 63 *Southern California Law Review*, 1990: 2.

23. *FRE* 801(a), (c).

24. *FRE* 801 (c).

25. *State* v. *Hargrave*, Supreme Court of North Carolina, 1887. 97 NC 457, 1 SE 774.

26. Austin, 13.
27. *Freeman* v. *Metropolitan Life Insurance. Co.* 468 F. Supp. 1269, 1271 (WD Va. 1970).
28. *Safeway Stores, Inc.* v. *Combs*, US Court of Appeals, Fifth Circuit, 1960. 273 F.2d 295.
29. *Hanson* v. *Johnson et al.*, Supreme Court of Minnesota, 1924. 161 Minn. 229, 201 NW 322.
30. *194th St. Hotel Corp.* v. *Hopf*, 383 So. 2d 739 (Fla.App. 1980).
31. See Peter Tiersma, 'The language of defamation', 66:2 *Texas Law Review*, 1987. Tiersma presents a speech-act analysis of defamation, where he defines defamation as the assertive illocutionary act of accusing.
32. For a linguistic analysis of the Clinton impeachment trial, see Lawrence M. Solan and Peter M. Tiersma, *Speaking of Crime: the Language of Criminal Justice*, Chicago, IL: University of Chicago Press, 2005: 221–33.
33. Franklyn S. Haiman, *Speech and Law in a Free Society*, Chicago: University of Chicago Press, 1970: Ch.3.
34. *Betts* v. *Betts*, 473 P.2d 403 (Wash. Ct. App. 1970).
35. The Gucci hypothetical is based on *Zippo Manufacturing Co.* v. *Rogers Imports Inc.* 216 F. Supp (SDNY 1963). Purchasers of cigarette lighters thought they were buying authentic Zippo.
36. Paul F. Rothstein, Myrna S. Raeder and David Crump, *Evidence in a Nutshell: State and Federal Rules*, 3rd edn, St Paul, MN: West Publishing Co. 1997: 439–43.
37. Christopher B. Mueller and Laird C. Kirkpatrick, *Federal Evidence*, 2nd edn, vol. 4. Rochester, NY: Lawyer's Cooperative Pub., 1994: 74, note 6.
38. Fenner, *Hearsay Rule* 175–6 discusses the utterance, 'I am afraid that my husband will kill me', along with two related sentences: 'I am afraid because my husband has threatened to kill me', and 'I am afraid of my husband because he has threatened to kill me'.
39. Fenner, 175.
40. Fenner, 176.
41. Fenner, 176.
42. Graham C. Lily, *An Introduction to the Law of Evidence*, 2nd edn, St Paul, MN: West Publishing Co., 1987: 192.
43. Rothstein *et al.*, 432.
44. *Mutual Life Insurance Co.* v. *Hillmon,* 145 US 285 (1892). For an in-depth discussion of the *Hillmon* and *Shepard* cases, see Irving Younger, *Hearsay: a Practical Guide through the Thicket*, Clifton, New Jersey: Prentice-Hall, 1988: 174–83.
45. The expression, 'state of mind merely relevant' is due to Younger, 177.
46. *Shepard* v. *US.*, 290 US 96 (1933).
47. 290 US at 105–6.
48. Younger, 1.
49. Lawrence Tribe, 'Triangulating hearsay', 87 *Harvard Law Review*, 1974: 957.

Chapter 4   Promise and Contract Formation

1. *Restatement of the Law Second Contracts 2d.* St Paul, MN: American Law Institute Publishers, 1981: Sect. 1, 5.
2. The quoted phrases are taken from the titles of two books dealing with the controversy over the nature of current contract theory: Charles Fried,

Contract as Promise, Cambridge, MA: Harvard University Press, 1981; Grant Gilmore, *The Death of Contract*, Columbus, OH: Ohio State University Press, 1974.

3. Arthur L. Corbin, *Corbin on Contracts*, one-volume edition, St Paul, MN: West Publishng Company, 1982: Sect. 1, 2.
4. Fried, Ch. 1.
5. John Austin, *How to do Things with Words*, Cambridge, MA: Harvard University Press, 1962: 10.
6. Fried, 16–17.
7. See especially, Gilmore; Morton Horwitz, *The Transformation of American Law, 1780–1860*. Oxford University Press, 1977; and P. S. Atiyah, *The Rise and Fall of Freedom of Contract*, Oxford: Oxford University Press, 1979.
8. P. S. Atiyah, *An Introduction to the Law of Contract*, 3rd edn, Oxford: Clarendon Press, 1981: 13–25.
9. There are two versions of the *Restatement*. The first one appeared in 1932; the second in 1979. All my citations and examples are from the revised second edition, student version, 1981.
10. Reference to 'promise' can be found in the *Restatement* definitions of 'bargain' (Sect. 3, 13), 'terms of promise' (Sect. 5, 16), 'mutual assent' (Sect. 18, 53), 'acceptance of offers' (Sect. 50, 128) and 'consideration' (Sect. 71, 172; Sect. 75, 189; Sect. 76, 192; Sect. 77, 194; Sect. 78, 198).
11. *Restatement* 2d, 71 (1), 172.
12. *Kirsky* v. *Kirksy*, 8 Ala. 131 (1845).
13. See the discussion in Corbin, Sect. 195, 282–3.
14. *Hamer* v. *Sidway*, Court of Appeals of New York, 1891. 124 NY 538, 27 NE 256.
15. *Mills* v. *Wyman*, 3 Pick. 207 (Mass. 1825).
16. *Stilk* v. *Myrick*, Court of Common Pleas, 1810. 2 Camp 317.
17. For discussion of the *Stilk* case, see Gilmore, 23–5.
18. *Restatement* 2d, Sect. 71, 5, 174.
19. John R. Searle, *Foundations of Illocutionary Logic*, Cambridge: Cambridge University Press, 1985: 57–61.
20. *Restatement* 2nd, Sect. 2, comment c, 9.
21. Searle, 58.
22. Searle, 59.
23. *Restatement* 2d, Sect. 76, 1, 193.
24. *Restatement* 2d, Sect. 2, 3, 11.
25. *Restatement* 2d, Sect. 75, 189.
26. Corbin, Sect. 210, 302.
27. For a discussion of the history of consideration within the common law, see Corbin, Sect. 110, 164–7.
28. *Restatement* 2d, Sect. 71, (1), 172; Sect. 79, 200.
29. *Restatement* 2d, Sect. 71 (4).
30. Some of the examples presented here first appeared in Schane, 'A speech-act analysis of consideration in contract law', Paul Pupier and J. Woehrling (eds), *Language and Law*, Montreal: Wilson & Lafleur, 1989: 581–90.
31. *Restatement* 2d, Sect. 71, 2, 174.
32. *Restatement* 2d, Sect. 86, 1, 224.
33. *Restatement* 2d, Sect. 73 (1), 181.
34. *Restatement* 2d, Sect. 73 (4), 181–2.
35. *Restatement* 2d, Sect. 73 (2), 181.

36. *Restatement* 2d, Sect. 80 (3), 205.
37. *Restatement* 2d, Sect. 79 (5), 202.
38. Peter Tiersma cites the anecdote of the professor and the student at the outset of his article, 'Reassessing unilateral contracts: the role of offer, acceptance and promise', 26 *UC Davis Law Review*, 1992: 1.
39. For a summary of these various viewpoints, see Tiersma, 5–13.
40. Clarence D. Ashley, 'Offers calling for a consideration other than a counter-promise', *Harvard Law Review* 1910: 160–1.
41. *Restatement* 2d, §45 (1979).
42. Arthur L. Corbin, 'Offer and acceptance, and some of the resulting legal relations', 26 *Yale Law Journal* 169: 195 (1917).
43. Tiersma, 18–41.
44. Fried, 41–3.
45. Michael Hancher, 'The classification of cooperative illocutionary acts', 5 *Language in Society*, 1979.
46. *Dickenson* v. *Dodds*, 2 Ch. D. 463 (CA 1876). For a discussion of the rationale for this seminal case, see Gilmore, 28–30.
47. *Restatement* 2nd, 32, 89.
48. Otto Jespersen, *A Modern English Grammar on Historical Principles*, Copenhagen: E. Munksgaard, 1961: Part 4, 251–3.

Chapter 5   Conclusion

1. Lawrence M. Solan and Peter M. Tiersma, *Speaking of Crime: the Language of Criminal Justice*, Chicago, IL: University of Chicago Press, 2005: 27.
2. Irving Younger, *Hearsay: a Practical Guide through the Thicket*, Clifton, NJ: Prentice-Hall, 1988: 1.

Index

An italicized page number refers to a chapter section devoted to the topic entry.